COLLEGE FOR HUMAN SERVICES
LIBRARY
345 HUDSON STREET
NEW YORK, N.Y. 10014

FOSTERING PSYCHOSOCIAL DEVELOPMENT IN THE CLASSROOM

FOSTERING PSYCHOSOCIAL DEVELOPMENT IN THE CLASSROOM

By

ANGELO V. BOY

Professor of Education
University of New Hampshire
Durham, New Hampshire

and

GERALD J. PINE

Dean, School of Human and Educational Services
Oakland University
Rochester, Michigan

CHARLES C THOMAS • PUBLISHER
Springfield • Illinois • U.S.A.

Published and Distributed Throughout the World by
CHARLES C THOMAS • PUBLISHER
2600 South First Street
Springfield, Illinois 62794-9265

This book is protected by copyright. No part of
it may be reproduced in any manner without
written permission from the publisher.

© *1988 by* CHARLES C THOMAS • PUBLISHER
ISBN 0-398-05422-3
Library of Congress Catalog Card Number: 87-18166

With THOMAS BOOKS *careful attention is given to all details of manufacturing and design. It is the Publisher's desire to present books that are satisfactory as to their physical qualities and artistic possibilities and appropriate for their particular use.* THOMAS BOOKS *will be true to those laws of quality that assure a good name and good will.*

Printed in the United States of America
Q-R-3

Library of Congress Cataloging in Publication Data

Boy, Angelo V.
    Fostering psychological development in the classroom.

    Bibliography: p.
    Includes index.
    1. Social psychology. 2. Social learning. 3. Social skills--Study and teaching--United States. I. Pine, Gerald J. II. Title.
LC192.3.B68   1988   371.8'1   87-18166
ISBN 0-398-05422-3

PREFACE

PSYCHOSOCIAL is a term applied to the behaviors exhibited by an individual which have a social bearing either in origin or in outcomes. This definition stresses that the individual can never cut the self off from others. Others are always there either causing one's behavior or being the recipients of behavior that originates in the individual. Because of the cause-and-effect relationship between the self and others, we must learn to live with each other, within our families, classrooms, schools, neighborhoods and communities. Indeed, the peace of our international community may depend on the humanness of the behaviors we learn during our formative years.

The approach presented in this book is intended to influence students to become persons who are: more interested in peace than in war; more interested in ethnic and racial harmony rather than conflict; more interested in preserving the concept of family rather than destroying it; more interested in preserving the rights of all because their own rights are secure; more interested in understanding and being understood than in being right; and more interested in being part of the solution to interpersonal problems rather than creating them. We visualize students who are psychosocially strong individuals and use the strength to improve the human condition for themselves and others.

The psychosocial approach presented in this book recognizes the following fundamental principles:

- Students possess individual psychological needs and equally important social needs.
- There is a reciprocal relationship between individual and social needs; each affects the other.
- The interaction between these needs forms our behavior.
- Behaviors which can be described as mature and stable come from persons whose psychosocial needs have been verbalized and balanced.

- Students gain more from an academic curriculum when their psychosocial needs are concurrently met.
- Schools are the major institutions in our society which have contact with those who might later be labeled as mentally ill adults.
- Schools have contact with students while problems of psychosocial development are in their early or formative stages; this access enables schools to prevent normal psychosocial problems from becoming incapacitating.
- Schools can help students learn to identify, integrate, and balance their psychosocial needs and carry that learning into more stable and fulfilling adults lives.
- The psychosocial development of students can best occur in the natural and familiar environment of the classroom.
- The psychosocial development of students occurs in proportion to the psychosocial maturity of teachers.
- Psychosocial development is meant to complement and improve academic learning, not replace it.

Many educators across our nation share a dream: To see an ever-increasing number of schools fulfill *both* their academic and psychosocial missions and to finally see an end to the debate over which is the more important mission; to have schools produce persons who are academically grounded in those skills necessary for adulthood and to be equally grounded in their psychosocial awareness so that they can live an adulthood characterized by behavioral maturity and stability; and to be persons who are responsible in their own behavior and in the behavior directed toward others.

To members of the National Mental Health Association Commission, this dream must become a reality. In their 1986 report, entitled, *The Prevention of Mental-Emotional Disabilities,* the commission emphasizes the following as a high priority: "Programs should be developed in schools (preschool through high school) that incorporate validated mental health strategies and competence building as an integral part of the curriculum. The commission emphasized the importance of academic mastery and the development of psychosocial skills in kindergarten and the early grades" (as reported in the July 1986 issue of the *American Psychologist).*

The authors hope that those who read this book will help this dream to become a reality by committing themselves to the importance of fostering the psychosocial development of students.

A. V. B.
G. J. P.

CONTENTS

Chapter   *Page*

    I. Rationale for Fostering Psychosocial Development............... 3
   II. Teaching and Educational Approaches to Foster Psychosocial Development....................................... 29
  III. The Teacher as a Counselor.................................. 81
  IV. The Reflective Process: Foundation for Effective Teacher Counseling..111
   V. Principles and Conditions of Learning: Their Application to Psychosocial and Academic Education.......................127
  VI. The Psychosocially Sensitive Teacher 141
 VII. Teaching for Psychosocial Development........................167
VIII. Fostering Psychosocial Development Through Career Awareness..189
  IX. Fostering Psychosocial Development Through Play 209
   X. Eclectic Activities to Foster Psychosocial Development 229

Name Index 247
Subject Index 253

FOSTERING
PSYCHOSOCIAL DEVELOPMENT
IN THE CLASSROOM

CHAPTER I

RATIONALE FOR FOSTERING PSYCHOSOCIAL DEVELOPMENT

THE STUDENT'S psychological and social development is more critically important today than at any time in the history of education. Today's students are faced with problems which are unprecedented in their severity. The world has changed and that change has produced deeper and more debilitating problems than those faced by any previous generation of students. The availability and use of alcohol and drugs is common and those who sell both find an eager market among young people. The physical and psychological abuse of children startles our standards of decency. The sexploitation of young people occupies an increasing amount of space in our newspapers. Children run away from home in growing numbers. Divorce is now commonplace, but the children of divorce are still not able to accept it as easily as their parents. Children are terrified about the possibility of nuclear war, and although some adults are comfortable about discussing death, many children remain frightened about its meaning and certainty.

A recent report released by the Business Advisory Commission of the Education Commission of the States finds growing numbers of youths of every class and race risking becoming alienated from school, society, and work. The resulting costs to business in lost labor and government in lost tax revenues and higher welfare expenses demand early intervention to reverse the trends. The report found that:

- Some 700,000 students drop out of school each year; another 300,000 become chronic truants.
- More than 3 million youths between 16 and 19 are looking for work; another 391,000 unemployed youths have given up looking.
- One million teens become pregnant each year, with teen pregnancy rates growing in all class and racial groups.

- Juvenile arrests jumped sixty-fold between 1960 and 1980; the number of high school seniors arrested for drunkenness skyrocketed by 300 percent during the same period.
- Suicides among white teens grew by 177 percent between 1950 and 1978; for non-whites, the suicide rate rose 162 percent (Schappi, 1985).

AMERICA'S PSYCHOSOCIAL CRISIS

Schools must lead the battle against the worst psychosocial epidemics that have ever plagued the children of this society (London, 1987). The most conservative statistics show that millions of children are at risk because of the psychosocial problems affecting them (London, 1986). The psychosocial problems challenging our schools and affecting the lives of children and adolescents have been well documented by London (1986, 1987), Hodgkinson (1985), Hofferth (1987), and others. The following examples illustrate the magnitude, complexity, and severity of the psychosocial problems which affect large numbers of America's next generation:

Family problems. Divorce has more than doubled since 1960, and the number of children affected by divorce now exceeds one million annually. The number of unmarried couples cohabiting has increased dramatically in the past quarter century, as has the number of children under age 15 living with them. The number of single-parent families has also risen (Emery, 1982; Espenshade, 1983). 38 percent of first marriages of women in their late twenties will end in divorce. Between 40 percent and 50 percent of children born in the 1970s will live in a single-parent family for five or six years. Forty percent of black children and 20 percent of all children in the U. S. already do. In 1984 more than 1.5 million children under the age of 18 were living with neither parent (Bumpass, 1984, Hofferth, 1985).

By 1984 almost half of the 10 million working mothers in the United States had children in nursery school or kindergarten. At the same time, there were as many as eight million "latchkey children" (Hodgkinson, 1985).

Sexual behavior and births to unwed females. 40 percent of the 29 million teenagers in the U. S. have had sexual intercourse (about five million girls and about 6.5 million boys). The average age of first sexual experience may well be below 16 (Baldwin, 1986).

Increased sexual activity among teens increased the pregnancy and child-bearing rates among unmarried American girls. Until 1965, barely 15 percent of teenage girls who gave birth were unmarried; by 1983 50 percent to 75 percent of them were unwed. Among 15 to 19 year olds in 1983, 37 percent of white girls and 87 percent of black girls giving birth were unwed. Moreover, between 1947 and 1982 the proportions of premarital births to postmarital conceptions nearly reversed among 15 to 17 year olds; in 1947 more than 57 percent of the births for this age group were conceived postmaritally; in 1982 more than 57 percent of the births for this age group were premarital. Among 25 to 29 year old mothers, the rates have held steady (3% to 4% premarital births, 91% to 93% postmarital conceptions).

More than 715,000 children were born to unwed females in 1982. In 1960 children under 16 bore 25,000 babies; in 1977 they bore 42,000. Girls under 20 were delivered of 92,000 babies in 1960 and 250,000 in 1977. Since 1978, 10 percent of all teenage girls in the United States become pregnant annually, half of them within the first six months of sexual activity (Morrison, 1985). The results are not always disastrous; however, over 50 percent of aid to families with dependent children starts when the mother is a teenager. Even when teenage mothers recover socially and financially, their children have higher-than expected rates of serious adjustment problems in the teen years (Furstenberg, Gunn, & Morgan, 1986).

Child neglect and abuse. More than a million cases of nonsexual child abuse and neglect are reported annually. This figure is more than double the number since 1978, and many cases still are not reported.

Alcohol and drug use by children. Since the 1950s, surveys of American children from age 12 through 12th grade report that from one-fourth to three-fourths or more of teenagers have used alcohol. In one study, more than 30 percent of children in grades 10 through 12 said that they have been drunk six or more times in the past year (Capuzzi and LeCog, 1983, Milgram 1983). Perhaps three million 14 to 17 year olds may be problem drinkers (Eckardt et al. 1981). In his interviews with high school students in upper-class, middle-class, and inner-city schools, (London, 1987) found that students estimates of drinking rates all support the survey data. And though these data may overstate the case, few students say that they know more than a handful of peers who totally abstain.

Children's suicide. The suicide rate of children in the United States has risen 300 percent in 25 years, reaching perhaps 6,000 suicides and about half a million suicide attempts annually (*Interim Report,* 1985; *Guidepost,* 1987; Strother, 1986). The true rate of youth suicide is probably even higher because an unknown number of lethal auto accidents and drug overdoses may be suicides.

High school dropouts. The high school dropout rates reported by the U. S. Census Bureau have actually diminished in the past two decades, especially for blacks. But the numbers still total almost half a million young people per year, and the rates are highest among 14 to 17 year olds and among the urban poor (Hahn, Danzberger, and Lefkowitz, 1987).

Child Poverty. The Children's Defense Budget (1987) indicates that thirteen million children in America are poor, nearly one out of every four children under 6 is poor, and more than half the children in families headed by females are poor. All the figures related to poverty must be viewed against the background that greater child poverty means worse nutrition, less health care, more homelessness, and greater despair as opportunities and options are foreclosed (Howe, 1986).

This list of psychosocial problems represents only the tip of the iceberg. Other problems which have been identified include: psychological stress (Stensrud and Stensrud, 1983), school violence and vandalism (Baker, 1985), no sense of relationship to and impact on the future (Wagschal and Johnson, 1986), racial, class, cultural and sex discrimination (Barriers to Excellence, 1985), increased social and psychological disabilities of poverty (Hodgkinson, 1985, Howe, 1986), and (*Children in Need,* 1987), and physical, emotional, and learning handicaps (Fagan and Wallace, 1979).

How many children and families are affected by these problems? What is the overlap among these problems? London (1987) suggests that a conservative estimate would yield several millon. He observes (p. 669):

> Using figures (chiefly those from the U. S. Census Bureau) for just a few problem areas to make extremely conservative, almost surely underestimates of how many children need special help, the total still runs to several million. Add in the full array of problems, even discounting the overlaps, and the number could double. And add to that total the number of children who must be addressed by prevention, not just intervention, programs—for it makes no sense to treat only the victims of an epidemic if we can inoculate others—and most of the school age population needs help of one kind or another.

In commenting about the problems of today's youngsters, Conley (1983), an experienced classroom teacher notes:

> They are scared to death about things that they see in the world. They are worried about nuclear war and many don't think that they'll live a

natural lifetime. One out of three is from a broken family and they are worried about getting sucked into the same mistakes as so many of the adults they see. Decisions are pushed on them and they are forced to grow up early; they are pushed into the pool before they are ready to swim. (p. 8.)

SCHOOLS AS CONTRIBUTORS TO PSYCHOSOCIAL DEVELOPMENT

Ginott (1972) makes the following commentary on the effect of schooling on some of our citizens:

> I visited a prison last week, and I came back bothered and burdened. I can't escape thinking about my responsibility as teacher. Every adult murderer was once a child who spent years in school. Every thief had teachers who presumably taught him values and morals. Every criminal was educated by teachers. Every prison is a dramatic demonstration of the failure of our system. (p. 29).

Ginott (1972) goes on to tell about a note sent to all teachers by a principal on the first day of a new school year. The principal said:

> I am a survivor of a concentration camp. My eyes saw what no man should witness:
> Gas chambers built by **learned** engineers.
> Children poisoned by **educated** physicians.
> Infants killed by **trained** nurses.
> Women and babies shot and burned by **high school** and **college** graduates.
> Your efforts must never produce learned monsters, skilled psychopaths, educated Eichmanns. (p. 317.)

Ellenburg (1985) wonders about what our schools are producing and calls for a national campaign to combat the problem.

> What are schools really producing? Just take a look at our newscast any evening, read the newspapers of any city, listen to employers, observe the behavior of people on any street, take a good look at motorists driving their vehicles, talk with teachers about pupil conduct in their classes, and yes, read about our nation's leaders, and it won't take much to be convinced that we indeed need to mount a national campaign to deal with our irresponsible conduct. (p. 10.)

Although psychosocial development has received very little attention in the recent educational reform movement it does appear in several reports. *Horaces' Compromise (Sizer, 1984); A Place Called School* (Goodlad,

1983); *High School* (Boyer, 1983); (Etzioni, 1984); and the report of *The Thanksgiving Statement Group* (1984); have made psychosocial development a priority. All those reports strongly imply that schools must be concerned with the many different aspects of students' psychosocial development that complement the development of cognitive skills. These aspects of psychosocial development include (Crisci, 1986):

1. Learning to appreciate one's own talents and potential and developing a sense of self esteem;
2. Learning to set personal and intellectual goals, to develop plans for achieving these goals, and to persevere;
3. Learning to postpone gratification;
4. Learning to make informed decisions;
5. Learning to accept responsibility for one's behavior;
6. Learning to make and adhere to commitments;
7. Learning to interact and communicate effectively with others;
8. Learning to resolve conflicts and solve problems.

Students who lack these skills have problems as severe as those faced by students who lack basic academic and cognitive skills. Bronfenbrenner (1986) reminds us that in other nations schools are not primarily places where only academic basics are taught. Both in purpose and in practice, they function instead as settings in which young people learn citizenship; what it means to be a member of society, how to behave toward others, what one's responsibilities are to community and to the nation.

Bronfenbrenner (1986:435) calls for a *curriculum of caring* arguing that the effort to make caring an essential part of the curriculum is rooted in our values as a nation. In a curriculum of caring students would not simply learn about caring they would engage in it. Just as many schools now train superb drum corps, they could also train "caring corps"—groups of young men and women who would offer caring school and community based services to the young, the sick, the old, the hungry, and the aliented. Our schools must help our young people to believe that their hearts are as important to the nation's future as their heads (Lewis, 1986). While activities which promote the development of psychosocial development would be deplored by some critics as diluting the academic purpose of schools (Howe, 1986:195) agrues "my guess is that these activities will promote more academic success and rescue more dropouts than all the new tests, higher standards, and required courses combined."

Some schools have been insensitive or unable to respond to the psychosocial dimensions of the child's world. Such schools expect the child to come to school prepared to learn academic facts and leave whatever problems which interfere with learning at home. They expect the child to put aside the realities of what's occurring in the child's life and pay attention to the acquisition of academic knowledge. They continue to promote the importance of doing well in school while remaining insensitive to the child's problems and how they impede the learning process. Some schools convey the message that they are only interested in the child's ability to learn facts and skills. They prefer not to be involved with those problems which interfere with learning and believe these problems are not part of the school's responsibility.

In other schools, these problems are seen as part of the school's responsibility if the child is to fully participate in, and profit from, the learning process. They realize that a student cannot be expected to learn unless the school addresses itself to alleviating or mitigating those problems which interfere with learning. Those problems must be concurrently dealt with if we expect the student to become motivated to learn. A student will respond to a school which shows that it cares for the student as a psychosocial person. A student will appreciate the school's sensitivity to those problems which interfere with learning. When that student walks into a classroom there is a reasonable interest in learning simply because the student knows that the school is *also* interested in the student's psychosocial development and, in some cases, the student's psychosocial survival.

The curricula of our schools have been good but insufficient. Certainly a student expected to make one's way in the adult world must be educated in those learning fundamentals which enable the journey to occur. But such an education deals only with a portion of the child's needs. It prepares persons to read, count, and write but it does not prepare them to handle the psychosocial realities of living in today's world or developing the capacity to live an adult life which is relatively free from incapacitating psychosocial problems.

The psychosocial development of students is not meant to replace academic education. It is meant to complement and enrich academic education so that, for the first time in our educational history, we will educate the whole person; not just the academic person but the whole person who has *both* intellectual and psychosocial needs. The whole person has a mind but also has inner feelings, emotions, and perceptions which influence when and how that mind functions.

There are too many boys and girls sitting in too many classrooms who are not learning subject matter. They are not learning, because we have not educated them to monitor those feelings, attitudes, and perceptions which influence the mind to be receptive to learning.

Students who have been exposed to psychosocial development programs in school have a higher level of motivation and interest in academics. They possess positive self-concepts and know how to act and react to the psychosocial requirements of a situation and its relationship to the enhancement or debilitation of the self. They are more complete persons. Their minds have been academically expanded but so has their psychosocial awareness. They have been educated in a school which recognizes the importance of a pupil's psychosocial development (Skovholt, 1977).

One of the teaching approaches identified in the next chapter for fostering the pupil's psychosocial development is student-centered teaching, which has been conceptualized and developed by Carl R. Rogers. In Rogers's *Freedom to Learn for the 80's* (Rogers, 1983), an expansion of his classic book, *Freedom to Learn* (Rogers, 1969), Rogers cites research done by Aspy and Roebuck (1977) and the National Consortium for Humanizing Education. The results, which cover seventeen years of research in forty-two states and seven foreign countries, examined the relationships between Rogers's facilitative conditions (empathy, congruence, positive regard) as possessed by the teacher and their effect upon students' academic achievement, attitudes, attendance, health, discipline and IQ. Students who are exposed to teachers who possessed high levels of empathy, congruence, and acceptance were found to:

- Make greater gains in academic achievement
- Possess improved self-concepts
- Miss fewer days of school
- Present fewer discipline problems
- Increase their scores on IQ tests
- Be more spontaneous
- Use higher levels of thinking

A psychosocial approach to education will produce results. It recognizes that the relationship between intellect and affect is indestructibly symbiotic and makes good use of this relationship. It is the deliberate and conscious process of integrating affective and cognitive elements in individual and group learning. It is a learning process designed to affect personal, social, behavioral, ethical, aesthetic, and philosophical development (Mosher & Sprinthall, 1971). It is educational experiences which encourage students to select their own goals, anticipate alternative experiences, choose among them, and develop effective ways for achieving goals (Ivey & Alschuler, 1971).

A basic objective of the process of psychosocial development is to make the student's affective development a prominent part of the schooling experience. It uses a variety of approaches and activities to enable the student to personalize the process of psychosocial development. In essence, this means consciousness-raising activities which enable students to become psychosocially aware, to be able to identify feelings, to accurately perceive people, and to better understand themselves. It also means assisting students to listen to others, to respond to the feelings of others, to make decisions, and to develop an individualized awareness of the psychosocial meanings contained in life experiences (Pine & Boy, 1977).

Until now, our schools have assumed that healthy self-concepts and positive psychosocial growth would be the natural outcomes of a carefully planned academic program. However, this has not been the case. Today, it seems, the longer students remain in school, the more students' intrinsic interest in learning may decline. In urban ghetto schools, negative self-concepts have tended to increase with the amount of time spent in schools. Schools appear to foster the decline of personal responsibility and prejudiced thinking. There is a continuing schism between young people and adult authority figures. Increasing unrest, incidents of violence, and an increased presence of the police in many of our schools constitute a reality in contemporary society.

The problems plaguing our society have impacted our youth. We have a breakdown of law and an increase in disorder; there is a disintegration of the sense of community and, at the same time, an erosion of marriage and family as a supportive societal unit; and there is an uprooting of past traditions, and values, accompanied by an increasing alienation from and "atomization" of the stabilizing influences of the past. These phenomena tend to generate anomie—a feeling of helplessness and hopelessness. And, because youth is in a state of profound psychosocial development during the school years, it can be deeply, and perhaps permanently, affected by such problems.

Until recently, we have misdiagnosed the human problems of society by treating the victims of insensitive institutions instead of making those institutions more humanly sensitive. In schools, we must mobilize ourselves to restructure learning and interpersonal and intergroup relationships so that there will be more psychosocially stable human beings and fewer casualties.

The school's strategic position in affecting the student's psychosocial development was accurately stressed by Arbuckle (1965), who said: "It is crucial to note that the school is the only social organization that for many years houses within its walls all of the individuals who might now or who will, later on, be described as mentally ill" (p. 141).

Boy and Pine (1963) indicated that much human potential has been lost, because unresolved psychosocial problems prevented youngsters from deriving the full benefit of a school's academic curriculum: "We may never know the untold number of boys and girls who could have achieved optimum benefits from their educational experiences but didn't because their emotional problems prevented them from doing so" (p. 223).

Schools are the one place in our society where virtually everyone at particular age ranges can be reached by helping professionals. Many of the current interventions of helping professionals with adults would have had a more profound effect if they had been delivered to younger age groups when these persons were in school (Shaw and Goodyear, 1984).

Since school has a deep and long-lasting effect on those who enter its doors, it follows that the greatest potential for change and improvement in the psychosocial stability of young people lies in the school. If we can focus some of what happens in schools on the student's psychosocial development, we may be able to contribute to the student's well-being today as well as preparing that student to live a psychosocially stable adult life.

Weinstein and Fantini (1970) see contemporary schools fulfilling a philosophical and moral mission which has practical outcomes:

> Education in a free society should have a broad human focus, which is best served by educational objectives resting on a personal and interpersonal base and dealing with students' concerns. This belief rests on philosophical and moral grounds, but it also has plainly practical implications in terms of the price a society pays for negative social behavior—crime, discrimination, tensions, and, ultimately, widespread pathology. (p. 88.)

What is being sought by including psychosocial development in schools has always been part of what an excellent teacher has done. Teachers who have attained high performance levels in their work have been those who have been able to influence both the academic and psychosocial development of pupils. As Brown (1971) has said: "Actually, affective techniques are not much different from what good teachers have done since teaching began. By promulgating confluent education and its affective dimension, we are only making explicit what has long been implicit in excellent teaching" (p. 249).

Educators, psychologists, and sociologists have recognized that schools which focus exclusively on the academic training of the mind have not produced citizens who are able to cope with the psychosocial demands of life. One may be a graduate of a prestigious college of engineering, but those credentials do not prevent the act of suicide. One may have graduated at the top of a medical school class, but that accomplishment does not prevent the physician from becoming addicted to drugs. An attorney's academic credentials are no insurance against performing acts of child abuse in the home. The influence of schooling upon one's psychosocial development has long been recognized, and the school's pivotal role in the development has long been emphasized. (Arbuckle, 1950, Ringness, 1968, Rogers, 1969, and Lyon, 1971). More recently, because of an increase in the intensity of psychosocial problems which youngsters bring to school, there has been a renewed thrust toward the critical importance of education as a vehicle for preventing students from becoming psychosocial casualties (Brown, 1975, Buscaglia, 1978, Sprinthall, 1980, Kremer, 1981, Carkhuff, 1982, Newberg and Love, 1982, Farley, 1982, Bardon, 1983, and Takanishi, DeLeon and Pallack, 1983).

Gelatt (1983) states that if we could imagine a future society where the development of the following human qualities is given equal priority to technological development, we would possess a new vision of what it means to be human. Teachers have an opportunity to contribute to that humanness by participating in the development of the following desirable psychosocial qualities while youngsters are still in school:

1. High confidence and positive attitudes toward living and learning. (Confidence)
2. Personal values and behavior based on the interrelatedness of things and people. (Connectedness)
3. Ability to establish and maintain caring and responsible relationships with others. (Compassion)
4. Competence in decision making, critical thinking, and other self management skills. (Choosing) (p. 5.)

FEELINGS INFLUENCE THINKING AND BEHAVIOR

One's ability to understand the critical importance of a pupil's psychosocial development will depend largely upon one's identification with the viewpoint developed in this section. This section serves as foundation for understanding the chapters which follow. If the reader sees the mind simply as a vessel into which facts are poured, then this section will be troublesome. If the reader feels that the purpose of schools is to educate the mind so that the student can enter college or get a job, then this section will not be easily understood. If the reader feels that the school should not become involved with the pupil's psychosocial problems, then this section will be a burden. If, however, the reader sees the school as an institution through which all future neurotic and psychotic individuals pass; as an institution with the potential to prepare its students for a psychosocially stable adulthood; and if the reader sees the mission and purpose of education as not merely exposing students to the fundamentals of reading, writing, and arithmetic but as serving a larger mission and purpose, then this section will be useful for understanding the rationale which supports the inclusion of psychosocial experiences in the educational process.

We like to think of ourselves as being very rational and, indeed, our ability to learn any subject matter is dependent on our rationality. Very often, however, we do not use our rationality. Intellectually, we know how we should respond, but somehow we don't end up responding the way that we should. We know that excessive speed on our highways is an invitation to death, but we insist on exceeding speed limits. We know that children should be emotionally nourished and physically protected, but the statistics tell us of the increasing rate that children are being abused. We know what constitutes proper schooling, but we insist on providing students with second-rate learning experiences.

Regarding our behavior, one clear and fundamental answer to why we behave as we do lies in the covert world of our feelings. We do not behave in a vacuum. We often behave as a response to feelings that have developed over a period of time. Feelings that have been nurtured and influenced by an entire range of life's experiences and events. An employer may insist on badgering an employee not because the worker is inefficient but because the employer has unresolved feelings of inadequacy. A student may act out in class not because the learning experience is inadequate but because of unresolved and angry feelings about the death of a parent. An adolescent boy may engage in abusive sexist language because he has unresolved feelings about his own sexuality.

We are not the rational persons that we think we are. Yes, the rationality exists, but it is often unused and hampered because our feelings get in the way. These feelings interfere with the use of our intellect and prompt us to behave in ways that are not good for ourselves or the well-being of others. Life would be good, simple, and clear if our thinking were based upon rational analysis. We'd have a world free from the threat of nuclear war, child abuse, murder, and rape. Our rationality would clearly indicate the inhumanity of these acts. But the reality of our world indicates that we do have these crimes, and the cause of these crimes is often unresolved feelings which were never expressed or dealt with — feelings which needed to be safely expressed but instead were expressed in inhuman ways. Each of the perpetrators of these crimes has a rational grasp of the difference between right and wrong, but their feelings overwhelm and block out that rationality. We all have the potential to use our minds well and reach logical conclusions — conclusions based upon the evidence of objective facts. But our ability to reach logical conclusions is influenced by feelings which interfere with the mind's ability to function logically. A teacher may logically explain the importance of studying mathematics to a student, but the student's feelings of intellectual inadequacy will prevent the teacher's message from being received. The student's feelings of inadequacy prevent the assimilation of the logical message that mathematics is a necessary life skill.

Feelings Affect Thinking

We all want to think well — to gather the facts, analyze those facts, and reach logical conclusions. But the thinking process is influenced by feelings. Clear thinking emanates from a person whose feelings are known and under control. Faulty thinking emanates from a person who is unaware of how feelings influence our ability to reason well.

If the logic of a work situation dictates that an employee should have an open and frank discussion with an employer, a subconscious fear of authority figures will result in that discussion never taking place. If logic dictates that one should not smoke cigarettes, the feelings which nourish the desire to smoke overpower the logic of not smoking.

We are not what we appear to be. As persons, we are supposed to be logical and rational. But leaf through the pages of any daily newspaper. There you will read stories that serve as prime evidence that we do not think well. But if these stories were examined in detail, we would find persons who engaged in illogical behavior not because they lost the ability to think but because their unexpressed and unresolved feelings obstructed that clarity of thinking.

Feelings Affect Behavior

Feelings affect thinking and thinking affects behavior. One's behavior is not random. It is caused by something. We often look at negative behavior and conclude that it's due to poor thinking. "If he had only used his head he wouldn't be in this mess!" This statement is true, but we often fail to identify what caused the person to think as he or she did.

Feelings lead to good or faulty thinking and the quality of that thinking leads to good or faulty behavior. Simply stated, *feelings influence thinking and thinking influences behavior.* Good behavior is preceded by good thinking which is influenced by good feelings; poor behavior is preceded by faulty thinking which is influenced by negative feelings.

Our ability to think is buffeted from two sides: our feelings on one side and our behavior on the other. The quality of our feelings, however, influences the quality of our thinking and the subsequent behavior. This chain reaction is put in motion by our feelings. When they are positive, then the thinking and behavior will be positive. When they are negative, then our thinking and behavior will be negative.

When examining any behavior and attempting to determine the cause of that behavior, we must avoid examining superficial causes (i.e. home conditions, physical handicap, family income, learning disability, cultural deprivation). The person may be a product of these conditions, but the deeper cause for the behavior is the person's unexpressed and unresolved feelings about these conditions. It is these feelings which caused the thinking which caused the behavior.

Repressing Feelings Leads to Interpersonal Conflict

Many of us keep our feelings bottled up inside. We smile, do our daily work, and try to come across as friendly and reasonable people. But too many other persons have unexpressed, antagonistic feelings toward others. We often tolerate an insensitive employer, spouse, parent, or politician. We do that by putting on a front. But if these negative feelings persist, they must eventually find expression. When they are expressed, they often come out in a torrent of bitterness, anger, and resentment. In some cases these repressed feelings eventually find their expression through some act of violence.

Some people attempt to deal with their repressed feelings through physical activity or fantasy. Runners and joggers are often able to release a buildup of negative and angry feelings. Other people find solace in their fantasies or daydreams of a better life. In both cases these persons may develop an ability to cope with life. But they may not. In far too many cases, when repressed feelings have built up over a period of time, they must be expressed more directly. This direct expression is most often toward another person and usually takes the form of "clearing the air." The benefit of doing this is enormous. But far too many people fear this exchange and prefer to hide behind a mask. They prefer to keep negative feelings to themselves. They fear coming out into the open because of a fear of the consequences. The problem with doing this is that there is a corresponding buildup of tension. And eventually that tension may reach a point where it has to be expressed and it sometimes becomes expressed in dehumanizing and harmful ways.

Repressing Feelings Leads to Negative Physical Consequences

When feelings are continually repressed the result can be nagging backaches, stomach disorders, migraine headaches, or low levels of energy. These are the less severe consequences. Medical research has now produced evidence which links one's psychosocial behavior to heart attacks and various forms of cancer (Levy, 1985). This is a logical outcome for the person whose life is filled with repressed feelings. Feelings were repressed in childhood, during adolescence, during marriage, and on the job. This buildup of unexpressed feelings, over the years, can only result in the eventual deterioration of the body and its normal functioning.

Medical research also indicates that a large percentage of patients who appear in a physician's office do not have physical problems which can be medically treated. They have psychosocial problems which produce pseudo-physical symptoms that have no medically discernible basis.

We pay little attention to our feelings, since we cannot see or touch them. We do pay attention to the swollen breast, the limp, and the back pain, because they are obvious. Feelings, however, are hidden from sight and touch. They're there, but we often label them as moods and figure that what we can't see or touch can't harm us. The consequences of negative feelings, however, are far more incapacitating than a broken leg. The leg can fully mend in a short period of time. Negative feelings, however, are not that easily mended. They linger, grow, cause us anxiety and tension, and affect not only our interpersonal behavior but our physical well-being.

Expressing Feelings Involves Risk

Repressed feelings often cause us to feel isolated, lonely, angry, and not understood. We'd like to turn to people in our lives in an effort to get help, but we often feel that they're too involved with their own problems to give us the time and understanding we need. Furthermore, getting help from them requires an enormous risk that we're often not willing to take. If we do express our feelings to relatives, co-workers and friends, there is the possibiliy that our human frailties will not be understood or accepted. So, instead of risking the expression of how we feel, we turn inward. We keep those feelings inside, since there is less apparent risk involved. The risk, however, of keeping those feelings inside is far greater than the risk of expressing them. Bottling up feelings can lead to psychosocial and physical consequences that can be far more painful and long-lasting than the risk involved in expressing those feelings. The decision, however, for most of us is not to say anything, to survive each day, to protect those feelings from being expressed and exposed to others.

Expressing Feelings Enables Us to Examine Motives

A person expressing previously inhibited feelings, however, feels a release from the bonds of such feelings. They feel free from the negative consequences of not having expressed feelings in the past, free from the anguish that accompanies not having responded to persons, situations, and events that require a feeling response. As a person becomes comfortable in expressing feelings, a desire also occurs to examine the motives which prompted the development of these feelings. The person is asking, "Why do I do these things? Why do I feel this way? Where did all of this come from?"

This self-examination of motives usually leads one to examine situations and events which influenced the development of certain feelings. Such an examination enables one to recall experiences that influenced the development of current feelings. The person often says, "Now I know *why* I feel as I do." By recalling the situations and events which caused current feelings, one is able to determine the rhyme and reason for those feelings. Current feelings are understood more deeply, especially the motives which prompt those feelings to exist.

There are motives for feeling as we do and these motives are usually linked to situations and events in which we felt either enhanced or diminished as persons. Debilitating experiences, whether they occurred yesterday or many years ago, leave us with psychosocial scars—repressions of feelings about what transpired and how we emotionally responded. We want to know what happened and why we responded as we did. We want to identify the motives which undergird our feelings.

Expressing Feelings Serves as a Release

If all of the feelings we've accumulated do not have an opportunity to be released, we create a reservoir of feelings that will eventually overflow its banks. The victim in such an overflow is often ourselves and those around us. We cannot expect to repress feelings and live a life that is free from tension, anxiety, and physical consequences. The bottling up of feelings, for too long, can only lead to negative physical and psychosocial consequences. The price that one pays for inhibiting feelings is too high.

When feelings are siphoned off as they begin to form, they are released. They no longer have the power to build up and incapacitate us. They no longer have the power to make us uncertain and insecure. When released, feelings have an opportunity to evaporate. Their expression releases us from the tension, anxiety, and anguish that retaining them requires. Keeping feelings inside requires an enormous effort. We have to carefully plan what we say, to whom, and the circumstances in which we'll say anything. Just saying how we feel does not require the same planning. We merely say it, feel better about having said it, and cleanse ourselves of feelings that have no opportunity to build up inside.

Expressing Feelings Leads to Self-Responsibility

A person who has learned to express feelings gains in self-responsibility. There is an enormous responsibility involved in expressing feelings. It is the dual responsibility toward self and others. It is obvious that the expression of feelings is beneficial. The person will feel released from the necessity of harboring certain feelings as well as the psychological and physical tensions that accompany such a repression. But the person will also develop a responsibility to examine feelings, to determine whether these feelings are legitimate and emanate from an objective situation or event or whether they are more related to an egocentric need to feel angry, misunderstood, lonely, or unloved. Often, we express feelings toward a person today that are totally unrelated to what the person is saying or doing. The feeling expressed often doesn't feel right and we know it. It is often more related to a past experience with *another* person, but we wait until today to express that feeling to an innocent bystander.

Being in touch with our feelings gives us an opportunity to examine their accuracy. The more practice we have with expressing our feelings, the better able we are to monitor their expression so that they'll be expressed to the right person in the right situation. We become less random in expressing feelings. We know more accurately how we feel and the persons to whom those feelings should be expressed. We become more responsible because we have a more accurate understanding of how we feel, why we feel that way, and identify the most appropriate person who needs to hear our feelings.

Expressing Feelings Leads to Personal Freedom

Persons who have learned how to express their feelings are in contact with an important ingredient of personal freedom. They feel alive, liberated, and whole. They feel connected to what it means to lead a life which is psychologically and socially stable. They have freed themselves from the negative consequences of unexpressed feelings. They can make free choices and decisions based upon the logic of what should be done rather than having those choices and decisions connected to unknown and unexpressed feelings.

Clearly, an important outcome for the person who has expressed feelings is the movement toward increased psychosocial freedom. The motives for certain choices and decisions are unrelated to unexpressed feelings. A certain house or car is purchased because of their reasonableness rather than being related to impressing others. A special cause is supported because of the importance of the cause rather than being a symbol of ego needs contained in unexpressed feelings. Choices and decisions are made because they are logically the best rather than being symbols of certain feelings which have not been expressed.

Personal freedom is not a luxury for the chose few. It is a way of living that is available to anyone who has learned to understand feelings, express them, and identify the relationship of this expression to one's sense of freedom and comfort in interpersonal relationships.

In conclusion, an assimilation of how feelings affect us will help the reader to understand the concept of psychosocial development that will be presented in this book. We also want to emphasize that when a school insists on just attempting to educate the mind, it will always be fighting against those feelings which inerfere with the mind's ability to function. Instead of fighting those feelings, dismissing them, or ignoring them, a teacher who deals with them and helps them to be expressed is making the best of all contributions to the psychosocial development of the student.

SELF-KNOWLEDGE EDUCATION: FEELINGS, THOUGHT AND BEHAVIOR

How do we deal with the relationship between and among feelings, thought, and behavior? How can we learn to understand and know how our inner experiences, emotions, and thoughts affect our behavior? Weinstein and Alschuler (1985) propose that we educate students for self-knowledge development. The goal of self-knowledge education is to develop students' competence in generating knowledge about the nature, causes, and consequences of their inner experiences. According to Weinstein and Alschuler (1985:24) "Daily problems are necessary events in the development of increasingly adequate self-knowledge. We are all natural students of our own experience. We are teachers whenever we assist others to increase self-knowledge."

Weinstein and Alschuler (1985:19) have adopted a scientific model of how people create self-knowledge. They see similarities between the way people solve problems of every day life and the way scientists search for solutions to objective problems in the external world. From their experience, people generate increasingly adequate self-knowledge that provides more accurate representations, predictions, and control. In less scientific terms these are the abilities to describe experience more fully, to anticipate experience more precisely, and to manage experience more intentionally and effectively. These naturally developing abilities to describe, to anticipate, and manage experience are generic goals for virtually all students.

Weinstein and Alschuler (1985) believe that a theory of how self-knowledge develops can suggest a variety of strategies for the teacher to use to increase the adequacy of student's self-knowledge. They argue (1985:24) that individuals, like inductive scientists, generate knowledge about themselves by gathering the raw data of experience, construing that experience in various ways, and expressing it as descriptions and hypotheses. While the process does not necessarily occur in discrete, sequential, conscious steps, it does approximate formal scientific procedures. More specifically, the raw data of experience consist of all sensations, feelings, thoughts, and actions in a person's conscious awareness. These data are construed through mental operations such as categorizing, assigning causality, and hypothesizing alternative actions and consequences. Mental operations are organized into coherent wholes called structures. As structures evolve into adequate, powerful processing mechanisms, they pass through an invariant sequence of hierarchical stages. Structures can only be inferred from systematic differences in their products. In their research these products have been descriptions and hypotheses that individuals have made about themselves. *Self-knowledge* refers to these descriptions, the external products of internally processed experience; it does not refer to unsymbolized, private awareness of one's own experience. In an analogy to computers, experience is the data entered into the machine. Stages are different programs that transform the data into statements, numbers, or figures on the computer screen.

Based on their study of people who have explicitly theorized about their experiences and produced samples of self-knowledge, Weinstein and Alschuler (1985:20-21) have identified four stages of self-knowledge: elemental, situational, pattern, and transformational.

Elemental Self-Knowledge. Memorable experiences are recounted in a fragmented list of juxtaposed elements. These elements are those that can be recorded by a camera and a tape recorder—overt, external, observable events. The person's inner states must be inferred by the listener. Usually, the only feeling words used are happy, sad, like, hope, and want. The elements are not causally linked, classified, or interpreted. There are no statements that summarize the elements as belonging to a single, coherent, named situation. This rudimentary self-knowledge lacks power, and descriptions of experience are incomplete. The absence of causal connections makes accurate predictions unlikely, even if the exact collection of elements were to recur. Consequently, learning to act internationally in subsequent similar situations is severely restricted.

Situational Self-Knowledge. At the stage of situational self-knowledge, people describe a whole situation. The time frame may be a few minutes, several months, or even years. In the example above, consequences such as the inability to work or having bad dreams extend over a long time. People refer to a single, coherent situation by depicting reactions to it and consequences of it or by using it to refer to the whole event (e.g., "It wasn't a pleasant experience.").

Although the phenomena described are still primarily external, internal states that go beyond the elemental five feelings are introduced ("funny dreams," "wasn't a pleasant experience"). Bodily sensations are described, such as being nervous, calm, steady, or numb. But descriptions of subjective states lack differentiated nuances and remain at a global, cliched level—heavy, out of sight, deal with, face up to, wiped out, in touch with. In contrast to the seemingly random ordering of events at the elemental stage, people at the situational stage name causal connections between external phenomena and internal states by simple connective phrases such as because, since, therefore, so, or although. Even though causation is present, it is relatively naive and "one-way." Situations are seen as causing feelings, but feelings are not reported as causing subsequent behavior or even a sequence of other feelings.

Pattern Self-Knowledge. Pattern self-knowledge contains descriptions of stable internal responses that are reactions to a class of situations or result in a class of situations. Freed from the time and space limits of each concrete situation, people are able to describe how they are consistent across situations: "Whenever I'm in trouble, I'm afraid to ask for help." Situations are described abstractly ("in trouble") rather than concretely ("in physics class without my homework completed"). People make predictive statements about probable reactions in classes of situations.

People see patterns of overt behaviors, but descriptions of covert patterns—personality traits, psychological characteristics, dispositions, ongoing inner conflict—are the hallmarks of this stage. These traits are named and seen as causes of behavior in types of social conditions.

People at the pattern self-knowledge stage retain their capacity to identify elements and describe the intricacies of a situation. They also can see beyond the moment, generalize across situations, more accurately anticipate events, and systematically modify their pattern of perceiving or responding to those situations.

Transformational Self-Knowledge. People at the transformational self-knowledge stage describe how they consciously monitor, modify, or manage their inner patterns of response: "I try to make my guilt work positively by setting realistic deadlines and then feeling anxious if it looks like I'm not meeting those deadlines." In the previous pattern stage, people describe their stable pattern of responses to a class of external situations. In the transformational stage, they can describe the repertoire of inner processes they use to alter their inner life. They are proactive in influencing inner states: "I know when and how to give myself permission to express my true feelings." People with tranformational competencies know that satisfaction and meaning are not solely dependent on situational determinants. They can stop their negative reactions, reinterpret situations, and confer new meanings on situations. They have the capacity to create their inner states.

The primary goal for self-knowledge educators is to extend students' existing stage of self-knowledge to new areas. Rather than pushing students through stages of self-knowledge the emphasis is on state elaboration over stage transition. This can be done by using stage specific objectives, choosing a specific content area, and employing a variety of psychoeducational approaches to encourage self-knowledge in that specific area. Weinstein and Alschuler (1985:23) suggest questions that teachers can ask directly or indirectly or that students can address in writing about a psychosocial problem area.

Ask people at the elemental stage: Where did it happen? When did it happen? What were you doing when it happened? How did people look? How did you look? Who was there? Who did what? What did you do? Who said what? What did you say? What happened right before that? What happened right after that? What did you want? What did they want? How did your body feel? What did you like or dislike about it?

Add the following questions for people at the situational stage: What started it all? What were some of the things you were saying to yourself during the time? What feelings were you experiencing? What made you feel that? What made you think that? What did you think would happen? What did you want more (or less) of? What made you say that? How did it affect the rest of your day (or anytime after)? What would a title be for that whole situation? What would be the moral of your story? In what situations could you get (or avoid) these things?

Add these questions for people at the pattern stage: How do your responses in this situation remind you of responses in similar situations? What kinds of situations make you think or feel that way? What is the same about those situations? What feelings and thoughts do you recognize about yourself in those situations? How is the way you respond typical, especially the feelings and thoughts you had? What does that response get for you or help you avoid? Would you like to change that type of response? What responses would be more beneficial? How could you practice these new responses?

Finally, add the following questions for people at the transformational state: When you know you're feeling that way, do, or can you do, anything about it? When you find yourself having those kinds of thoughts, do you do anything about it? What things do you say to yourself or do that interrupt and alter what you are thinking? How do your beliefs about yourself affect your attitude? What could you believe about yourself that could change the way you think and feel?

While they caution that their theory of self-knowledge is limited, Weinstein and Alschuler (1985:23) have provided a paradigm for organizing psychoeducational approaches. They suggest that a variety of psychoeducational approaches reflecting experiential, affective, cognitive, or behavioral strategies can be used to facilitate self knowledge. Inherent in their work is an affirmative view of human nature and a respect for the potential power of psychoeducational approaches to enhance the full development of human beings.

REFERENCES

Arbuckle, D. S. (1950). *Teacher-Counseling*. Cambridge, MA: Addison-Wesley.

Arbuckle, D. S. (1965). *Counseling: Philosophy, theory and practice*. Boston: Allyn & Bacon.

Aspy, D. & Roebuck, F. (1977). *Kids don't learn from people they don't like*. Amherst, MA: Human Resources Development Press.

Baldwin, W. (1986). *Adolescent Pregnancy and Child Rearing-Rates, Trends, and Research Findings*. Washington, D. C. NICHD.

Bardon, J. I. (1983). Psychology applied to education: A speciality in search of an identity. *The American Psychologist*, 38, 185-196.

Berg, C. D. (1978). Helping children to accept death and dying through group counseling. *The Personnel and Guidance Journal*, 56, 169-172.

Boy, A. V. & Pine, G. J. (1963). *Client-centered counseling in the secondary school*. Boston: Houghton Mifflin.

Bronfenbrenner, V. (1986). Alienation and the four worlds of childhood. *Phi Delta Kappan*, 67, 6, 430-436.

Brown, G. I. (1971). *Human teaching for human learning*. New York: Viking.

Brown, G. I. (1975). *The live classroom*. New York: Viking.

Bumpass, L. (1984). Children and marital disruption: A replication and update. *Demography* 21, 71-82.

Buscaglia, L. (1978). Affective education: A means to a beginning. *School Psychology Digest*, 7, 4-7.

Capuzzi, D. & LeCog, L. L. (1983). Social and personal determinants of adolescent use and abuse of alcohol and marijuana. *The Personnel and Guidance Journal*, 61, 199-205.

Carkhuff, R. R. (1982). Affective education in the age of productivity. *Educational Leadership*, 40-484-487.

Committee for Economic Development (1987). *Children In Need*. New York.

Conley, J. E. (1983). Many paths, one call. *At home with Holy Cross*. Notre Dame, IN: University of Notre Dame.

Courtois, C. A. & Leehan, J. (1982). Group treatment for grown-up abused children. *The Personnel and Guidance Journal,* 60, 564-567.

David, H. P. and Baldwin, W. P. (1981). Childbearing and child development: Demographic and psychosocial trends. *American Psychologist,* 34, 866-871.

Drake, E. A. (1981). Children of separation and divorce: School policies, procedures, problems. *Phi Delta Kappan,* 62, 27-28.

Eckardt, M. J. (et. a.) (1981). Health hazards associated with alcohol consumption. *Journal of the American Medical Association,* 246, 648-666.

Ellenburg, F. C. (1985). Society and schools must teach responsible behavior. *Education,* 106, 9-11.

Emery, R. E. (1982). Interparental conflict and the children of discord and divorce. *Psychological Bulletin,* 98, 538-568.

Espenshade, T. (1983). Black-white differences in marriage. Paper presented at the Annual Meeting of the Population Associaton of America.

Etzioni, A. (1984). *Self Discipline, Schools, and the Business Community.* Washington, D. C. National Chamber Foundation.

Fagan, T. & Wallace, A. (1979). Who are the handicapped? *The Personnel and Guidance Journal,* 57, 215-220.

Farley, J. R. (1982). Raising student achievement through the affective domain. *Educational Leadership,* 40, 502-503.

Foster, C. D. & Miller, G. M. (1980). Adolescent pregnancy: A challenge for counselors. *The Personnel and Guidance Journal,* 58, 236-245.

Furstenberg, F., Brooks-Gunn, J. and Morgan, S. P. (1986). *Adolescent Mothers in Later Life.* New York: Commonwealth Fund.

Gelatt, H. B. (1983). The counselor's new clothes. *ACES Newsletter,* 2, 5.

Ginott, H. G. (1972). *Teacher and child.* New York: Macmillan.

Guidepost (1987). Suicide epidemic spreading among nation's teenagers. *Guidepost.* Alexandria, Virginia. American Association for Counseling and Development, 30, 3, 1.

Hahn, A., Danzberger, J., and Lefkowitz, B. (1987). *Dropouts in America: Enough Is Known for Action.* Washington, D.C.: Institute for Educational Leadership.

Hodgkinson, H. (1985). *All One System.* Washington, D.C.: Institute for Educational Leadership.

Hofferth, S. L. (1985). Updating children's life course. *Journal of Marriage and the Family,* 47, 93-115.

Hofferth, S. L. (1987). Implications of family trends for children: A research perspective. *Eduational Leadership,* 44, 5, 78-84.

Howe, H. (1986). The prospect for children in the United States. *Phi Delta Kappan,* 68, 4, 191-196.

Ivey, A. & Alschuler, A. S. (Eds.) (1973). Psychological education: A prime function of the counselor. *The Personnel and Guidance Journal,* 51, 586-691.

Jeghelian, A. (1976). Surviving sexism: Strategies and consequences. *The Personnel and Guidance Journal,* 54, 307-311.

Kirkpatrick, J. S. (1975). Guidelines for counseling young people with sexual concerns. *The Personnel and Guidance Journal,* 53, 144-148.

Kremer, B. (1981). *Mental health in the schools.* 2nd ed. Washington, DC: University Press of America.

Lee, E. E. (1978). Suicide and youth. *The Personnel and Guidance Journal,* 56, 200-204.

Lee, R. E. & Klopfer, C. (1978). Counselors and juvenile delinquents: Toward a comprehensive treatment approach. *The Personnel and Guidance Journal,* 53, 144-148.

Levy, S. M. (1985). *Behavior and cancer.* San Francisco, CA: Jossey-Bass.

Lewis, A. C. (1987). Their hearts are as important as their heads. *Phi Delta Kappan,* 68, 8, 572-573.

Lifton, W. M., Tavantis, T. N. & Mooney, W. T. (1979). The disappearing family. *The Personnel and Guidance Journal,* 57, 161-165.

London, P. (1987). Character education and clinical intervention: A paradigm shift for U. S. schools. *Phi Delta Kappan,* 667-673.

London, P. (1986). *Character Education, Social Conscience and Clinical Training.* Cambridge, Mass: Harvard Graduate School of Education.

Lyon, H. C. (1971). *Learning to feel-feeling to learn.* Columbus, OH: Charles E. Merrill.

Mayer, G. R. & Butterworth, A. (1979). A preventive approach to school violence and vandalism: An experimental study. *The Personnel and Guidance Journal,* 57, 436-441.

Morrison, D. M. (1985). Adolescent contraceptive behavior: A review. *Psychological Bulletin,* 98, 538-68.

Mosher, R. & Sprinthall, N. (1971) Deliberate psychological education. *The Counseling Psychologist,* 18, 3-82.

National Coalition of Advocates for Students (1985). *Barriers to Excellence: Our Children at Risk.* Boston, Mass: NCAS.

Newberg, N. A. & Love, W. E. (1982). Affective education addresses the basics. *Educational Leadership,* 40, 498-500.

New York State Governor's Youth Suicide Prevention Council (1985). *Interim Report.*

Norton, F. H. (1981). Foster care and the helping professions. *The Personnel and Guidance Journal,* 59, 156-159.

Pine, G. J. & Boy, A. V. (1977). *Learner-centered teaching: A humanistic view.* Denver: Love.

Ribner, N. & Ginn, R. (1975). Overcoming and managing depression. *The Personnel and Guidance Journal,* 53, 222-224.

Ringness, T. A. (1968). *Mental health in the schools.* New York: Random House.

Rogers, C. R. (1969). *Freedom to learn.* Columbus, OH: Charles E. Merrill.

Rogers, C. R. (1983). *Freedom to learn in the 80s.* Columbus, Charles E. Merrill.

Ryan, K. (1986). The New Moral Education. *Phi Delta Kappan,* 68, 4, 228-233.

Schappi, A. C. (1985). Report says millions of youths disconnected from society. *The Guidepost,* 28, 1 and 7.

Shaw, M. C. & Goodyear, R. K. (1984). Introduction to the special issue on primary prevention. *The Personnel and Guidance Journal,* 62, 444-445.

Skovholt, T. (1977). Issues in psychological education. *The Personnel and Guidance Journal,* 55, 472-475.

Sprinthall, N. A. (1980). Psychology for secondary schools: The saber-tooth curriculum revisited? *The American Psychologist,* 35, 336-347.

Stenstud, R. & Stenstud, K. (1983). Coping skills training: A systematic approach to stress management counseling. *The Personnel and Guidance Journal,* 61, 214-218.

Strother, D. B. (1986). Suicide among the young. *Phi Delta Kappan,* 67, 10, 756-759.

Takanishi, R., Deleon, P. H. & Pallack, M. S. (1983). Psychology and education: A continuing productive partnership. *The American Psychologist,* 38, 996-1000.

Thompson, A. P. (1982). Extramarital relations: Gaining greater awareness. *The Personnel and Guidance Journal,* 60, 101-105.

Wagschal, P. H. and Johnson, L. (1986). Children's views of the future: Innocence almost lost. *Phi Delta Kappan,* 67, 9, 666-668.

Weinstein, G. & Fantini, M. D. (1970). *Toward humanistic education.* New York: Praeger.

Weinstein, G. & Alschuler, A. (1985). Educating and counseling for self-knowledge development. *Journal of Counseling and Development,* 64, 1, 21-25.

Woods, E. (1977). Counseling minority students. *The Personnel and Guidance Journal,* 55, 416-418.

Woody, R. H. (1976). Sexism in child custody decisions. *The Personnel and Guidance Journal,* 54, 168-170.

Wynne, E. (ed.) (1984). *Developing Character and Transmitting Knowledge: Sustaining the Momentum for Reform in American Education.* Chicago: The Thanksgiving Statement Group.

CHAPTER II

TEACHING AND EDUCATIONAL APPROACHES TO FOSTER PSYCHOSOCIAL DEVELOPMENT

TEACHERS committed to meeting the psychosocial needs of students must be able to energize that commitment through teaching. This chapter describes teaching and educational approaches which can contribute to the psychosocial development of students. Each of these approaches can be applied independently or can be integrated with established patterns for teaching subject matter.

Teachers interested in applying these approaches can use this chapter as an overview or as a beginning point. The effectiveness of a particular approach will be realized when the original works of the approach are read, understood, applied, and adapted. Using short cuts in the application of psychosocial teaching approaches typically will not yield satisfying results. Satisfying results will occur when the teacher's application of a particular approach is based on an educated understanding and internalization of the approach. Fostering the psychosocial development of students cannot be accomplished solely by good intentions to humanize the teaching and learning processes. Love is not enough. Good intentions must be matched by an assimilation of the theory and practice behind the psychoeducational approach being utilized.

ACHIEVEMENT MOTIVATION

Alschuler (1973) is concerned with student motivation and indicates that a lack of motivation has led many students to waste their intellectual and psychosocial resources. They sit in our schools daring teachers and staff to detract them from their lack of interest in schooling and life. Without the intervention of the schools, these students all too often grow into depressed adults who can find little meaning from family life or their occupations. An undernourished desire to achieve in school finds its expression in an unmotivated adult life.

McMullen (1973) indicates that when a person's achievement motive is charged up: "People appear to use alert, self-confident, and going about the business of meeting realistic but challenging goals they've set for themselves. They are doing something better than they have done it before, or competing hard against someone else, or working on new approaches to solving tough problems. They are driving and competitive" (p. 642).

McMullen (1973) outlines a sequence of six steps which characterize an experience in achievement motivation. The purpose of such an experience is to encourage the student to engage in personal goal setting and attainment. The six steps are summarized as follows:

Step 1: Attending. The teacher must get the attention of students by developing a "grabber" which will interest students. Identifying and developing a "grabber" requires teacher sensitivity to the psychosocial needs of students.

Step 2: Experiencing. Through a competitive game or role-playing experience, students identify the behavior, thinking, or feeling that is associated with the achievement motive. They participate and talk about the degree to which they are motivated to compete.

Step 3: Conceptualizing. Students learn to label the thoughts, feelings, and behaviors that accompany achievement motivation. They use a special vocabulary to enable them to recognize certain motivation and achievement elements in themselves and others: achievement goals, world obstacles, personal obstacles, moderate risks, using concrete feedback, fear of failure, and hope of success.

Step 4: Relating. Students explore the relevance of this new motivation knowledge of their own values, goals, and behaviors. They discuss the need for affiliation and power and how they affect their interrelationships.

Step 5: Applying. Students are encouraged to apply their knowledge of their own personal achievement motive to their lives. They plan self-improvement projects based upon a clarified and improved achievement motive.

Step 6: Internalizing. Students internalize their achievement motive and apply it through practice. The teacher works out a schedule with students to enable them to keep track of their progress toward certain goals.

The effectiveness of an achievement motivation experience will largely depend upon a teacher's ability to explain its rationale to students and solicit their active participation. Stimulating student interest in achievement motivation will require teacher creativity, commitment, and leadership.

ADAPTIVE EDUCATION

What Ever Happened to Individualized Instruction?

Individualized instructional programs seemed to reach their peak in the mid-1970s. The term *individualized instruction* has fallen out of favor and interest in individualized instruction has declined in the past several years (Rothrock, 1982). Part of the problem in implementing individualized instruction has been the confusion surrounding the term itself. *Individualized instruction* has been defined as independent study, individual pacing, individual diagnosis, the achievement of individual outcomes, or a combination of these. Despite the diminution of interest in programs labeled as individualized the need for adapting education to individual differences remains an essential ingredient of quality education (Fenstermacher and Goodlad, 1983; Wang and Walberg, 1985). *Adpative education or adaptive instruction* are now terms in vogue which describe programs which attempt to use a variety of curricula and instructional strategies in a manner best suited to each student, teacher, and class. (Waxman, Wang, Anderson, and Walberg, 1985).

Adaptive instruction is based on two premises: (1) students learn in different ways and at different rates, and (2) identification and accommodation of these individual differences are necessary for efficient learning to take place. Adaptive programs use a variety of curricula and a wide range of instructional strategies that have proven to be effective in many types of classroom settings and with diverse students.

Adaptive instruction is characterized by the following (Waxman, Wang, Anderson, and Walberg, 1985):

1. Instruction is based on the assessed needs and capabilties of each student.
2. Materials and procedures permit each student to progress at a pace suited to his or her abilities and interests.

3. Periodic evaluations to inform students of their progress toward achieving skills, knowledge, and understanding.
4. The assumption by each student of responsibilty for diagnosing his or her current needs and abilities; for planning individual learning activities; for pursuing those planned activities, and for evaluating the learning outcomes.
5. The provision of alternative activities and materials to help each student acquire essential academic skills.
6. Students have a choice in selecting educational goals, outcomes, and activities.
7. Students help one another to pursue individual goals and cooperate in achieving group goals.

A quantitative synthesis of thirty-eight research studies conducted over a ten year period shows that adaptive instruction significantly improves student learning and psychosocial development. Adaptive instruction programs achieved similar outcomes despite differences in specific program features, social context, grade level, or type of students.

Strong and consistent effects were noted in the research synthesis findings. Adaptive instruction produced substantial positive result in students' cognitive outcomes but had even stronger effects on affective and behavioral outcomes. (Waxman, Wang, Anderson, and Walberg, 1985). The findings of the research synthesis on adaptive instruction suggests that individualizing instruction to respond to the learning characteristics and needs of individual students can be much more effective in obtaining psychosocial and academic outcomes than whole group instruction.

The literature on effective teaching tends to regard as ineffective such features of adaptive instruction as choice for students. Yet Wang and Wolberg (1985) found that these features actually facilitate student learning. Moreover, they found that adaptive instruction produced superior outcomes in psychosocial areas that many students, parents, and educators value: constructive student interactions, independent work, individual self diagnosis and prescription, cooperative learning, and exploration by students. Strother (1985) in examining these result concluded, "The findings . . . emphasize the striking differences that exist between conventional teacher-directed, group paced instruction in large and small groups and instructional approaches that give students an active role in mediating their own learning."

The research indicates that adaptive instruction is advancing technically, becoming more practical, and its theory becoming more refined. Based on the findings of ten years of research Wang and Walberg (1985) offer several generalizations about adaptive instruction:

1. Information about individual differences in learning should guide instructional planning.
2. Learners' differences are best described in terms of the knowledge and competence they possess for specific learning tasks and the ways in which they process information, not in terms of their performance on tests or other traditional evaluative measures.
3. The learning needs of individual students can be identified through analyses of students' characteristics, cognitive operations, and affective responses as they acquire and seek to retain knowledge and skills.
4. Adaptive instruction is feasible in regular school settings.

In summary, the findings of the studies on adaptive instruction are grounds for optimism about the value of individualizing instruction. They affirm that a number of instructional features combined and carefully coordinated to adapt to individual needs and capacities yield significant cognitive and psychosocial outcomes.

ADLERIAN APPROACH

The application of Adlerian psychology within the classroom to address problems of discipline, learning, and social and emotional development was pioneered by Dinkmeyer and Dreikurs (1963) and has been systematically developed by Dinkmeyer into practical training and curricula materials (Dinkmeyer & McKay, 1976, 1983, Dinkmeyer, McKay, Dinkmeyer Jr., 1980, Dinkmeyer, 1970, 1973).

According to Dinkmeyer (1980) certain principles are basic to understanding human behavior. Once we accept and internalize these principles, tensions are reduced, and we are able to contribute to the development of students. The following Adlerian principles about human behavior provide directions for the analysis of the interactions which occur on a daily basis in classrooms in teacher-student transactions and also in the interaction between members of groups:

(1) Behavior is understood on a holistic basis and comprehended in terms of its unity and pattern.

(2) The significance of behavior lies in its social consequences.
(3) The individual is understood as a social being whose behavior makes sense in terms of its social content and social context.
(4) Motivation is best comprehended by observing how the individual seeks to be known or become significant.
(5) Behavior is goal-directed and purposeful. We are led by our goals, not driven by causes.
(6) Belonging is a basic requisite for human development.
(7) Behavior is always understood in terms of the internal frame of reference of the individual, the individual's perceptual field.

Dinkmeyer and Dreikurs (1963) and Dreikurs, Greenwald, and Pepper (1971) indicate that students' misbehavior reflects one of four goals. Children usually misbehave because they (a) want attention, (b) seek power, (c) are looking for revenge, or (d) have chosen to display their inadequacy.

These goals can be diagnosed by a teacher who is aware of his or her own feelings. If you feel annoyed, the goal of misbehavior is attention. If you feel angry, the goal is power. If you feel hurt, the goal is revenge. And if you feel like giving up, the goal is inadequacy. Each goal indicates specific ways the teacher can learn to respond more effectively to misbehavior. The teacher's goal is to help students increase self-esteem and feelings of worth so they are free and motivated to cooperate in the give and take of life (Dinkmeyer and Dinkmeyer, Jr., 1980)

Destructive goals can be directed to positive goals, thus

From: Attention getting	To: Involvement Belonging by contributing
From: Power	To: Autonomy Responsibility of one's behavior Self-discipline Resourcefulness
From: Revenge	To: Justice Fairness Cooperation
From: Display of inadequacy	To: Withdrawal from conflict Ignoring provocation

The task of the teacher is to build a relationship in which the teacher's and the student's goals are aligned (working in the same direction). This necessitates that teachers understand the goals of misbehavior and are skilled in motivating and redirecting children toward the positive goals. Dinkmeyer indicates that the teacher who is effective in discipline:

1. Understands the meaning of behavior. All psychological movement has a purpose. The teacher's feelings and the student's response to correction will clarify the goal.
2. Pinpoints the real issue. Educators do not merely deal with symptoms but with the real issue, which is usually the goal of attention getting, power seeking, revenge, and the display of inadequacy.
3. Involves the student in considering the alternatives and choosing, thereby developing self-evaluation.
4. Gets a commitment to a specific course of action; a contract for motivation modification.

Central to the Adlerian approach in working with children and their families is the process of *encouragement*. *Encouragement* is the process of increasing the individual's self-esteem and feelings of worth, and thereby enhancing the self-concept.

The encourager is a talent scout who is able to identify and affirm any possible resource. When we encourage we can see how even a negative trait, such as stubbornness, has the potential to become positive (e.g., determination) or that the other side of the coin to being aggressive can be being involved. Think of a specific liability in a person. Can you see a way it can become a resource?

Through encouragement, one conveys support and the attitude: You can do it. Go ahead, give it a try. Mistakes are only guides for learning.

Adlerian Approach: C-Groups

Dinkmeyer and Losoncy (1980) suggest that an essential skill each teacher needs is the ability to encourage. Teacher training and teacher in-service programs should be focusing on a competency-based curriculum in encouragement.

Such a curriculum would include the following skills: listening and empathy; focusing on strengths, assets, and resources; the development of perceptual alternatives; focusing on efforts and contributions; identifying and combatting discouraging fictional beliefs; and encouraging commitment and movement. Dinkmeyer and Carlson (1973, 1975) have developed the "C" group as a procedure for helping teachers to change and become more effective in developing students. The C-group recognizes a basic learning principle: If one is to assist another to learn and change, there must be access to the affective and cognitive domains. Feelings, values and attitudes must be openly revealed and considered when discussing facts and theory. The dichotomy between one's emotions and intellect, often present in learning, cannot be permitted. There must be a combination of the didactic and experiential approaches, which enables the teacher to understand what is preventing effective functioning.

The C group approach is not to be confused with a T-group in that it goes beyond consideration of the process and self to examination of the transaction between teacher and student and the application of specific procedures. It also causes the teacher to see how attitudes and feelings may keep the teacher from changing. A process which combines the didactic and experiential approaches is thereby achieved.

The new approach was labeled C-group because so many of its components begin with the letter C.

Collaboration: The group works together on mutual concerns.

Consultation: The interaction within the group helps the members to develop new approaches to relationships with children.

Clarification: The group clarifies for each member what it is he really believes and how congruent or incongruent his behavior is with what he believes.

Confidential: Discussions are not repeated outside the group.

Confrontation: The group expects each individual to see him/herself, his/her purposes, and his/her attitudes and to be willing to confront other members of the group.

Communication: Members communicate not only ideas, but personal meanings and feelings.

Concern: The group shows that it is involved both with its members and with children.

Commitment: The group develops a commitment to change. Participants are concerned with recognizing that they can really change only themselves. They are expected to develop a specific commitment which involves an action they will take before the next C-group to change their approach to a problem.

Teachers are taught through the "C" group experience to utilize four procedures for improving communication. Teachers learn to recognize that in most communication with children, they are sending messages with emotional as well as intellectual content. Thus, the procedure in communication involves:

(1) Indicating that the teacher understands their feelings. Through reflective listening the teacher clarifies that the teacher got the message. "You feel angry; you are very disappointed."
(2) Indicating how their behavior and feelings are affecting the teacher. Teachers state their own feelings and how the student's behavior comes over to them.
(3) Utilizing conflict resolution to come to an agreement by reaching a solution that is agreeable to the teacher and the child, taking into account the thoughts, feelings, and behavior of both parties.
(4) When agreement cannot be reached through the hearing and sharing of feelings and conflict resolution procedures, the teacher permits the child to experience the logical consequences. This is done in a friendly but firm fashion which does not interfere or contrive to make the teacher a winner.

Adlerian Approach: DUSO

One of the most popular applications of Adlerian psychology in fostering the psychosocial development of students is DUSO. DUSO (Developing Understanding of Self and Others) is an educational program consisting of kits of activities and materials designed by Dinkmeyer (1970, 1973) and Dinkmeyer and Dinkmeyer (1982) to facilitate the social and emotional development of children. The kits come in two levels: DUSO Kit D-1 (Kindergarten and Lower Primary) and DUSO Kit D-2 (Upper Primary and Grade 4).

The DUSO programs are based on Adlerian psychology and the premise that every child, in the process of growing up, is confronted with normal developmental problems and that the classroom teacher can help children with these problems. To be most effective in this role, the teacher needs the assistance and direction provided by programs of planned experiences and materials. The two DUSO kits provide such programs which can be carried out with a minimum of preparation.

The DUSO activities make extensive use of listening, inquiry, and discussion approaches to learning.

The wide variety of materials and activities provided in the DUSO kits, allows the teacher to select the approach which is most appropriate for each unique group of children.

DUSO Kit D-1

The program for this kit is organized around the following eight unit themes:

   I. Understanding and Accepting Self
  II. Understanding Feelings
 III. Understanding Others
  IV. Understanding Independence
   V. Understanding Goals and Purposeful Behavior
  VI. Understanding Mastery, Competence, and Resourcefulness
 VII. Understanding Emotional Maturity
VIII. Understanding Choices and Consequences

The activities of the program have been designed to achieve three basic goals: (1) learning more words for feelings; (2) learning that feelings, goals and behavior are dynamically related; (3) learning to talk more freely about feelings, goals, and behavior. The D-1 program is presented in a teacher's manual containing enough activities for an entire year. It also contains general guidelines for presenting the various types of activities as well as specific guidelines for individual day-to-day activities. Each group of activities, approximately one week in length, contains a problem situation, a story, a role playing activity, a puppet activity, a list of supplementary activities and supplementary reading.

Included in the kit are: two story books, posters, records and cassettes, puppet and role playing cards, puppets, puppet props, and group discussion cards.

DUSO Kit D-2

The D-2 program is built around the following eight unit themes:

   I. Toward Self-identity
  II. Toward Friendship
 III. Toward Responsible Interdependence
  IV. Toward Self-Reliance
   V. Toward Resourcefulness and Purposefulness
  VI. Toward Competence
 VII. Toward Emotional Stability
VIII. Toward Responsible Choice Making

The foregoing themes are interrelated by the following general objectives: (1) to develop understanding and positive valuing of one's unique self; (2) to develop understanding of interpersonal relationships; (3) to develop understanding of the purposive nature of human behavior; (4) to develop understanding of dynamic interrelationships among ideas, feelings, beliefs, and behavior in order to express one's feelings accurately; (5) to develop understanding of competence and the components of accomplishment.

The D-2 manual contains enough activities for an entire year. It presents general guidelines for the program as well as specific guides for day-to-day activities. Each cycle of activities, which is about one week's program contains a story, problem situation, role playing activity, puppet activity, discussion picture, career awareness activity, supplementary activities, and supplementary reading.

Included in the kit are: self- and social development activity cards, discussion pictures, posters, puppet and role activity cards, cassettes, puppets, career awareness cards, and discussion guide cards.

CHALLENGE EDUCATION

The shifting circumstances in post-industrial America that are changing daily life, the nature of work, and the futures our studens will face are profoundly affecting education. These circumstances demand that the schools prepare students to cope with the crucial issues of work, social ethics, change, and survival and offer an education which will build a sense of community, a sensitive civility, and a cooperative future. In response to the failures of the traditional educational paradigm, Maurice Gibbons reawakens us to the possibilities created by a totally new conception of schooling—Challenge Education (Gibbons, 1984).

According to Gibbons the continuing failures of the traditional paradigm require that we shift into a new paradigm which will: produce better education with fewer resources and restore the education profession to a place of pride in the community; make public education a highly desirable alternative that meets the challenge of new technology, enable students to deal with a rapidly changing society and workplace, and prepare them to deal with the incredible national and global problems we now face. In addition the new paradigm must teach high-order skills through high-impact teaching methods, develop the talents of all individuals as fully as possible, cultivate social skills and responsibility, encourage students to develop their inner drives and express them through their learning activities, and insure that students are well-equipped for a lifetime of learning.

Gibbons (1984:594) calls for an educational paradigm that meets several criteria. The new paradigm must be a process that enables students to design and manage their own learning. The process must be eminently practical, adaptable to all grade levels, and appropriate for use throughout life.

The paradigm proposed by Gibbons in Challenge Education and is built on the Walkabout philosophy which he articulated in the seventies (Gibbons, 1974). Challenge Education reflects the principle that we learn and grow best when we are challenged. Challenge Education teaches students to carry out a five part process (Gibbons, 1984:594).

(1) Goal setting—reviewing the choices for learning, making decisions about what is important to learn, and setting a clear goal to pursue; (2) strategic planning—outlining exactly what has to be learned and accomplished, selecting those methods of learning that are appropriate for the task and for one's learning style, and organizing a plan of action for achieving the goal; (3) self-management—learning to organize and manage time and effort by recognizing and solving such personal problems as disorder and lack of self-discipline, when they arise, and by securing the resources necessary for implementing the learning plan; (4) self-evaluation—determining in advance what would constitute a high-quality learning outcome, seeking and using information about one's progress, and making a final judgment about one's success; and (5) review—looking back over what was learned and achieved, considering what worked well and what didn't (in order to focus on key improvements in the next cycle), and only then making decisions about the next goal and endeavor.

This process can be introduced in a simple form with any easy task at any level of schooling. As students progress, they can apply the process to tasks of increasing complexity and duration, until eventually they are designing and carrying out major portions of their own learning programs. In the years following school, the process will still be appropriate for learning and doing, for personal and professional development, and for strategic planning in business, industry, and government. It is the basic process for effective action and continuous improvement.

To help students learn and internalize the five part process Challenge Education organizes instruction, learning activities, practices, and context in ways that have a significant impact not only on students' ability to direct their own learning but also, holistically, on all aspects of their development. To manage student learning so that students become self directed, learners depends upon a balance between reflection and action. This balance can be developed through the working journal. In the working journal (Gibbons 1984:597) students record what they are learning, explore their talents and budding interests, examine the struggles they are facing, describe their emerging visions of what they want to accomplish and in what ways they wish to be different, tell the stories of their experiences, and outline the ideas they are beginning to shape. The working journal is not only a record of the students' personal journey toward responsible, self-directed maturity, but also a means of shaping that journey. From this recorded reflection, the student's goals and plans emerge.

In order to help students transform their reflections into strategies for action, the teacher can show them how to write formal proposals, contracts, or plans that outline what they intend to do and how they intend to do it. With a detailed plan of action in hand, a student can negotiate his or her proposal with the teacher and, perhaps, with a parent or other adult who will be involved. This negotiation enables the teacher to consult with the student, to confirm the student's intentions, to offer appropriate assistance, and to protect the student from dangerous risks. But always the prevailing spirit will be to confirm and enhance, not to rescue and control. In the pursuit of a personal goal, failure is another opportunity to learn and a guide to future decisions.

The plan then becomes the student's agenda for action, and the teacher's record of mutually negotiated agreements becomes a reference for monitoring the student's progress. Beginners who are developing plans for brief activities may simply state an intention and a procedure. Later, students may be required to negotiate detailed proposals that deal with all aspects of the strategic planning process, from vision and goal to demonstration and celebration.

Challenge Education (Gibbons, 1984: 598-599) features a three-block four-mode program structure. Schooling is divided into three blocks of four years each. The first four years are referred to as the Incoming Block, the second four years as the Developing Block, and the third four years as the Outgoing Block. In any given year of the block students are exposed to four basic modes of teaching and learning: directed, assigned, self directed, and open.

These modes represent a progressive increase in students' control over the program and a progressive change in the role of the teacher. In the directed mode, the teacher plans and presents all instruction. In the assigned mode, the teacher assigns a goal or purpose, but students plan their own programs to achieve it. In the self-directed mode, students choose their own goals and the plans for achieving them—but all within the framework of a specific subject, course, or field of study. In the open mode, students choose their own goals and fields of study and establish their own learning plans—with negotiation, but not restriction. The open mode begins in the first year and grows in importance until, in the 12th year, it becomes the basic mode. The assigned, directed, and self-directed modes serve as preparation for the open mode, in which students clarify and pursue their own intentions, conducting their own searches for meaning and becoming.

Throughout the three blocks and in all four modes, students regularly work in large groups, small groups, and individually—balancing the public and the private, the active and the reflective, the social and the personal. Throughout the program, teachers are open with students about decisions, sharing why and how they made their plans, often including students in their planning sessions, and leading students through planning sessions of their own.

In the Developing Block, the emphasis is on focused competence. The four modes now become four aspects of each field of study. There are six such fields: scientific and logical inquiry; creative expression; the development of practical and vocational skills, mastery of an academic field, the practice of service to others, and lifestyle development, which includes fitness, adventure, and recreation. The seventh field of study is the student's own invention, using the open mode. Here the student continues to explore, but he or she now plans longer projects and is expected to focus on at least one area in which to become demonstrably expert. The focus in the fields of study is on becoming active in them and knowledgeable about them.

Challenge Education has been implemented and adapted in more than 150 schools. Several of these schools have won statewide awards for improvement and excellence. Challenge Education is a significant educational approach because it embodies the integration of cognitive and affective development to produce students who can take charge not only of their learning but also their lives. It teaches students powerful ways to learn and teaches them to think, to act, and to contribute.

Challenge Education is holistic, developing in concert both desirable inner states and the strateties for successful learning and action. It is the appropriate form of education for citizens of a participatory democracy. It involves members of a community in clearly defined ways that make education an enterprise that they share with school.

It involves teachers in high-teach roles that no high-tech device can replace—roles that enable them to make significant, observable differences in the lives of their students. Challenge Education provides excellent preparation for students entering a world where there are many personal and public problems to solve and where the only certainty is change.

CLASSROOM MEETINGS

Glasser (1969) indicates that the major problem of the schools is that of failure. Ways must be discovered so that more children can succeed. Too many children find their identity through withdrawal or delinquency. Glasser recommends several approaches for reaching failure or negatively oriented children, including no punishment (but discipline), no excuses, positive involvement, and individual responsibility. Among Glasser's most significant procedures is the use of the class, led by the teacher, as a discussion group, which daily spends some time developing the social responsibility necessary to solve behavioral and educational problems within the class. Glasser's concept of "the classroom meeting" has been implemented in classrooms and is a prominent approach for fostering students' psychosocial development.

There are three types of classroom meetings: *the social-problem solving* meeting, concerned with the students' social behavior in school; the *open-ended* meeting, concerned with intellectually important subjects; and the *educational-diagnostic* meeting, concerned with how well the youngsters understand the concept of the curriculum. Glasser (1969) recommends the following guidelines for conducting these meetings.

1. All problems relative to the class as a group and to any individual in the class are eligible for discussion. A problem can be brought up by an individual student or by the teacher.
2. The discussion itself should always be directed toward solving the problem; the solution should never include punishment or fault finding. The orientation of the meetings is always positive, always toward a solution. It is important in class meetings for the teacher but not the class to be non-judgmental. The teacher may feed back to the class the class attitude, but should give opinions sparingly.
3. Meetings should always be conducted with the teacher and all the students seated in a tight circle. Classroom meetings should be short (10 to 30 minutes) for children in the lower grades and should increase in length (30 to 45 minutes) for older pupils. The duration of a meeting is less important than its regular occurrence and the pertinence of the problems discussed.

4. The teacher sits in a different place in the circle each day and makes a systematic effort to arrange seating so that the meeting will be most productive. Boys who squirm and nudge one another can be separated. Boys and girls are interspersed as are the vocal and quiet children.
5. Subjects for open-ended discussion may be introduced by the teacher or by the class. The teacher encourages the class to think of relevant subjects.
6. Disciplinary meetings should not be repetitive. Discussing a problem-child day after day does more harm than good. Open-ended discussions that are interesting enough to attract the participation and cooperation of problem children lead to improved behavior.
7. With primary grade children, meetings are more effective if they are held before recess, before lunch, or before the school's closing time. No meeting should be prolonged and become an excuse for the children to avoid other responsibilities during the day.
8. A teacher avoids interrupting a student to correct affective ideas or perceptions. A student corrected while struggling to express an idea or perception may withdraw and never volunteer again.
9. All students must be accepted as potentially capable, not as handicapped. We cannot change their past, but we can give them the opportunity to have a more personally satisfying educational experience in the present. (pp. 122-160.)

Sorsdahl and Sanche (1985) indicate that classroom meetings can help students to enhance their problem-solving skills, decision-making skills, accept responsibility, and improve their interpersonal skills. They also state that classroom meetings have significant potential for providing preventive counseling services to large numbers of children through their regular classroom teachers.

CURRICULUM OF CONCERN

Borton's (1970) affective learning model is three-tiered. He was concerned with follow-up learning after evaluating his experience with a summer project in Philadelphia which made great use of affective learning techniques in combination with open education approaches. The experience for teachers and students was a good one, but some problems were identified through feedback from students who had participated in the program. As one girl put it, she was happier but uncomfortable outside of the summer project school, because she was not free as she had learned to be there and did not know how to be happy when she was not free. This suggested to Borton that something had to be added to the learning experience to help students carry through and resolve problems connected with the changes in themselves.

Borton (1970) developed the *What-So What-Now What* system of learning. *What* connotes sensing a new stimulus or experience; *So What* is the transforming of the stimulus into some kind of meaning for the individual; *Now What* is the "Acting function that rehearses possible actions and picks one to put into the world as an overt response" (p. 78). He concluded that teaching students how to handle their concerns and feelings and to understand and be responsive to others around them is not enough. "Bringing such concerns to the surface without providing a means (a process) for dealing with them can turn a curriculum of concerns into a curriculum of anxiety" (p. 80). He cites the example of a boy who after going through the summer project had trouble convincing his father he was mature enough to take responsibility for a theater group in addition to his other responsibilities. Through roleplaying the conflict at a reunion with other students from the project, he was able to see how his father perceived him and the problem and worked out ideas for a successful solution.

Borton suggests that pressure juxtaposed with a quiet contemplative time produces insight and learning. "The combination of the two modes creates an effect similar to that which a person experiences when hours of difficult work on a problem get him nowhere and then suddenly the missing link pops into his head while reading Dr. Seuss to the children" (p. 89).

DELIBERATE PSYCHOLOGICAL EDUCATION

Mosher and Sprinthall (1971), with several colleagues, developed a curriculum consisting of systematic experiences designed to directly influence the psychological development of adolescents. The curriculum draws from developmental, counseling, and educational psychology and from the humanities and the result is a series of coordinated courses focusing on various stages of the human life cycle. Adolescent students study the principles of early childhood development, child development and care, middle childhood, adolescence, interpersonal relations and marriage, career decision making, and the psychology of aging. A significant part of the curriculum is experiential and adolescents learn through such activities as tutoring peers who are handicapped.

A prominent component of the curriculum is the seminar and practicum in counseling which teaches high school students the simple fundamentals of the counseling process. This component is intended to make the student's psychological development a primary objective of a school's curriculum. The model for instruction is essentially a didactic seminar and a supervised practicum. In the first phase of a 4-to-6-week course, students role play the counseling process using tape recordings. In the second phase the student's role-playing experiences are replaced by real talk about themselves. In the last phase the students shift from counseling each other to counseling peers. Supervision, seminars, audiotape and videotape feedback and peer critique are tools used throughout the course.

Another major component in the curriculum is cross-age teaching and learning. Adolescent students are provided with the opportunity to teach elementary school children individually and in groups, inside the classroom or outside. Students in this component learn about themselves, as well as about teaching young children, and the course is seen as an alternative way of studying psychology. Students have a supervised teaching experience coupled with ongoing seminars and reading in contemporary education and pedagogical methods. The teaching skills which the students learn, and the effect on their self-perception and sense of competence in perfroming an adult job, are important concomitants. The program is designed not to train classroom helpers but as a component of deliberate psychological education for adolescent students.

Improvisational drama is another approach in deliberate psychological education. It offers students an opportunity to study the individual's expressive behavior—both verbal and physical—and thus gain insights into their own positive and negative attitudes. By employing dance and drama techniques, the teacher helps students bring forth the dramatic content which is highly personal and typically is very relevant to what adolescents currently are thinking and feeling. Students learn how they are perceived by other people, they discover feelings about what it means to be male or female, and they explore alternative ways of responding in psychologically threatening situations.

The improvisational drama curriculum concentrates on three basic objectives: (1) to help students achieve more self-knowledge through a study of their expressive behavior; (2) to free people to enjoy responding capacities they might not have known they had; and (3) to help people learn to relate more candidly and effectively to other people. To achieve these objectives the teacher focuses on the four bases of the curriculum through a series of activities: physical freeing, concentration, believability, and relationships.

In the child development component of deliberate psychological education teenage students assume a variety of roles in a nursery: helper, storyteller, someone to talk to, participant, initiator, and observer. In seminars students discuss assigned reading materials and films on child development, share observations of children, study videotapes of children's behavior in the nursery, and occasionally participate in workshops on materials and activities used with nursery school children.

The overall strategy for improving deliberate psychological education involves the steps of clinical research: a cyclical process involving the framing of a course of action after reflection, the implementation of it, evaluation of the outcomes, and the framing of a new course of action. The method is an alternating cycle of reflection and action, of hard thinking, and exacting practice so that conceptualization and practice is validated one against the other.

While deliberate psychological education has been developed and tested primarily with high school adolescents, its potential for application in the middle and elementary schools are obvious. More recently (Hatfield, 1984), attention has focused on preparing pre-service and in-service teachers in a variety of cognitive and experiential learning experiences designed to familiarize them with the goals and processes of the approach.

GESTALT APPROACH

Perls, Hefferline, and Goodman (1951) fathered the Gestalt approach to individual and group counseling. Perls is most associated with the approach, and he believes that one's awareness to self and others is the foundation for psychological stability and indicated that this lack of self-awareness causes one to be insensitive to those life experiences which can disrupt our psychosocial stability. He indicates that psychosocial growth and maturity occurs when one is first in touch with personal psychosocial needs. Perls also states that we learn to wear masks and hide our feelings from outselves and others. Eventually, such a repression results in the true self being lost and a multitude of feelings, especially anger, eventually becoming bottled up inside. This repression of feelings can simmer over a period of years and eventually explode and cause emotional harm to the self and others. According to the Gestalt view, it is better for the individual to siphon off these feelings (express them) during their formative stages so that they will not be psychosocially incapacitating during later stages of life. There are many adults who are frustrated and angry because they do not possess the ability to express their feelings in safe ways. They have never learned to do so. Unfortunately, for themselves and others, they have explosive expressions of these feelings at home, at work, and in their neighborhoods. Gestaltists want school-age youngsters to learn how to identify these feelings and learn how to express them, as they develop, in safe ways which contribute to one's psychosocial stability. Passons (1975) indicates that Gestalt approaches can develop self-awareness and understanding and promote a responsible and safe process for expressing feelings.

Remer and Schrader (1981) have developed Gestalt units for classroom use designed to increase awareness of one's emotional environment, internal feelings, and teach students how to be more aware of these external and internal emotions and their effective expression. They identify three important units which teachers can use with students.

UNIT 1: External Awareness

Awareness of the five senses:
1. Introduction to the word "aware"
2. Visual awareness
3. Awareness of smells
4. Tactile awareness
5. Sound awareness
6. Taste and the other four senses

UNIT 2: Internal Awareness

1. Awareness of the outside of the body
2. Awareness of the inside of the body
3. Fantasy trip
4. Discussion

UNIT 3: Expressing Feelings

1. Body trip
2. Freeze activity
3. Sharing (of feelings)

In a Gestalt approach the teacher participates with students in each of the preceding units and learns more about the students as experiencing persons as well as the students learning about the teacher. This increased awareness of each other enables a respectful and accepting bond to develop among those in a classroom. When academic units are introduced they are better absorbed by the mind because negative emotions are not impairing its ability to learn.

THE HUMAN DEVELOPMENT PROGRAM

The Human Development Program (HDP), developed by Bessell and Palomares (1967), with the aid and sponsorship of the Institute of Personal Effectiveness in Children (IPE), is designed to promote psychosocial growth in children. Growth in self-understanding, self-confidence, and social interaction is facilitated by structured learning experiences which utilize the techniques of group dynamics. Through small group experiences, the student progresses through the planned Human Development Program and develops greater personal and social effectiveness.

The Human Development Program is designed to facilitate learning in the affective domain, especially in three areas of emotional development: self-understanding (awareness), self-confidence (mastery), and human relations (social interaction).

The program was developed with a focus on beginning with preschool children and continuing through the grades in order to determine if effective, large-scale prevention measures could be taken that would assure normal, healthy psychosocial growth, much as a sound, balanced diet can ensure the development of children who are physically normal and healthy. The program capitalizes on the basic drives of children to achieve mastery and gain approval. It seems that persons who have not had the HDP experience at the preschool and elementary levels can still profit from an equivalent experience geared to their present stage of development.

The approach employs cumulative, sequential activities on a regular basis as outline or suggested by HDP guides or manuals. Its major vehicle is the "Magic Circle" (8-12 members) which meets for 25-50 minutes per session. Responding to statements like "Something that makes me feel good" (awareness), "I can do something well" (mastery), and "I did something that someone liked" (social interaction), the participant learns to practice awareness, to dispel the delusion of uniqueness, to be an effective communicator, to develop independence and the ability to influence environment, and to discover what works and what doesn't work with people (personal/social effectiveness).

The thrust of an HDP is on prevention. It is a circle or group of children sharing and listening and communicating which is structured to promote and develop self-confidence, and social understanding and interaction — ingredients believed to be necessary to become a psychosocially stable adult.

The leader supplies the statement which can later be discussed by the circle or group. The leader facilitates sharing, listening, feedback and acceptance. The leader does not prove, analyze, or evaluate and prohibits (in a gentle, but firm way) participants from engaging in this behavior. While both similarities and differences as well as both positive and negative aspects of affective experience are the foci of HDP, the atmosphere is one of acceptance, communication, and listening. Each student has an opportunity to participate in each session and is gently encouraged to do so, but is also made to feel comfortable if there is a reluctance to participate.

HUMANISTIC EDUCATION

Weinstein and Fantini (1970) identified three important concerns shared by most children: Concerns about self image, disconnectedness (how one fits or does not fit into one's world or the whole scheme of things), and control over one's life. These may be shown in different ways, depending on a student's cultural background or developmental level, but they are evident in all school-age children. Part of the teacher's job is to discern how these concerns are expressed and to respond to them during the process of teaching. Many examples could be cited, but most people are able to think of several where an item of immediate concern to the students was ignored or squelched by a teacher as a digression from the lesson, even when it could easily have been incorporated into the lesson as a complementary learning experience. Weinstein and Fantini indicate that students are more interested in these "digressions" because they often relate directly to important issues and decisions in their lives. Moreover, their subsequent classroom behavior is more likely to be affected directly by such "digressions." The process of learning, then, becomes a matter of linking the curriculum to the basic intrinsic concerns and feelings of students.

Following are the major elements in a humanistic approach for fostering the psychosocial development of students (Weinstein & Fantini, 1970).

1. *Identifying the learning group:* the teacher must analyze the social, economic, geographic, cultural and ethnic, as well as the developmental level of the class.
2. *Identifying shared concerns:* what concerns does the class have as a group?
3. *Understanding underlying factors:* how do the children manifest their concerns and their behavioral changes, what different ways do they have of expressing them?
4. *Organizing ideas:* teachers may construct lessons around core themes. "Hooks" or dideas help to clarify the children's experiences and help the teacher to give a discussion a focus.
5. *Content vehicles:* may be traditional or non-traditional subjects, such as classroom or out-of-classroom incidents affecting the students, media or field trip experiences, or the chidlren themselves.
6. *Learning skills:* examples include evaluating, problem solving, hypothesizing, planning, predicting, finding alternatives, and awareness of others. Useful steps in the process are:
   - recognition and description of what is happening
   - understanding of how others do the same
   - comparison of responses and feelings
   - analyze varied responses and consequences
   - test altneratives
   - make decisions
7. *Teaching procedures:* procedures should be based on the pupils' learning style. Whatever the procedures selected, teachers should develop interaction systems that support the learner emotionally and strengthen feelings of self-worth.
8. *Evaluation:* the teacher evaluates the teaching and learning experience periodically. Questions the teacher may ask are: Have behaviors

changed? Were the discussion topics the most appropriate or are there better ones that could have been used? Were the skills and the teaching procedures the best to achieve the goals originally set?

Shapiro (1985), in his empirical analysis of operating values in humanistic education, has identified fifteen value principles which characterize a humanistic approach to teaching:

1. Process oriented ("How" more important than "what" or "why")
2. Self-determination (autonomy, self-direction and self-evaluation)
3. Connectedness (empathy, pluralism, relationships)
4. Relevancy (personal meaning and readiness to learn)
5. Integration (affect with cognition, living with learning)
6. Context (awareness of environment, politics, and culture)
7. Affective (experiential) bias (preference for concrete feelings and sensing)
8. Innovation (social change orientation, anti-authoritarian)
9. Democratic participation (equity, consensus, collaboration)
10. Personal-growth oriented (self-actualization through self-awareness)
11. People oriented (people over production)
12. Individualism (authenticity, freedom, person over state)
13. Reality claims (defines "reality" as concrete and pragmatic)
14. Evaluation ("formative" over "summative," quality over quantity)
15. Variety-creativity (spontaneity, originality, diversity) (p. 99).

Signs of Creative Teaching: Research Hypotheses for Humanistic Education

One of the best resources for testable research hypotheses of humanistic education is ASCD's 1962 Yearbook, *Perceiving, Behaving, Becoming* regarded as a classic contribution to humanistic education. (Aspy and Hicks, 1978). The yearbook offers a guideline for humanistic education and principles about humane people and facilitative schools. In Chapter 14 it delineates fourteen signs of creative teaching and learning (Coombs, 1962) which have been translated into effective research hypotheses by Aspy and Hicks (1978).

Sign I: Less teacher domination; more faith that children can find answers satisfying to themselves.

Rationale—Domination lessens when teachers use fewer controlling behaviors. Student initiation increases when students are more satisfied with their classwork.

Sign II: Less teacher talk; more listening to children, allowing them to use the teacher and the group as a sounding board when ideas are explored.
Rationale—The less the teacher talks and the more students talk, the greater the possibility that both teachers and students are listening to students.

Sign III: Less questioning for the right answers; more open-ended questions with room for different and the exploration of many answers.
Rationale—The measurement of this sign is very straightforward. The greater the number of open-ended questions, the more the interaction is characteristic of creative teaching.

Sign IV: Less destructuve criticism; more teacher help which directs the child's attention back to his or her own feelings for clarification and understanding.
Rationale—The measurement of this sign is straightforward. The greater the rate of destructively critical remarks the higher the possibility that the student learns that there is something bad about him or her as a person.

Sign V: Less emphasis on failure; more acceptance of mistakes. More feeling on the part of the child that when he or she makes a mistake it is done, accepted, and that is it. As one child said, "She doesn't rub salt in."
Rationale—The larger (numerically) the ratio of "good try" to "bad try" answers, the greater the possibility that students will learn not to feel "put down" by their failures.

Sign VI: Children's work is appreciated, but praise is not used to put words in the mouths of children.
Rationale—The larger (numerically) the ratio between the invitational and manipulative remarks by the teacher, the greater the possibility that the student will learn that he or she is appreciated but not manipulated.

Sign VII: Goals are clearly defined; structure is understood and accepted by the group.
Rationale—The greater the percentage of students who (a) know the goals of the class and (b) like them, the greater the possibility that the class is meaningful to them.

Sign VIII: Within appropriate limits, children are given responsibility and freedom to work. "For once a teacher told us we could do it ourselves and really meant it."
Rationale—The larger (numerically) the ratio between the assisting and interfacing behaviors, the greater the possibilty the student will learn that he/she does have responsibility and freedom to work.

Sign IX: Children are free to express what they feel and seem secure in their knowledge that the teacher likes them as they are.
Rationale—A student indicates that his or her expressions of feeling are accepted when he or she expands on them as a result of the teacher's re-

sponse to the original expression of feeling. It is important to identify the sequence of behaviors. Each triadic sequence (A-B-C) is scored as on behavioral incident. One piece of the sequence is not scored in this approach.

Sign X: Ideas are explored; there is an honest respect for solid information, an attitude of "let's find out."
Rationale — The larger (numerically) the ratio between thinking and memory ratio, the greater the possibility that a student will learn that ideas are important in the classroom.

Sign XI: There is a balance of common tasks and individual responsibility for specific tasks which are unique and not shared.
Rationale — The more the ratio between time in individual tasks and time in group tasks approaches 1.0, the great is the possibility that a student learns to value both his or her individual and group responsibilities.

Sign XII: The teacher communicates clearly to children that learning is self-learning. Faith is demonstrated that all children want to become and pupils show satisfaction as they become aware of their growth.
Rationale — The greater the rate of quadric of ABCD sequences, the higher the possibility the student will learn that his or her learning is self-learning and experience joy in this learning.

Sign XIII: Evaluation is a shared process and includes more than academic achievement.
Rationale — The larger (numerically) the ratio, the greater the possibility that evaluation is a shared process and includes more than academic achievement. A corollary is that both of these factors increase the possibility that evaluation is a shared responsibility and that non-academic factors are also important.

Sign XIV: Motivation for learning is high and seems inner-directed; pupil activity seems to say, "I've got a job I want to do."
Rationale — The larger (numerically) the ratio between the teacher's use of student initiated behaviors and the teacher's rejection or blockage of those behaviors, the higher the possibility that students are motivated to accomplish their own goals. It is felt that the students' initation of questions and/or suggestions is a symptom of their being "turned on" by school. Additionally, the teacher's use of the students' behaviors is thought to be a stimulus for them.

INTENTIONALITY AND HUMAN RELATIONS

The central objective of a human relations curriculum in the school is the development of the intentional individual (Ivey & Alschuler, 1973). The person who acts with intentionality has a sense of capability, can generate alternative behaviors in a given situation, and "come at" a problem from different vantage points. The intentional student is not bound to one course of action but can respond in different ways to changing life situations.

In *academic* life, intentionality may be demonstrated by the student who is faced with a complex problem in science. Not knowing exactly how to solve the problem, the student tries a method to find a solution; if it doesn't work, the student backs up and attacks the problem from a new direction. The student learns that there is more than one avenue to problem solution. In *social* life, intentionality may be demonstrated in the case of a child who has to deal with bullies or excessive teasing. Some children react by crying, hitting, or perhaps pass on their frustration to their younger brothers and sisters. The youngster who acts with intentionality has many responses available in such a situation. The youngster may tease the large individual back, may ask quietly that a stolen hat be returned, may totally ignore the larger person, and may even point out the immature behavior of the larger child. At another level, the youngster may want to help smaller children when they are bullied.

Teachers have always taught human relations in the classroom. Reading material, discussions of issues in social studies, good sportsmanship on the playing field, etc., are often focused on how people can work together more effectively and comfortably.

It is possible to further general human relations aims by linking them to classroom units which relate to present school life and problems. As an example, the study of one's community might also give children the opportunity to learn about the different work roles and points of view in their community. A unit on the food chain in science could be correlated with a unit on the "behavioral chain" (general principle, "When I get hit, I tend to hit someone else"). There are a number of creative ways one could teach important concepts of human relations in conjunction with regular academic work.

A major focus of this approach is the encouragement of intentionality; the generation of alernative behaviors in order to help one achieve both short-term and long-term goals. Too many of us have only one or two responses to frustration or a single route toward our goals. This program is designed to familiarize children with the wider range of possibilities open to them in the belief that the child will select what is individually appropriate as the child learns about these possibilities.

Following are some examples of how to teach human relations in the classroom:

1. A specific area of concern within human relations may be identified. It might be listening skills, self-expression, authority, decision making, brainstorming, handling a bully, etc.
2. A lesson plan developed as a "performance unit" would be completed by a teacher. The lesson plan typically would include: (a) a definition of objectives; (b) suggestions; (c) organization of lesson; (d) opportunity for participation by students at more than a listening level; and (e) follow-up work in the form of "homework," murals, or small group projects.
3. Lesson plans would be developed by teachers at all grade levels and placed in a central location. Lessons on listening, for example, have relevance at all grade levels with appropriate adaptations for the level. Eventually, it would be possible to develop a large number of units in human relations education. Lessons could be designed as supplementary units for academic class sessions or as an integral part of a human relations curriculum.
4. The development of one skill or concept area might be exemplified by a unit taught in "What it means to be big." The teacher first reads the students a selection from a book in which a small child learned that bigness could be determined in more ways than size. The teacher discussed the concept with the children for a short time. The teacher then had pupils role play a situation at the school bus stop in which a larger child teased a smaller child. The teacher asked the child who was "big" and who was "small" in this situation. The children were pleased and surprised when they realized that "big" people are not always physically big. They discussed this for a short time and then they were asked to observe an incident in which they saw someone who was big and report on it the next day. The next day they drew pictures of their stories. During the next several days, the teacher reported that children commented frequently on seeing examples of people being bigger than their size.
5. This approach stresses individuality and alternative ways to demonstrate competence. Children learn that there are several "right" answers in human relations. They also have the opportunity to learn about the perceptions and opinions of other children.
6. Children are encouraged to develop units for use with other children. A child with artistic skills, for example, might develop a unit illustrating a human relations experience through the use of this

medium. Giving children a chance to share themselves and their ideas with one another is a useful method of fostering improved human relationships.
7. Students can be taught how to attend to the psychosocial needs of others. For example, the process of listening to and responding to the concerns of others can be taught to students and enable them to listen more deeply and care more affectively about friends and family.

THE INTERACTIVE PROCESS OF EDUCATION

Gorman's (1974) emphasis is on developing group process skills. He scores the old one-way communication where the teacher lectures and solicits questions about the material from students. In the group process approach strong multi-way conversation about content and personal concerns is encouraged and facilitated with the teacher acting as moderator, guide, and observer, the teacher responds as a facilitator when the students need the teacher's resources but is not dominant in the classroom.

Gorman (1974) protests the overly formal and distrustful relationships between teachers and students and asserts that when teachers and students come to know each other through the interactive process of education that they become more accepting of each other and real learning (academic and psychosocial) occurs. Through the group process of learning students not only learn subject matter but they also learn about themselves, how they react to each other, and to the subject matter. To accomplish group learning students and teacher develop an awareness of the behaviors that make up an effective interactive process and try to model those behaviors during group interactions.

Gorman (1974) reminds all who teach of the reality of the affect inherent within each of us. His position is that teachers must be communication experts who transform the aggregate of a class into a cooperative supportive group, capable of fostering cognitive and affective understanding. His approach integrates a philosophy of education and a conceptualization of communication theory into a student-centered approach to learning.

The Interactive Process of Education combines structured human relations training, group process, old fashioned progressive education discussion skills, and practical evaluative devices to help both students and teachers assess the process. It reflects a considered examination of the proper role of education in a democracy and a concern for helping students overcome years of dependency training.

INVITATIONAL EDUCATION

Purkey and Novak (1984) subtitle their invitational education approach as *a self-concept approach to teaching and learning.* They emphasize the importance of a positive self-concept and its influence on successsful outcomes. When teachers and learners develop positive self-concepts, academic learning and teaching occurs more deeply and the goals of psychosocial development are well served. Rogers (1942, 1951, 1969, 1970a, 1980), in his landmark contributions to our understanding of the human condition, focused on the self-concept as the primary influence on human behavior. When that self-concept is positive, persons behave in a manner which is consistent with that self-concept. When it is negative, persons behave in a manner which is consistent with that self-concept. Persons who feel good about themselves will behave in ways that are psychosocially nourishing for themselves and others. The teacher who fosters positive self-concepts among students lays the foundation for carrying such self-concepts into adult life.

Purkey and Novak (1984) see good teaching as "the process of inviting students to see themselves as able, valuable, and self-directing and of encouraging them to act in accordance with these self-perceptions. Rather than viewing students as physical objects to be moved around like puppets on strings, the teacher's primary role is seeing students in essentially positive ways and inviting them to behave accordingly" (xiii).

Purkey and Novak (1984) go on to indicate that invitational education is based upon four principles:

1. people are able, valuable, and responsible and should be treated accordingly;
2. teaching should be a cooperative activity;
3. people possess relatively untapped potential in all areas of human development; and
4. this potential can best be realized by places, policies, and programs that are specifically designed to invite development, and by people who are personally and professionally inviting to themselves and others (p. 2).

Invitational education develops learning environments that are anchored in "attitudes of respect, care, and civility, that promote positive relationships and encourage human potential" (Purkey & Novak, 1984, p. 2).

Chapters by Purkey and Novak (1984) focus on self-concept development, self-concept as a personal guidance system, the significance of positive self-regard, viewing students as able, perceiving students as valuable, seeing students as responsible, viewing oneself positively, and perceiving education affirmatively.

PEER COUNSELING AND PEER MODELING

The ability of one person to help another to overcome psychosocial problems was an unexpected outcome of the group counseling movement. In the early stages of this movement, the process of group counseling was leader-centered. That is, the leader set the group's agenda by determining what would be discussed and furnished the group with specific directions regarding the best method for solving a psychosocial problem. It was essentially a cognitive process which had all of the qualities of a lecture.

During this early period, some group counseling leaders, who exercised less control over the group, began to observe the emergence of a phenomenon whch was both personally and professionally threatening as well as being therapeutically effective for group members. When involved in a group which was less structured and less leader centered, certain group members responded to other group members in a manner which was therapeutically helpful. By using an intuitive and natural response to the concerns and problems of other group members, certain participants were able to render facilitative and therapeutically positive assistance. This was surprising, since the participants who were helpful to others had no formal training in counseling and psychotherapy. They were lay persons using very human and spontaneous interventions to help group members.

Hobbs (1951), in describing the general values of group counseling, noted this occurrence when he said, "The individual group member may be a giver of help while receiving help" (p. 293). Rogers (1970a) confirmed this observation when he stated: "There is a development of feedback from one person to another, such that each individual learns how he appears to others and what impact he has in interpersonal relationships" (p. 7).

This observation led others to provide experimentation and research which confirmed the observation. Carkhuff and Berenson (1967) developed research evidence which supported the concept that the natural and intuitive abilities to counsel others, possessed by lay persons, could be refined and expanded through mini courses or workshops. This new knowledge enabled lay persons to effectively assist and counsel persons who were having developmental problems.

In school settings, the outcome of this new understanding has resulted in the development of peer counseling. Peer counseling is the process of students assisting each other by applying fundamental counseling skills which they learn in a course, laboratory, or workshop setting.

Sprinthall (1973) describes a peer counseling program he conducted in a school setting:

> The counseling psychology class was essentially a practicum and seminar in peer counseling. The instructional procedure was parallel to a graduate school program. The pupils engaged in role play counseling, listened under supervision to their tape recorded efforts at listening and responding to their peers, discussed aspects of the helping relationship, and examined some readings, such as *Dibs* by Virginia Axline, *Gestalt Therapy* by Fritz Perls, and *Freedom to Learn* by Carl Rogers. At the same time we also found it helpful to structure some learnings especially on specific listening skills. (p. 365).

Sprinthall (1973) went on to report the outcomes of the counseling practicum and seminar in teaching teenagers to become peer counselors: "Using pretest-posttest measures of skills such as empathy, positive regard, and immediacy, the teenagers demonstrated not only statistically significant change, but also achieved higher levels on these scales than commonly achieved by professional trainees in graduate schools" (p. 366).

Fink and his colleagues (1978) researched the effectiveness of a secondary school peer counseling program. Effectiveness was based on global ratings of client improvement and from the client's perspective of the adequacy of the peer counselor's skills. Both peer counselors and the school's faculty rated most of the students who had received peer counseling as either "very improved" or "improved."

In addition to peer counseling research findings suggest that peer modeling has promising applications for fostering psychosocial development in the classroom (Schunk, 1987). Peer models can promote social interaction rates of withdrawn children and facilitate mainstreaming efforts by enhancing handicapped children's acceptance by their peers

(Gresham, 1981; Peck et al., 1981). Social skill training programs typically combine modeling with other components (e.g. coaching, behavioral rehearsal of skills). Videotapes or live models are used to portray peers in different play and work situations (Gresham, 1981). Studies that include school situations in the training scenarios and have students practice skills in actual school situations help to promote the maintenance and generalization of prosocial behaviors.

One classroom application of peer models involves selecting some children as the targets of teacher reinforcement for prosocial behaviors. Strain, Kerr, and Ragland (1981) note that "spillover" effects, or generalization to other children, may occur. Even though the latter are not participating in the intervention, their social behaviors may improve. Other applications involve training peers to initiate social interactions with students. In research by Strain and his colleagues (Strain et al., 1981), peers are trained to initiate social play with withdrawn children by using verbal signs (e.g., "Let's play blocks") and motor responses (handing child a toy). Students have shown that initiations increase children's subsequent social initiations and gains often generalize to classrooms, but the amount of gain typically relates to children's entry-level social repertoires. Although training of peer initiators is time-consuming, it seems minimal compared with teacher methods of remedying social withdrawal (prompting, reinforcement) requiring near-continuous teacher involvement (Schunk, 1987).

Peer models may be especially helpful with students who hold self-doubts about their capabilities for learning, performing well, or coping with stressful situations. Observing capable peers helps them to learn that they also can improve. Self-efficacy for learning can enhance motivation and is subsequently validated as students succeed at the task (Schunk, 1985; Schunk & Hanson, 1985).

Teachers often apply these ideas by selecting one or more students to demonstrate a skill to other class members. The typical practice is to choose peers who master skills readily (i.e. mastery models). This arrangement may help teach skills to learners but may not have much impact on the self-efficacy of students who are experiencing difficulty learning. For these students, low achievers who have mastered skills may be excellent models. Peers also could model such coping strategies as increased concentration and hard work.

Peer modeling promotes students learning skills, rules, and concepts. Students with learning or other handicaps benefit most from one to one or small group instruction. Peers often serve as useful adjuncts to support regular classroom instruction (Schunk, 1987; Schunk, Hanson, & Cox, 1987). A common use of peers as instructional agents involves tutoring. Research demonstrates that tutoring can lead to academic and social gains among tutors and tutees (Feldman et al., 1977). There is evidence that a greater age differential may lead to higher tutee performance, but the nature of the interaction may be better when tutor and tutee are peers.

Using peers to help correct skill deficiencies also seems appropriate where peer teaching strategies fit well with learners' capabilities or the skills being taught. Whereas child teachers tend to use modeling and nonverbal demonstrations and to link instruction to specific items, adults typically employ more verbal instruction and relate information to be learned to other material (Ellis & Rogoff, 1982). Peer instruction may be quite beneficial with learning disabled students and other learners who do not process verbal material particularly well, as well as for any student on tasks that do not require teaching or superordinate rules or concepts.

QUEST

The *Skills for Living Program* has become known as Quest since it was the first program developed by the Quest National Center in Findlay, Ohio. The Quest National Center was formed over a decade ago to equip youngsters between 10 and 18 with skills for successful living. Quest has developed a wide range of programs and materials, including teacher manuals, student workbooks, and textbooks for grades 6 through 12; curriculum components on learning through community service; materials on leadership training for non-traditional leaders; in-service training workshops for teachers; and seminars for parents. The *Quest* programs are in use in more than 1,200 schools (Crisci, 1986).

The content for the *Skills for Living Program* emanated from the concerns of adolescents identified through a survey of more than 2000 students in 120 U. S. high schools. The survey conducted by Rick Little, the founder of *Quest,* led to a conference of nationally recognizes experts on character education and social skills development. These individuals went on to help Little create *Skills for Living* (Crisci, 1986). An offshoot of the *Skills for Living Program* is *Skills for Adolescence: A New Program for Young Teenagers* (Gerler, 1986).

Kirschenbaum and Glaser (1982), in their *Skills for Living* program for teachers to use with students, indicate that:

> In our society, the evidence of stress, emotional pain, loneliness, and destructive action toward self and others is common in schools, families, and the community. These problems have been widely recognized throughout the nation. Increasing crime, drug abuse, health problems, suicide, child abuse, divorce, and other social problems abound. Individuals are having more and more difficulty establishing life goals, finding meaning and purpose in life, and committing themselves to vocations, interpersonal relationships, and the betterment of the human condition (p. 5).

They go on to indicate that youngsters attending schools today are less psychologically stable and education has a responsibility to do something about this condition just as it has a responsibility to teach reading, writing, and arithmetic. As the world becomes more threatening, survival may depend more upon psychosocial awareness than upon academic skills. Today's young people are faced with low or poor family interaction, a more heterogeneous value system, dissonant role models, few intergenerational associations, high technology, little sense of community, and many broken homes (38-42 percent).

In 1979 The World Health Organization investigated the age in which young people across the world reached functional adulthood or the daily requirements of being an adult. It was found that in all urbanized and technologically-advanced nations of the world, other then the United States, it was 16 to 17 years of age. For the United States it was 24 years of age.

Kirschenbaum and Glaser (1982) are alarmed not only at the acceleration and depth of the human problems that youngsters bring to school, but that schools ignore their existence and insist on gearing the curriculum to the acquisition of academic facts. They identify five overlapping areas of skills for living for those teachers who want to improve the psychosocial condition of youngsters and prepare them for a stable adulthood: Thinking, Feeling, Decision-making, Communicating, and Acting (Action):

> Some of the skills involved in the *Thinking* dimension are: thinking at different levels, from memorizing to analyzing to evaluating; logical and mathematical thinking; critical thinking such as distinguishing fact from opinion, analysing advertising, etc.; and creative thinking.
>
> Skills involved in the *Feeling* area are: being aware of one's feelings and inner states, including knowing what one prizes and cherishes; dealing wih distressful feelings, such a anger, fear, and emotional hurt; and developing a positive self-concept.

The *Decision-making* process involves: goal-setting; data gathering; generating alternatives; examining consequences of alternatives and their pros and cons; choosing freely, and evaluating the results of a decision.

Communication skills involve: sending clear messages—expressing one's feelings, thoughts, and meanings through verbal, non-verbal, and written communication; empathic listening—accurately receiving the communication of others, through verbal and non-verbal messages and reading; and conflict resolution.

The *Action* dimension refers to developing observable competence in both academic and psychosocial skills.

The curriculum helps to promote the values of self discipline, respect for others, compassion, good judgment, responsibility, honesty, family cohesion, trustworthiness, involvement, friendship, openness, and liberty. These values are developed through units on the self-concept, feelings, friends, family, marriage, parenting, financial management, life planning and life philosophy.

The *Skills for Living Program* has been cited by the Pyramid Project of the National Institute on Drug Abuse as one of the top three drug abuse prevention programs in the United States even though drug abuse is dealt with only indirectly through such topics as decision making, resisting negative peer pressure, and developing a strong self concept.

Empirical evaluations have confirmed the effectiveness of *Skills for Living* (Crisci, 1986:441). The most recent study conducted in 1983-84 involved 892 students in 30 schools located in four states. Of these 892 students, 560 took part in the Quest program and 332 did not. On post tests, the students who participated in Skills for Living showed statistically significant gains on six of the seven scales: family relationships, self-esteem, self-concept within the family, feelings about school, communication skills, and goal setting and problem solving. The data collected on *Skills for Living* and *Skills for Adolescence* indicate that participants in these programs improve their attitude toward schools and their teachers, feel more comfortable accepting responsibility, and more able to say no to peer pressure, feel better about themselves and are better able to solve the problems of adolescence.

Quest also has developed a program to prepare high school students for community service. *Project LEAD* (Leadership Experience and Development) enables students, working closely with adult mentors to make meaningful contributions to their communities and, in so doing, to develop important leadership and development skills.

Each Project LEAD team consists of six people: an adult team leader, a teacher or counselor, and four students. Through a formal training program, each team learns to conduct a needs assessment in its community, to develop broad support for its goals, to recruit other students, and to implement its service project in the school or the community (Crisci, 1986:441).

Among the goals of Project LEAD are: to identify non-traditional leaders—those students who have leadership potential but are not the kinds of students who are usually chosen for leadership roles, e.g. star athletes, straight A students; and, to develop a commitment among young people to volunteerism and community service. Service projects conducted under the LEAD program have involved adolescents in cleaning up and beautifying their communities, tutoring and caring for younger children, establishing a crime prevention program, and adopting senior citizens.

Quest programs exemplify Ryan's (1986:233) observation that "the role of the school is not simply to make children smart, but to make them smart and good. We must help children acquire the skills, the attitude, and the dispositions that will help them live well and that will enable the common good to flourish. For schools and teachers to do only half the job puts the individual child and all the rest of us in danger."

THE RATIONAL-EMOTIVE APPROACH

How can rationale-emotive psychology be employed in the classroom? To answer this question, The Institute for the Advanced Study in Rational Psychotherapy started a private school for childen, The Living School, which it operates in New York City. The purpose of the school is to teach children the regular elements of academic education but, at the same time, to combine that with emotional education.

The school was started as a laboratory school in which materials and procedures in rational-emotive education could be developed and used with elementary school children. The approach is derived from the rational-emotive theory of counseling initiated by Ellis (1962). Children are taught concepts of how people think, feel, and behave. This is accomplished through regular "lessons" in emotional education, through role-playing demonstrations, and in the course of actual problems that may arise in the classroom during the day.

Parental involvement is an integral part of The Living School, with parents learning rational-emotive skills along with their children. They are given guidance by the school's staff to enable them to deal with their children's, as well as their own, dysfunctional beliefs and behavior so as to enable them to deal with their children's, as well as their own, dysfunctional beliefs and behavior so as to enable them to follow through at home. In addition, they attend monthly workshops dealing with such topics as problems with siblings and parental nagging.

Although the school's unique contribution is in the area of rational-emotive education, it also has an academic program of individualized learning, geared to the needs and interests of each student. The model is an open classroom, with teachers and students sharing warm and close relationships with each other.

Ellis (1972) believes that children *naturally* acquire several basic irrational ideas which they tend to perpetuate and which sabotage their lives forever. They religiously, devoutly believe that they absolutely *need* and utterly *must have* others' approval; that they've *got to* achieve outstandingly and thereby prove how worthwhile they are; that people who act unjustly or inconsiderately to them are bad, wicked, or villainous and should be severely condemned and punished for their villainy: that it is awful and catastrophic when things are not the way they would like them to be; that obnoxious situations and events *make them* feel anxious, depressed, or angry; that if they endlessly worry about something they can control whether or not it happens; that it is easier for them to avoid than to face certain life difficulties and responsibilities; and that they absolutely *need* a well-ordered, certain, pretty perfect universe. These are the same kinds of irrational ideas which most human adults more or less tend to believe, but children often believe them more rigidly and profoundly.

The rational-emotive approach to teaching involves the student in recognizing and working against these irrational ideas and beliefs and replacing them with an existential presence and control over how one is responding. The approach indicates that what causes us psychosocial trauma is not the events or experiences of life but how we respond to those events and experiences. We can respond in a way which diminishes our psychosocial stability or respond in a way which strengthens our psychosocial stability. The rational-emotive approach wants the student to recognize the different ways of responding and elminate those which denegrate the self and replace those responses with ones which strengthen the self.

SELF-INSTRUCTION: A CURRICULUM FOR COUNSELING

Martin (1983) suggests a life skills curriculum that could be incorporated into the schools to train students in skills such as problem solving decision making, planning, self motivation, and self planning. Martin and Martin (1983) referred to these skills as self-instruction skills i.e. an organized body of skills, knowledge, and attitudes that assist people to exercise influence over their human environmental system. Martin (1984) developed a theory of self-instruction which describes three levels of self-instruction competence for individuals.

The first level consists of a single schema that maps the major procedural phases of counseling in a generic process of self-instruction. Phases in this schema are setting goals, creating, information structures, preassessing, mapping task domains and objectives, planning, maintaining action, and evaluating. The other two levels of schema in Martin's (1984) theory of self-instruction detail the cognitive and metacognitive tasks subsumed by the phase in the first level.

Martin (1984) suggested that self-instructional schemata are activated by information from three primary sources (a) *declarative knowledge structures* that contain information in substantive areas associated with specific self-instructional efforts (e.g. information about exercise, calories, metabolism, life style in relation to a self-instructional attempt to learn and practice weight reduction methods), (b) *procedural knowledge* required for the operation of specific programs of self-instruction, e.g. (knowledge of procedures such as stimulus control, self-management, self-reward that would facilitate weight reduction) and (c) *situational contextual* information internalized and processed from the immediate situation confronting the individual (e.g. an invitation to a pig roast). Most of the work associated with teaching self-instruction has focussed on the procedural phases of goal setting, planning, evaluating, preassessing, mapping objectives, maintaining action, and creating information structures and activities (Martin, 1985).

In each of the procedural phases of goal setting, creating information structures, preassessing, mapping task domains and objectives, planning, maintaining action, and evaluating there is a variety of cognitive behavioral skills and strategies which can be taught (Martin 1985). Groups can be used to teach students these specific skills and strategies of self-instruction. Curriculum packages have been designed to teach self-instructional skills and strategies to high school students using the self-instruction curriculum packages showed statistically reliable improvements from pre-test to post-test in knowledge of self-instructional skills and strategies, in abilities to transfer such skills and strategies, and in significant increase in locus of control. A matched control group showed no change from pre-test to post-test on any of the experimental measures.

Martin (1985) indicates that metacognitive skills (i.e. thinking skills used to monitor cognitive processes and strategies) are crucial to the ability to self-instruction. Knowing what one knows, knowing when and how one comes to know it, being able to think and plan strategically, acquiring the ability to represent knowledge effectively, and being able to monitor and evaluate one's own competence are essential to self-instruction.

STUDENT-CENTERED TEACHING

Client-centered theory is a counseling theory, but early adherents saw it as being logically applicable to the process of education. Soon after the appearance of Rogers's first major contribution, *Counseling and Psychotherapy* (1942), there quickly emerged an awareness that the viewpoint was also applicable to teaching (Blocksma & Porter, 1947; Gross, 1948; Schwebel & Asch, 1949; Faw, 1949). Rogers (1951) confirmed this interest in his book, *Client-Centered Therapy,* by devoting Chapter 9 to "Student-Centered Teaching." This applicability to teaching was further extended by Rogers (1969) in his book, *Freedom to Learn,* is evident in Part Three of his book, *A Way of Being* (Rogers, 1980), and is reconfirmed in his latest work, *Freedom to Learn in the 1980s* (Rogers, 1983). The convertibility and applicability of the client-centered counseling view has also been recognized in organizational behavior, families, parenting, groups, marriage and its alternatives, leadership, pastoring, and general interpersonal relationships.

Rogers (1951) has traditionally recognized the applicability of the concepts of client-centered counseling to the teaching and learning process: "If the creation of an atmosphere of acceptance, understanding, and respect is the most effective basis for facilitating the learning which is called therapy, then might it not be the basis for the learning which is called education?" (p. 384).

Rogers (1951) identified certain characteristics of student-centered teaching which he presented as principles and hypotheses:

1. We cannot teach another person directly; we can only facilitate his learning. (p. 389.)
2. A person learns significantly only those things which he perceives as being involved in the maintenance of, or enhancement of, the structure of self. (p. 389.)

3. Experience which, if assimilated, would involve a change in the organization of self tends to be resisted through denial or distortion of symbolization. (p. 389.)
4. The structure and organization of self appears to become more rigid under threat; to relax its boundaries when completely free from threat. Experience which is perceived as inconsistent with the self can only be assimilated if the current organization of self is relaxed and expanded to include it. (p. 390.)
5. The educational situation which most effectively promotes significant learning is one in which threat to the self of the learner is reduced to a minimum and differential perception of the field of experience is facilitated. (p. 391.)

Rogers (1962) indicates that teaching is a process in which the psychosocial development of the student can emerge. He places the creation of such an atmosphere directly in the hands of the teacher, who must be free from the facades generally characteristic of the endeavor we call education: "We would also endeavor to plan the educational program for these individuals so that they would come increasingly to experience empathy and liking others, and that they would find it increasingly easier to be themselves, to be real." (p. 420.)

For the teacher who believes that the concept of student-centered teaching has merit theoretically but is not operative because of the limitations imposed by a particular institution, Rogers (1951) offers the following: "Every group has some limitations, if only the fact that they meet for a limited rather than an unlimited number of hours per week. It is not the fact that there are limitations, but the attitude, the permissiveness, the freedom which exists within those limtiations, which is important" (p. 396).

In describing the interpersonal relationship that facilitates teaching and learning, Rogers (1970b) indicates that it is characterized by the teacher's possession of a humanistic attitude which includes realness, prizing, acceptance, trust, and empathic understanding. These characteristics are identical to those which Rogers has described as being characteristic of an effective counselor or psychotherapist.

Unlike other approaches, student-centered teaching does not rely on pre-planned strategies, techniques, or exercises. It instead relies on the fully developed personhood of the teacher. The psychosocial development of the pupil occurs because of the student-centered humanness of the teacher and the teacher's ability to naturally and spontaneously communicate this humanness to students in the teaching-learning process. As Pine and Boy (1977) indicate, it is applicable in proportion to the caring human qualities of the teacher. It occurs when the teacher has a genuine commitment to be attitudinally student-centered and express the human qualities of the approach in what the teacher feels, says, and does. This demands an attitudinal evolvement on the part of the teacher. The teacher must evolve toward being more respectful of others and their rights; more stable in his or her own psychosocial development; more committed to values which enrich others; more trustful of human behavior; more open to experience; and more initiatory, natural, and spontaneous.

The catalyst for effective student-centered teaching is clearly the *gravitas* of the teacher who is student-centered in both attitude and behavior. It is an approach to fostering psychosocial development which requires a high level of psychosocial maturity, since the teacher's human attitude and values are fully visible (what is felt is what is said). If the student-centered teacher expects students to be more real, prizing, acceptant, trustful, and empathic with each other, then the teacher must be able to model these behaviors during the teaching-learning process (Boy & Pine, 1982).

Rogers (1951) further clarifies the attitudinal and value commitments required of the student-centered teacher when he says:

> He creates a classroom climate which respects the integrity of the student, which accepts all aims, opinions, and attitudes as being legitimate expressions of the student's internal frame of reference at that time. He accepts the feelings and emotionalized attitudes which surround any educational or group experience. He accepts himself as being a member of a learning group, rather than an authority. He makes learning resources available, confident that if they meet the needs of the group they will be used. He relies upon the capacity of the individual to sort out truth from untruth, upon the basis of continuing experience. He recognizes that his course, if successful, is a beginning in learning, not the end of learning. He relies upon the capacity of the student to assess his progress in terms of the purposes which he has at this time. He has confidence in the fact that, in this atmosphere which he helped to create, a type of learning takes place which is personally meaningful and which feeds the total self-development of the individual as well as improves his acquaintance with a given field of knowledge. (p. 427.)

VALUES CLARIFICATION

Values clarification attracted the attention of educators and the public as a consequence of the turmoil which surrounded the collision of values during the 1960s and into the 1970s. The focus of the collision was the Vietnam War and the heated and sometimes violent conflicts between those who supported the war and those who did not. Debate and conflict over Vietnam, however, was just the beginning. It evolved into values conflicts over other value-laden issues: the effects of marijuana, premarital sex, abortion, homosexuality, euthanasia, nuclear power, and the socioeconomic rights of ethnic and minority groups. It was a turbulent period which some perceived as the sunrise of enlightenment regarding certain moral issues; others saw the period as the twilight of the moral foundations of our civilization.

This clash of values spilled over into our nation's schools. Students began to experiment with drugs and sex; racial conflicts erupted into riots; schools were being destroyed; and teachers were being physically assaulted. These behaviors alarmed politicians, school boards, parents, teachers, and the community at large.

An attitude of "we've got to do something about this" quickly emerged and Raths, Hamrin, and Simon (1966) stated that American education had better start paying attention to the degree to which one's values influence and affect behavior. They indicated that behaviors do not occur in a vacuum; that one's behavior are a reflection of values that often fulfill one's psychosocial needs. Simon, Howe, and Kirschenbaum (1972) elaborated on this viewpoint and the concept that schools needed to help students clarify values gained in momentum. The concept was in the right place at the right time.

Educators implementing values clarification procedures in the classroom are quick to point out that they are not interested in influencing students to select one set of values over another. The aim of values clarification is to prompt students to investigate and understand how values influence behavior. The fundamental process of values clarification is to help students to identify values which enhance the self and respect the dignity and rights of others. Understanding personal values must be accompanied by an understanding of the values of others so that conflicting values are mitigated and harmonized in a pluralistic and democratic society.

Simon (1973) suggests the following strategies for a teacher desiring to involve a group in values clarification. These strategies serve as catalysts to enable a group to identify and clarify personal values and understand how these values affect behavior:

Strategy 1: Either-Or Forced Choice. Students are requested to choose between two conflicting alternatives. In the process of choosing, students are asked to examine their feelings, self-concepts, and, of course, their values.

Strategy 2: Spread of Opinion. Students are asked to identify the range of opinions that might exist within our society on value issues like population control, premarital sex, legalization of marijuana, or open marriage. Students are then asked to identify and clarify their own values regarding these topics.

Strategy 3: Alternative Search. Identifying which alternatives exist when considering a certain issue of values is an important reflection of what we have to do in adult life. Choosing from among the available alternatives is a vital process in values clarification. This strategy provides students with practice in searching out the different value alternatives available in attempting to solve a problem.

Strategy 4: Twenty Things You Love to Do. In this strategy, the identification is accompanied by consideration of the values which influenced the choices. Sometimes, what we choose reveals values which validate the self at the expense of the rights of others.

Strategy 5: "I learned" Statements. This strategy enables the student to summarize and bring closure to a certain values clarification experience. It can be oral or written and the usual format is to have the student complete a number of "I" sentences: I learned that . . . I was disappointed that I . . . I see that I need to.

Strategy 6: Opposite Quadrangles. Students are asked to divide a piece of paper into four sections. In the upper-left section they are asked to list the people they most like to be with; in the upper-right section they are asked to list the places they enjoy going to; in the lower-left section they are asked to list the people they least like being with and in the lower-right section they are asked to list the places they least enjoy going to. As students examine their opposite quadrangles, they are asked to identify the values which influenced their selections rather than revealing the selections.

Sprinthall and Mosher (1978), in their co-edited book, *Value Development as the Aim of Education,* focus on moral and democratic development as a critical need in our nation's schools. None of the articles in their book identify the morals which should be promulgated. Instead, the articles indicate that the moral and ethical foundations of our behavior must be examined and understood if students are to be fully educated.

In their article, Sullivan and Dockstader (1978) identify events which prompted public interest in including values and moral education in a school's curriculum:

> The Watergate scandal with its cast of intelligent, well-educated individuals who knew or cared little about personal and political ethics was one national crisis which aroused people's concern for values and moral decision-making. Large corporations have made illegal campaign con-

tributions and bribed foreign governments to gain advantage over competitors. Congressmen have also been suspected of accepting bribes from Korean representatives. These highly publicized national events occurred at the same time that medicine, science, politics, and rapidly changing social conditions have been presenting us with new, preplexing moral questions which must be resolved. (pp. 136-137.)

Sullivan and Dockstrader (1978), who administer the Ethical Quest in a Democratic Society Project in the Tacoma, Washington Public Schools, go on to present sample lesson plans, which a teacher can use to stimulate student discussion of the moral and ethical foundations of certain decisions. For elementary school children "I wonder why" pertains to school rules and how the moral dimensions of these rules might be perceived by a student, teacher, principal, and parent. At the junior and senior high school levels moral reasoning lesson plans are presented which focus on the behavior of "Kino," a character in John Steinbeck's novel, *The Pearl*. A moral action lesson plan for senior high school students enables them to discuss the ethical behaviors of the main character in Herman Wouk's play, *The Caine Mutiny Court Martial*.

Kohlberg (1967) stimulated interest in moral education when he conceptualized and researched the following six stages of moral development. Teachers, parents, school boards, and the community responded positively to the concept of moral education because of the obvious desire to have students function at a higher stage of moral development.

Stage 1: Obedience and punishment orientation
Stage 2: Egoistic orientation
Stage 3: Orientation to approval and to pleasing and helping others
Stage 4: Authority and social-order maintenance orientation
Stage 5: Contractual, legalistic orientation
Stage 6: Conscience or principle orientation (pp. 347-380).

Hersch (1980) indicates that our schools must include moral education within the curriculum if we expect students to behave ethically and morally as adults. Students need to learn a process of examining ethical and moral behavior that they can carry over into their adult lives as they fulfill the responsibilities of citizenship in a free society.

THE EFFECTIVENESS OF PRIMARY PREVENTION APPROACHES

Do the primary prevention approaches, strategies, and programs described in this chapter work? Two comprehensive studies offer empirical evidence supporting the effectiveness of primary prevention. Baker, Swisher, Nadenichek, and Popowicz (1984) conducted a meta analysis of 40 primary prevention studies to determine the cognitive and psychosocial effects of primary prevention strategies and programs in schools. Methods for converting outcome data to effect-size statistics were taken from Smith, Glass, and Miller (1980). Using Cohen's (1969) criteria for judging effect size (.20 to .49 = small, .50 to .79 = medium, and above .80 = large) they found that overall preprimary prevention strategy effect size (.01) and the effect sizes for career maturity enhancement (1.33), communication skills training (3.90 and .93), deliberate psychological education programs (1.43), and deliberate psychological education and moral education programs combined (.83) were large. The overall effect size for values clarification programs (.69) and all values clarification programs combined (.51) were medium. These results statistically validate positive significant effects of prevention programs on intellectual and psychosocial outcome measures.

In a major three year study sponsored by the National Institute of Mental Health to implement primary prevention training and research programs involving 10,000 students and 600 teachers Aspy, Roebuck, and Aspy (1984) reported the following outcomes:

1. There is a positive and significant relationship between teachers' gains in levels of functioning on interpersonal process measures and their participation in training programs designed to enhance these skills.
2. There is a positive and significant relationship between teachers' levels of interpersonal functioning and students' gains on achievement test scores.
3. There is a positive and significant relationship between teachers' levels of interpersonal functions and student attendance.
4. There is a positive and significant relationship between teachers' levels of interpersonal functioning and enhanced self concept of students.
5. There is a positive and significant relationship between principals' levels of interpersonal functioning and the tendency of their teachers to employ interpersonal skills in the classroom.

The two comprehensive studies indicate that teachers using counseling skills and employing some of the primary prevention strategies described in this chapter positively and significantly affect the intellectual and psychosocial development of students. The significance of these findings is more important today than ever. The current situation regarding primary prevention is summarized cogently by Aspy, Roebuck, and Aspy (1984:458).

"In speaking of effective corporations Peters and Waterman (*In Search of Excellence* 1982:95) state 'The overwhelming failure of the human relations movement was precisely its failure to be seen as a balance to the excesses of the rational model, a failure ordained by its own equally silly excesses!' This same assessment can be made of most human relations programs for schools, as most of them have failed to demonstrate their relationship to the hard-nosed indices that are considered the major concern of schools by most observers. This is regrettable because the relationship between academic gain and effective interpersonal skills has been demonstrated."

REFERENCES

Alschuler, A. (1973). *Developing achievement motivation in adolescents; Education for Human Growth.* Englewood Cliffs, NJ: Educational Technology Publications.

Aspy, D. N. and Hicks, L. H. (1978). Research on humanistic objectives. In A. W. Coombs, *Humanistic Education: Objectives and Assessment.* Washington, D. C. Association for Supervision and Curriculum Development.

Aspy, D., Roebuck F. and Aspy, C. (1984). Tomorrow's resources are in today's classrooms. *Personnel and Guidance Journal,* April 62, 8:455-459.

Baker, S., Swisher, J. D., Nadenichek, P. E. and Popowicz, C. L. (1980). Measured effects of primary prevention strategies. *Personal and Guidance Journal,* April, 62, 8:459-464.

Bessell, H. & Palomares, U. (1967). *Methods in human development.* El Cajon, CA: Human Development Training Institute.

Blocksma, D. D. & Porter, E. H. (1947). A short-term training program in client-centered counseling. *Journal of Consulting Psychology,* 11, 55-60.

Borton, T. (1970). *Reach, touch and teach.* New York: McGraw-Hill.

Boy, A. V. & Pine, G. J. (1982). *Client-centered counseling: A renewal.* Boston: Allyn and Bacon.

Crakhuff, R. R. & Berenson, B. G. (1967). *Beyond counseling and therapy.* New York: Holt, Rinehart, and Winston.

Cohen, J. (1969). *Statistical Power Analysis for the Behavioral Sciences.* New York: Academic Press.

Coombs, A. W. (Ed) (1962) *Perceiving, Behaving, and Becoming.* Washington, D. C.: Association for Supervision and Curriculum Development.

Crisci, P. (1986). The Quest National Center: A focus on prevention of alienation. *Phi Delta Kappan,* 67, 6, 440-442.

Dinkmeyer, D. (1970). *Developing understanding of self and others (DUSO, D-1).* Circle Pines, Minn.: American Guidance Service.

Dinkmeyer, D. (1973). *Developing understanding of self and others (DUSO, D-2).* Circle Pines, Minn.: American Guidance Service.

Dinkmeyer, D. & Carlson, J. (1973). *Consulting: Facilitating human potential and change processes,* Columbus, Ohio: Charles Merrill.

Dinkmeyer, D. & Carlson, J. (1975). *Consultation: A book of readings.* New York: John Wiley.

Dinkmeyer, D. & Dinkmeyer, D., Jr. (1980). Alternative: affective education. *The Journal of Humanistic Education and Development,* 19, No. 2, 51-58.

Dinkmeyer, D. & Dreikurs, R. (1963). *Encouraging children to learn: The encouragement process.* New York: Hawthorn.

Dinkmeyer, D. & Losoncy, L. (1980). *The encouragement book: On becoming a postive person.* Englewood Cliffs, N.Y.: Prentice Hall.

Dinkmeyer, D. & McKay, G. D. (1976). *Systematic training for effective parenting (STEP).* Circle Pines, Minn.: American Guidance Service.

Dinkmeyer, D., McKay, G. D. & Dinkmeyer, D., Jr. (1980). *Systematic training for effective teaching (STET).* Circle Pines, Minn.: American Guidance Service.

Dinkmeyer, D. & Dinkmeyer, D., Jr., (1982). Developing understanding of self and others (rev. ed.). Circle Pines, Minn: *American Guidance Service.*

Dinkmeyer, D. & Dinkmeyer, D., Jr., (1984). School counselors as consultants in primary prevention programs. *Personnel and Guidance Journal,* 62, 8. 484-466.

Dreikurs, R., Grunwald, B. & Pepper, F. (1971). *Maintaining sanity in the classroom.* New York: Harper & Row.

Ellis, A. (1962). *Reason and emotion in psychotherapy.* New York: Lyle Stuart.

Ellis, A. (1972). *Emotional education.* New York: Julian Press.

Ellis, S. & Rogoff, B. (1982). The strategies and efficacy of child versus adult teachers. *Child Development* 53, 730-735.

Faw, V. E. (1949). A psychotherapeutic method of teaching psychology. *The American Psychologist,* 4, 104-109.

Feldman, R. S., Devin-Sheehan, L. & Allen, V. L. (1976). Children tutoring children: A critical review of research. In V. L. Allen (Ed.) *Children as teachers: Theory and research on tutoring* (pp. 235-252). New York: Academic Press.

Fenstermacker, G. D. & Goodlad, J. L. (Ed.) (1983). *Individual Differences and the Common Curriculum, Eighty Second Yearbook of the National Society for the Study of Education.* Chicago: National Society for the Study of Education.

Fink, A. M., et al. (1978). Service delivery and high school peer counseling system. *The Personnel and Guidance Journal,* 56, 80-82.

Gerler, E. (1986). Skills for adolescence: A new program for young teenagers. *Phi Delta Kappan,* 67, 6, 436-439.

Gibbons, M. (1974). "Walkabout: Searching for the right passage from childhood and school. *Phi Delta Kappan,* 55, No. 9, 596-602.

Gibbons, M. (1984). "Walkabout ten years later: Searching for a renewed vision of education. *Phi Delta Kappan* 65, No. 9, 591-600.

Glasser, W. (1969). *Schools without failure.* New York: Harper & Row.

Gorman, A. (1969). *Teachers and learners; The interactive process of education.* Boston: Allyn and Bacon.

Gresham, F. M. (1981). Social skills training with handicapped children: A review. *Review of Educational Research*, 51, 139-176.

Gross, L. (1948). An experimental study of the validity of the nondirective method of teaching. *Journal of Psychology*, 26, 243-248.

Hatfield, T. (1984). Deliberate psychological education revisited: A conversation with Norman Sprinthall. *The Personnel and Guidance Journal*, 62, 294-300.

Hersch, R. (1980). *Models of moral education*. New York: Longman.

Hobbs, N. (1951). Group-centered psychotherapy. In C. R. Rogers, *Client-centered therapy*. Boston: Houghton Mifflin.

Ivey, A. & Alschuler, A. S. (Eds.) (1973). Psychological education: A prime function of the counselor. *The Personnel and Guidance Journal*, 51, 586-691.

Kirschenbaum, H. & Glaser, B. (1982). *Skills for Living*. 2nd ed. Findlay, OH. Quest National Center.

Kohlberg, S. (1967). Stage and sequence: The cognitive development approach to socialization. In D. Goslin (Ed.), *Handbook of socialization theory and research*. Skokie, IL: Rand McNally.

McMullen, R. S. (1979). The achievement motivation workshop. *The Personnel and Guidance Journal*, 57, 436-441.

Martin, J. (1983). Curriculum development in school counseling. *Personnal and Guidance Journal*, 61, 406-409.

Martin, J. and Martin, W. (1983). Personal development: Self instruction for personal agency. Calgory, Alberta: Detselig.

Martin, J. (1984). Toward a cognitive schema theory of self instruction. *Instructional Science* 13, 159-180.

Martin, J. (1985). Self instruction: A curriculum for counseling. *Journal Counseling and Develoment*, 64, 126-129.

Mize, J., Ladd, G. W. & Price, J. M. (1985). Promoting positive peer relations with young children: Rationales and strategies. *Child Care Quarterly*, 14, 221-237.

Mosher, R. & Sprinthall, N. (1971). Deliberate psychological education. *The Counseling Psychologist*, 18, 3-82.

Passons, W. R. (1975). *Gestalt approaches to counseling*. Atlanta: Holt, Rinehart, and Winston.

Peck, C. A., Cooke, T. P. & Apolloni, T. (1981). Utilization of peer imitation in therapeutic and instructional context. In P. S. Strain (Ed.). *The utilization of classroom peers as behavior change agents* (pp. 69-99), New York: Plenum.

Perls, F., Hefferline, R., & Goodman, P. (1951). *Gestalt therapy*. New York: Dell.

Peters, T. J. & Waterman, R. H. (1982). *In Search of Excellence*. New York: Harper & Row.

Pine, G. J. & Boy, A. V. (1977). *Learner-centered teaching: A humanistic view*. Denver: Love.

Purkey, W. W. & Novak, J. M. (1984). *Inviting school success: A self concept approach to teaching and learning*. 2nd ed. Belmont, CA: Wadsworth.

Remer, R. & Schrader, L. A. (1981). Gestalt approach to classroom guidance. *Elementary School Guidance and Counseling*, 16, 15-33.

Rogers, C. R. (1942). *Counseling and psychotherapy*. Boston: Houghton Mifflin.

Rogers, C. R. (1951). *Client-centered therapy*. Boston: Houghton Mifflin.
Rogers, C. R. (1962). The interpersonal relationship: The core of guidance. *Harvard Education Review*, 32, 416-429.
Rogers, C. R. (1969). *Freedom to learn*. Columbus, OH: Charles E. Merrill.
Rogers, C. R. (1970a). *Carl Rogers on basic encounter groups*. New York: Harper & Row.
Rogers, C. R. (1970b). The interpersonal relationship in the facilitation of learning. In J. T. Hart & T. M. Tomlinson (Eds.), *New directions in client-centered therapy*. Boston: Houghton Mifflin, 468-483.
Rogers, C. R. (1980). *A way of being*. Boston: Houghton Mifflin.
Rogers, C. R. (1983). *Freedom to learn in the 1980s*. Columbus, OH: Charles E. Merrill.
Rothrock, D. (1982). The rise and decline of individualized instruction. *Educational Leadership* 39, 528-531.
Ryan, K. (1986). The new moral education. *Phi Delta Kappan*, 68, 4, 228-233.
Schunk, D. H. (1985), Self-efficacy and classroom learning. *Psychology in the Schools*, 22, 208-223.
Schunk, D. H. & Hanson, A. R. (1985), Peer models: Influence on children's self-efficacy and achievement, *Journal of Eduational Psychology*, 77, 313-322.
Schunk, D. H., Hanson, A. R. & Cox, P. D. (1987). Peer model attributes and children's achievement behaviors. *Journal of Educational Psychology*. 79, 54-61.
Schunk, D. H. (1987). Peer models and behavioral change. *Review of Educational Research*. 57, 2, 149-174.
Schwebel, M. & Asch, M. J. (1948). Research possibilities in nondirective teaching. *Journal of Educational Psychology*, 39, 359-369.
Shapiro, S. B. (1985). An empirical analysis of operating values in humanistic education. *Journal of Humanistic Psychology*, 25, 94-108.
Simon, S., Howe, L. & Kirschenbaum, H. (1972). *Values clarification: A practical handbook of strategies for teachers and students*. New York: Hart.
Simon, S. (1973). Values clarification: A tool for counselors. *The Personnel and Guidance Journal*, 51, 614-618.
Smith, M.S., Glass, G. V. & Miller, T. I. (1980). *The Benefits of Psychotherapy*. Baltimore: John Hopkins University Press.
Soradahl, S. N. & Sanche, R. P. (1985). The effects of classroom meetings on self concept and behavior. *Elementary School Guidance and Counseling*, 20, 49-55.
Sprinthall, N. A. (1973). Curriculum for secondary schools; Counselors as teachers for psychological growth. *The School Counselor*, 20, 361-369.
Sprinthall, N. A. & Mosher, R. L. (Eds.). (1978). *Value development as the aim of education*. Schenectady, NY: Character Research Press.
Strain, P. S. (Ed.) (1981). The Utilizaiton of Classroom Peers as Behavior Change Agents. New York: Plenum.
Strain, P. S., Kerr, M. M. & Ragland, E. U. (1981). The use of peer social initiations in the treatment of social withdrawal. In P. S. Strain (Ed.), *The utilization of classroom peers as behavior change agents* (pp. 101-128). New York: Plenum.

Sullivan, P. J. & Dockstrader, M. F. (1978). Values education and American schools: Worlds in collision. In N. A. Sprinthall & R. L. Mosher (Eds.), *Value development as the aim of education.* Schenectady, NY: Character Research Press, 135-156.

Wang, M. C. and Walberg, H. J. (Eds.) (1983). *Adapting Instruction to Individual Differences.* Berkely, California: McCutchan, 1985.

Waxman, H. C., Wang, M. C., Anderson, K. A. and Walberg, H. J. (1985). Synthesis of research on the effects of adaptive education. *Educational Leadership* 43, No. 1 27-29.

Weinstein, G. & Fantini, M. D. (1970). *Toward humanistic education.* New York: Praeger.

CHAPTER III

THE TEACHER AS A COUNSELOR

THE TEACHER who is committed to the psychosocial development of students has three major role functions which require attention. One requires teaching subject matter. Certain knowledge, information, facts, and skills must be taught in order to insure that students become employable adults and discerning citizens. There are also countless adult avocational activities whose enjoyment depends upon one's ability to apply the fundamentals of reading, writing, and mathematics.

The teacher who is committed to the psychosocial development of students must engage in two additional role functions which activate that commitment. The teacher must be able to contribute to the psychosocial development of students within the classroom structure or group setting and also be available to students outside that setting as a counselor. The previous chapter introduced the reader to some basic approaches whereby the teacher can contribute to the psychosocial development of students in the classroom or group setting. This chapter will introduce the reader to the concept of the teacher functioning as a counselor. This separation of the teacher's psychosocial functioning in and outside of the classroom is basically for the purpose of helping the reader to understand the difference in processes when the teacher is implementing psychosocial development in two different settings. In actuality, however, the teacher who contributes to the psychosocial development of students is functioning basically as a counselor, whether working with students within a classroom or outside of it.

The teacher's application of counseling fundamentals has had an interesting history. Arbuckle was the first to write about the teacher functioning as a counselor (Arbuckle, 1950). The teacher was selected as the one who should counsel students, because the formal profession of school counselors had not yet materialized. During the time of Arbuckle's book and prior to its publication, it was a natural course of events for the teacher to do the needed counseling with students.

School counseling became formalized as a profession when the United States Congress passed the National Education Defense Act of 1958. Part of the funding contained in the act was given to colleges and universities so that they could formally prepare persons to become school counselors. School counselors were needed to identify students who were academically talented and to develop their interests in science and engineering. In 1957, the Soviet Union had launched the first vehicle into space, *Sputnik,* and Congress was alarmed that the United States did not have the scientific talent to get into space before the Soviets. The National Defense Education Act was quickly passed so that the United States could begin the catching-up process. Over a ten-year period, the United States Congress provided several billion dollars for university-based training institutes which prepared enrollees to become school counselors.

Once on the job, the initial salaries for school counselors were paid with federal funds which were allocated for that purpose through the states. Over a period of years the proportion of federal support funds was decreased until the local school system eventually absorbed the full salaries of school counselors they employed.

While school counselors were designated to identify and encourage those students with scientific talent, they were also realizing that, within any student population, there was a startling percentage of students who had problems of psychosocial development. Many school counselors decided that the scientific talents of students could never be utilized because of the psychosocial problems which obstructed their use. This discovery is much like the viewpoint developed in the first chapter of this book in the section on *Feelings Influence Thinking and Behavior.* Students with scientific talents weren't able to use those talents (whose use required academic thinking and performance), because personal problems (with an emotional or psychosocial basis) were obstructing the use of those scientific talents. With this emerging awareness among school counselors, accompanied by an equivalent awareness in university-based National Defense Education Act Counseling and Guidance Training Institutes, school counselors began to do more and more personal (psychosocial) counseling with scientifically talented students; and because of the requirements of equity, which characterize a democratic society, personal counseling was also made available to all members of a student body instead of being restricted to those with scientific talents.

When school counselors began to do more personal counseling with students and school counselors became more professionalized, the need for teachers to counsel students became less necessary, since the school counselor was viewed as the one best trained to furnish students with counseling. Teachers were now officially unburdened from the need to counsel students. There was now a trained person in almost all schools whose specialized training in counseling made teachers' involvement in the process unnecessary.

During the 1960s and 1970s, however, there was a cultural upheaval occurring in the United States (see the section "Values Clarification" in Chapter II). The values of the past were being challenged and replaced. The deterioration of the family, rising divorce rates, the epidemic increase in the use of alcohol and drugs, and a new sexual freedom, all had a negative effect on the psychosocial stability of students. They came to school against the background of a society engaged in a public and excruciating debate over values which were at opposites ends of a liberal/conservative continuum. Many of these debates continued into the home and added to the normal and developmental psychosocial confusion of young people. Youngsters became uncertain where they stood on value issues which had become polarized. Others used the atmosphere of a new liberalism to experiment with new life-styles, alcohol, drugs, and sex. Stimulating experiences outside of school prompted many students to question the relevance of education: to question whether it was dealing with life's issues or merely perpetuating itself as an institution.

Teachers began to see youngsters coming into their classrooms who were troubled by what was occurring in their homes, neighborhoods, and the nation and had become uncertain about their own values. Teachers with an inclination toward the psychosocial well-being of students saw that these problems were obstructing the students' ability to learn. They gave these problems their attention because of the realization that these problems were being brought into the classroom and needed to be addressed in the classroom. The number of students who had psychosocial problems had increased because of what was occurring in the larger society. Because of the times, many teachers felt that what school counselors were doing for these students was adequate but insufficient. There weren't enough counselors for all of the classrooms of the nation. Someone had to help the increasing percentage of students with psychosocial problems and the teacher, out of both inclination and necessity, returned to the role once held: that of being a teacher-counselor.

The post-Arbuckle (1950) movement toward the classroom teacher embodying the attitudes and communication skills of a counselor took on many names. Some movement titles were humanistic education (Weinstein & Fantini, 1970), psychological education (Mosher & Sprinthall, 1971), open education (Barth & Rathbone, 1971), emotional education (Ellis, 1972), affective education (Flynn & LaFaso, 1974), and moral education (Hall & Davis, 1975).

The concept of the teacher as a counselor has gone through many ideological journeys through the years. But the concept, initiated by Arbuckle (1950), is returned to Arbuckle for conceptual ownership. The concept has merit, has been practiced by a countless number of teachers through the years, and students have had their psychosocial development improved because of the help provided by such teachers. This chapter will introduce the reader to a client-centered approach for performing the counseling dimension of the teacher's role.

As was indicated, the concept of the teacher as a counselor has had different ideologies competing for how the concept becomes applied. But all of the ideologies agree on one fundamental issue: effective teaching depends upon the counselor embodying the attitudes and communication skills of a counselor. The ideological debate is over what those attitudes and skills should be. So the concept of the teacher-counselor is renewed. This renewal is founded upon the realization that today's students have such large numbers of psychosocial problems that the responsibility for helping them cannot be limited to the small number of professionals available within the school and outside of it. Further, the process of helping students may be made more natural and effective by having it integrated with the teaching of subject matter. Arbuckle's concept (1950) is alive and well today as evidenced by this book and recent Canadian publication which indicate a contemporary interest in the topic's importance (Hiebert, Martin, & Marx, 1981; Martin & Hiebert, 1982).

A PERSON-CENTERED PERSPECTIVE

The counseling approach outline in this chapter is a renewed and adapted version of client-centered counseling which was initiated and developed by Carl R. Rogers (1942, 1951, 1954, 1961, 1967, 1979, 1970, 1972, 1974, 1975, 1977, 1980, 1983). What started as a process that was only applicable to one-to-one counseling has become applicable to an ever-widening range of human interactions: teaching, organizational behavior, families, parenting, groups, marriage and its alternatives, leadership, pastoring, the physician/patient relationship, and interpersonal communication in general.

We have been identified with the literature of client-centered counseling since 1963 (Boy & Pine, 1963) and have renewed and refined our Rogerian perspective in a more recent book (Boy & Pine, 1982). The application of client-centered counseling to teaching has been one of our enduring professional commitments (Boy, 1958; Boy & Pine, 1979; Pine & Boy, 1976; 1977a & b; 1979a & b).

Client-centered theory indicates that in order for a person to think and to profit from any learning activity that requires the use of the mind, the person must first be emotionally free to think. That is, our feelings, emotions, and personal problems often interfere with our ability to reason. If we expect students to learn academic subject matter, we must first attend to their emotional problems so that their minds possess the freedom to function and absorb that subject matter.

The teacher-counselor is committed to having students learn subject matter and does not neglect that commitment. What the teacher-counselor does, however, is also attend to those psychosocial problems which interfere with the student's acquisition of subject matter. The teacher realizes that academic learning will not occur until the student is emotionally free to participate in that learning.

If students sitting in class are victims of child abuse, divorce, drugs, neglect, or any other of the dozens of incapacitating problems that are chronicled in our daily newspapers, then we cannot expect them to be much interested in acquiring academic knowledge. Their interest in academics, however, can be increased if the teacher-counselor gives attention to those psychosocial problems which interfere with learning academic content.

RATIONALE FOR APPLYING CLIENT-CENTERED COUNSELING

When client-centered counseling is applied to teaching, it is called student-centered teaching. Client-centered counseling itself possesses the generic attitudinal and skill qualities to enable a teacher to counsel students. If the teacher has attitudinally and intellectually absorbed the content of client-centered theory, the realization emerges that it is applicable in meeting the psychosocial needs of students. It does not require the teacher to diagnose, evaluate, judge, or manipulate the student. It focuses on the individuality of the student and the student's definition, perception, and solution of a problem. It is *student-centered* in its philosophy, goals, and processes, and outcomes. It is an *applied* empathic human attitude toward students. The student-centered teacher feels that empathy is a fundamental attitude necessary to activate the helping process.

A competent student-centered teacher is able to counsel different students. A student-centered teacher is not frustrated by these differences, since the theory has always compelled the teacher to understand the uniqueness of the student from the student's internal frame of reference rather than from an external frame of reference furnished by the opinions of others.

Client-centered counseling is a generic process that has the strength and flexibility to be translated into student-centered teaching. Adopting the principles of client-centered counseling eliminates the need to confuse the counseling process by mechanically applying skills which may be applicable to one problem and have no carryover value when applied to a different problem. The student-centered teacher uses one fundamental empathic caring attitude for all students and tailors the helping process according to the psychosocial needs of the individual or group.

Why client-centered counseling? The following observations reinforce the thesis that client-centered counseling prossesses generic qualities and characteristics which make it applicable to a wide variety of students in many different settings.

It Possesses a Positive Philosophy of the Person

Client-centered counseling views the person as having basic impulses of love, belonging, and security which influence the person to be cooperative, constructive, trustworthy, forward moving, rational, socialized, and realistic. These human qualities tend to become actualized in classroom environments which encourage their emergence and tend to be dormant in classroom environments which inhibit their expression. Counseling, then, is the process of liberating a capacity which is natural to the person but has been inhibited by negative or confused life experiences.

It Articulates Propositions Regarding Human Personality and Behavior

These propositions regarding human personality and behavior (Rogers, 1951) form the philosophic core of client-centered counseling and provide the teacher-counselor with a generic conceptual framework for understanding different students.

These propositions view the person as:

- being the best determiner of a personal reality
- behaving as an organized whole
- desiring to enhance the self
- goal-directed in satisfying perceived needs
- being influenced by feelings which affect rationality
- best able to perceive the self
- interested in maintaining a positive self-concept
- behaving in ways that are consistent with the self-concept
- not owning behavior which is inconsistent with the self-concept
- producing either psychosocial freedom or tension by admitting or not admitting certain experiences into the self-concept
- responding to threat by becoming psychosocially rigid
- admitting into awareness experiences which are inconsistent with the self if the self is free from threat
- being more understanding of others because of a positive self-concept
- moving from self-defeating values toward self-sustaining values

It Possesses Achievable Human Goals for the Student

The goals of client-centered counseling are very personalized and human goals *for the student* rather than being goals designed to simply support the theory, society, or its institutions; but in achieving these personalized goals, the student will behave in ways that contribute to the well-being of society and its institutions. Although the goals of client-centered counseling are general, they are transmitted to the student by the teacher-counselor's attitude during, and outside of, the counseling relationship. The goals of client-centered counseling are aimed at helping the student to:

- realize how feelings influence thinking and behavior
- engage in behavior which liberates, actualizes, and enhances the self
- engage in the discovery of previously denied feelings and attitudes
- become more acceptant and trustful of the self
- engage in self-assessment
- engage in reorganizing the self
- become more self-reliant

- become more responsible for the self
- engage in self-determined choices, decisions, and solutions
- achieve individuality while being conscious of social responsibilities
- become sensitive to the process of becoming which involves a new and self-actualizing way of being

It Possesses a Definition of Teacher's Role Within the Counseling Relationship

The teacher-counselor's client-centered attitude toward the student finds its expression in the following behaviors. The teacher-counselor is understanding, liberal, acceptant, empathic, a sensitive listener, authentic, and possesses a sense of presence, emergence, and knows how to equalize the relationship with the student.

The term "concrete" (Carkhuff & Berenson, 1967) is added to the preceding desired teacher-counselor behaviors, because after the counseling relationship has been established with the student, the teacher-counselor is able to move toward responses which are related to the specific needs of the individual student. These responses are more concrete and represent an individualization of the counseling process which coincides with the experiential third period (1957 to the present) in the historic evolution of client-centered thinking (Hart, 1970; Corey, 1986).

While identifying the necessary teacher-counselor behaviors for effective counseling, the client-centered viewpoint also indicates teacher-counselor behaviors which must be avoided. The teacher-counselor is not a moralist, questioner, diagnostician, or authority figure.

It Has Research Evidence Supporting Its Effectiveness

Although client-centered counseling is more of an art than a science, any theory of counseling must also satisfy the requirements of science by possessing both qualitative and quantitative research evidence which confirm the effectiveness of the theory. Client-centered counseling does possess the desired research evidence which supports its effectiveness. In fact, it goes far beyond the requirements in this area. As Patterson (1973) has observed: "It must be noted that the client-centered approach has led to, and is supported by, a greater amount of research than any other approach to counseling or psychotherapy" (p. 412).

Corey (1986) also acknowledges the attention that has been paid to developing the research evidence which supports client-centered counseling." "Perhaps more than any other single approach to psychotherapy, client-centered theory has developed through research on the process and outcomes of therapy" (p. 57).

It is Comprehensive

Client-centered counseling can be applied beyond the one-to-one counseling relationship. The comprehensive nature of the client-centered view is seen in its application to teaching, organizational behavior, family relationships, parenting, groups, marriage and its alternatives, leadership, pastoring, the physician-patient relationship, and interpersonal relationships, in general.

Another indication of its comprehensiveness is that the generic principles of client-centered counseling can be applied to widely different persons—"normals," "neurotics," and "psychotics" (Corey, 1986).

It Can Be Applied

Client-centered counseling is clear and precise enough so that it can be applied. At the process level, it is an understandable concept that is applicable in proportion to the teacher-counselor's grasp of why it is done and how the process contributes to the student's psychosocial development. There is no difficulty in applying client-centered counseling *if* the teacher-counselor is *attitudinally* student centered. When a teacher-counselor is not *attitudinally* student centered, then that teacher has difficulty in accepting and applying the process.

It Focuses on the Student as a Person Rather Than on the Student's Problem

In terms of the philosophy, process, and goals of client-centered counseling, it has much to say about the person and the process for improving the human condition. It is person centered rather than being technique centered, process centered, skills centered, or teacher centered. It focuses on *the student as a person* rather than on the student's problem. It requires that the teacher possess the best of human qualities and be able to express those qualities in interpersonal relations with students.

When the teacher-counselor is able to assist a student to become a more adequate and better functioning *person*, this improvement will enable the student to solve other problems. When the person is psychosocially stable, that person is able to deal with problems because that stability produces clear and implemenable rational solutions. When one is psychosocially stable, insights and attitudes emerge which influence the identification of rational behaviors needed to solve specific problems.

If Focuses on the Attitudes of the Teacher-Counselor Rather Than on Techniques

The teacher-counselor's facilitative attitudes come from the personhood of the teacher. If we desire students to become psychosocially stable, we must also expect the teacher-counselor to exhibit the qualities of psychosocial stability. We cannot expect the student to become a more adequate and better functioning psychosocial person if the teacher-counselor does not model these qualities.

The personhood of the teacher-counselor, when expressed through counseling or teaching, becomes the primary influence which prompts the student to move toward more enriching psychosocial behavior. The teaching profession has neglected to focus on the psychosocial modeling influence that the teacher has on students. But the influence is present and will be emulated by students if it is positive.

It Provides the Teacher-Counselor With a Systematic Response Pattern

Client-centered counseling presents the most clear and well-defined response pattern to guide the teacher-counselor in the process of communicating with students: *reflecting the student's or group's feelings*. This response pattern is well established as a necessary counseling fundamental and enables the teacher-counselor to penetrate and understand the student's perceptions, values and attitudes and how these affect the student's behavior; it enables that student to perceive the teacher-counselor as a caring person who is able to understand the student's problem from the student's viewpoint; it serves to free the student to communicate values and attitudes which the student was not able to disclose in other interpersonal relationships; and it serves to establish a bond of trust between the student and the teacher-counselor. The reflective process will be more carefully examined in the following chapter.

It Provides Flexibility for the Teacher-Counselor to Go Beyond Reflection of Feelings

Reflecting the student's feelings does not have to be bland; the process can be lively, penetrating and expanding in proportion to the teacher-counselor's ability to read the feelings of students and maintain a disciplined commitment to the reflective process. A pure reflection of the student's feelings possesses impact, in that it prompts the student to investigate previously denied feelings and bring them into awareness.

In the refinement of client-centered counseling by Boy and Pine (1982), a second phase has been added to the basic client-centered counseling process. After an effective helping relationship has been developed with the student in phase one, the teacher-counselor can move to a second phase and individualize counseling according to the specific psychosocial needs of the student. This phase two individualization is accomplished by any one of the following: (1) a continuation of the process (reflecting the student's feelings) started in phase one, (2) making additives to the phase one process, (3) incorporating techniques from other process models of counseling, and (4) making a responsible judgment to do something which is logically concrete and helpful to students. The existence of phase two enables the teacher-counselor to be flexible in meeting the specific psychosocial needs of different students. The modern student-centered teacher-counselor would have no difficulty with the following viewpoint (Copeland, 1977): "If feelings of inadequacy are derived from within, the client-centered approach may be helpful initially, but if the client's problem has resulted from an impossible environment, the counselor has a moral responsibility to serve as an advocate or mediator and to actively attempt to alter the environment" (p. 400).

It Can Be Individualized According to the Psychosocial Needs of Different Students

The flexibility of the student-centered approach enables it to be individualized according to the psychosocial needs of each student. The theory has no grandiose message which the teacher-counselor has to deliver to students. What the theory does require is the development of a relationship in which *the student* can identify the problem and a relationship in which *the student* can choose the attitudes and behaviors that will enable the problem to be solved. A student-centered relationship is an open and flexible relationship, because the student is the one who determines the scope, depth, and intensity of a problem, and once this recognition has occurred, the student is in the best position to determine what needs to be done to solve the problem.

It Enables Student Behavior to Change in a Natural Sequence of Events

In student-centered counseling, the teacher-counselor establishes a relationship with the student in which repressed feelings can be expressed, thereby mitigating or eliminating their influence on behavior. The teacher-counselor accomplishes this by reflecting the student's feelings. If the teacher-counselor's reflections are accurate and penetrating, the student becomes more comfortable in the relationship and feels secure enough to go more deeply into these feelings and explore previously denied feelings.

Once a student has fully expressed previously repressed feelings and feels released from their debilitating behavioral effects, the student's rationality begins to take over as the student begins to think about a solution to a problem. At this stage, because the student does not feel emotionally repressed, confused, or burdened, the student moves away from the emotional foundations and expressions of a problem toward a rational consideration of a problem. Once the student begins to look at a problem rationally, the solution to the problem is close at hand. The resources of the student's mind, clouded by emotions in the past, are now free to function rationally and move toward a solution.

THE COUNSELING PROCESS

There are two basic phases which characterize an effective counseling relationship. In the first phase, the teacher must become involved in building a human and facilitative relationship with the student. Building such a relationship is the foundation from which future interactions with the student can be productive. That is, when a teacher has a caring relationship with a student, that student has a positive response to the relationship. The teacher's human credibility is the catalyst for the student's positive movement in the counseling process.

If the teacher has been effective in the relationship building first phase of counseling, then what the teacher says or does in the second phase tends to produce a positive response from the student. What is done in phase two, then, becomes effective essentially because the student has trust in the teacher; a trust which was initiated and developed by the teacher in the phase one process of relationship building. Therefore, if the teacher concentrates on first building a relationship with the student, then the outcomes of counseling will tend toward the positive.

Any approach to counseling can yield more positive results if it is founded upon a caring and human relationship with the student. It is the existence of such a relationship which enhances the effectiveness of any approach applied to the second phase of counseling. When the teacher has developed a caring human relationship with a student, that teacher is able to implement any natural and logical approach to counseling in phase two. Without a relationship, the teacher's effectiveness is greatly impaired in the second phase of counseling. Students respond to persons (Aspy & Roebuck, 1977). When the teacher is able to establish human credibiliy in the first phase of counseling, it is this credibilty which enables the second phase of counseling to occur and be effective.

The development of a substantive relationship requires that the teacher possess identifiable positive human attitudes and that they be communicated to students through the teacher's verbal and non-verbal behavior. The possession of a caring human attitude will contribute to building a facilitative relationship, so crucial in the first phase of counseling. Without the demonstrated possession of these attitudes, the teacher cannot expect the second phase of counseling to be productive.

Relationship building between the teacher and student is one beneficial outcome of phase one. Another equally valuable outcome is the accurate assimilation of the student by the teacher. By assimilating or absorbing the meaning and intention of the student's attitude and behavior, the teacher is able to gain an awareness of the student's hopes, fears, desires, motives, life-style, self-concept, and defenses. Such as assimilation enables the teacher to have a more accurate understanding of which approach will yield the best results with a particular student during phase two. Far too many teachers proceed with strategies which are based upon only a partial understanding of the student's psychosocial values and the result is a poor connection between the needs of the student and the teacher's response pattern. Phase one will enable the teacher to assimilate the student's life-style, and such as assimilation will result in the teacher making a far more accurate judgment regarding which approach will be most beneficial for a particular student during phase two.

The two distinct advantages of phase one are that it provides the teacher with a meaningful vehicle for building a helping relationship while also enabling the teacher to more deeply and accurately assimilate the student's psychosocial motives. An effective phase one will contribute significantly to the knowledge base needed for the teacher to meet the needs of the student in phase two.

PHASE ONE TEACHER ATTITUDES

More than any other theory of counseling, the client-centered approach focuses on the teacher-counselor's *attitude* toward the student as being the primary influence for establishing an effective counseling relationship. The attitudinal foundations of the client-centered view are:

Empathic understanding. The ability of the teacher-counselor to deeply penetrate how the student feels, from the student's viewpoint. This requires a selfless attitude on the part of the teacher-counselor: an attitude which is neither moralistic nor judgmental; an attitude which perceives the student's inner world of meanings from the student's frame of reference.

Acceptance This is ability of the teacher-counselor to respect students who are different from the teacher in values, behavior, and psychosocial experiences. Poets, philosophers, and theologians have called this an attitude of love. An attitude of accepting and respecting others comes from teacher-counselors who are secure enough not to hide their love and acceptance.

Sensitive listening. This attitudinal quality requires that the teacher-counselor be sensitive to the student's inner world of meanings. It requires a selfless attitude in which the teacher is willing to give up talking *at* students. It requires a patience that influences the teacher to be more interested in hearing what the student is feeling and saying rather than being interested in pontificating.

Authenticity. A student has a positive response to a teacher-counselor who is genuine; a teacher-counselor who does not use or manipulate the student. An attitude of authenticity enables the student to respond in an authentic manner and be free from the facades which too often characterize the student's interaction with teachers.

Presence. The attitude of presence means that the teacher-counselor is focusing on the relationship with a student and is not distracted. In lay terms, this has been called "giving a person your undivided attention." In other circles, it has simply been called "concentration." It means being so present and committed to the importance of a dialogue with a student that the student feels very special and important.

Emergence. This attitude requires a sophistication for timing and pacing on the part of the teacher-counselor. It is a realization that a change in attitude and behavior is a very individual process that occurs at different time intervals among students because of their very individualized reactions to the influences in their lives (parents, siblings, peers, the learning environment, community values, etc.).

Equalizing. Equalizing is the attitude which enables the teacher-counselor to form a relationship with a student in which there is a balance of power between them. There is too often an imbalance of power in the typical relationship between a teacher and student. The teacher typically has the upper hand and the student knows it. An attitude of equalizing enables the student to deal with the teacher as an equal and power games become eliminated from the relationship (Boy & Pine, 1976).

PHASE ONE COMMUNICATION

The teacher's basic response pattern in developing a helpful counseling relationship with a student is *reflection of feelings*. This chapter will briefly deal with the process of reflecting feelings, while the following chapter will examine the process in greater detail.

Reflection of the student's feelings enables the teacher to enter the student's pivate perceptual world; to understand and empathize with what it means to be *this* student, with *this* background, undergoing *this* set of experiences, with *this* combination of attitudes and feelings. When the teacher is able to communicate empathy to the student by reflecting the student's feelings, the student is influenced to express previously hidden or denied feelings. The student feels an expanding self-understanding in this process and identifies closely with the teacher who is enabling it to occur. The student develops a sense of trust for the teacher and an increased feeling of closeness to the authenticity, empathy, and *gravitas* of the teacher. This is an important and supportive feeling for the student to have, because, finally, in a fast-paced technological world there is someone who cares enough to listen and empathize. Being understood is an enriching experience for the student, and the student who receives understanding develops a bond with the teacher who is furnishing it. The teacher helps the student to feel this bond by engaging in the process of reflecting the student's feelings. Not the words, but the inner feelings that undergird the words and give affective meaning to the words. Such a reflective response pattern is the foundation for building a helpful counseling relationship. When a teacher develops a counseling relationship by using reflective responses in phase one, the teacher increases the chances of phase two being effective.

FROM PHASE ONE TO PHASE TWO

If the teacher makes the necessary investment in the relationship building required in phase one, then what follows in phase two will be a natural and helpful process. In phase two the teacher bases the interactions with the student on clearly identified student needs; and these needs are clearly known by the teacher as an outcome of the first phase of counseling.

The identification of student needs in phase one will enable the teacher to determine what specific behavior needs to come from the teacher in phase two in order to help the student. Without an investment in relationship building in phase one, the teacher is unable to know what clearly has to be done in phase two. The teacher doesn't really know the student. Phase one enables phase two to meet student needs, naturally and accurately.

In phase two the teacher has a number of different response patterns which can be used with students. The authors recommend that the teacher use a response pattern which is human, helpful, and logical and is connected to the student's psychosocial needs identified in phase one (Coulson, 1970).

This means that in phase two the teacher can continue reflecting a student's feelings, because of doing this best meets the needs of *this* particular student, or the teacher can use a non-reflective response pattern with another student because *it* best meets the needs of *that* student. Phase two must be tailored to the individual psychosocial needs of the student which became known to the teacher in phase one.

If the teacher decides that a more directive approach would better meet the needs of a student in phase two and if these needs have been identified as an outcome of phase one, then what the teacher does in phase two will be *heard, internalized, and acted upon by the student*. The teacher insures such a response if the relationship-building components of phase one were adequately applied. All teachers who are inclined toward more directive approaches to counseling desire that what they say to students will be heard, internalized, and acted upon. Such teachers will have a greater assurance that students will respond to them if those teachers have made an investment in building a phase one substantive counseling relationship. Persons hear and respond to friends, not strangers. This simple principle indicates that the more directive teacher must first achieve an affective communication process (reflecting feelings) in phase one if the teacher's interventions are to have any influence upon the student in phase two.

The length of time that it takes a teacher to build a phase one relationship will vary according to the relationship-building skills of the teacher and the needs of the student. Teachers with a high degree of natural relationship-building skills will be able to achieve a working relationship with a student in a relatively short period of time, perhaps even in the first counseling session. Other teachers may have to invest in six or more phase one counseling sessions, especially if the teacher has not yet achieved a high level of relationship credibility or if the student is inclined to be distrustful of anyone trying to help. Teachers need keen judgment in order to determine how many phase one counseling sessions are needed as a buildup for phase two. When to make a transition from phase one to two will become more clearly known as the teacher gains experience in the counseling process. It typically occurs when the student moves away from emotionally based dialogue and replaces it with rational dialogue.

PHASE TWO CHOICES

Before the teacher reaches the phase two point of using a particular approach to meet the specific needs of a student, the teacher must engage in a transition from phase one to phase two. The teacher needs to make an informed decision regarding which phase two process should be used to meet the needs of *this* student with *this* problem. The success of phase two depends upon both the effectiveness of phase one and the accuracy of the teacher's judgment regarding which approach will be most beneficial for the student in phase two.

When the teacher has only a limited and partial awareness of a student's psychosocial needs, the teacher should not move ahead with phase two. Moving ahead with phase two would not be beneficial for the student, because the teacher has limited knowledge upon which to base a phase two process judgment. In such a case, the teacher should continue phase one until an improved knowledge base about the student has been developed; a knowledge base that will enable the teacher to make a sound judgment regarding which phase two process will be best for the student. The basis for this judgment must always be the needs of the student; that is, which phase two process will yield the highest psychosocial gain for the student?

PHASE TWO GUIDELINES

The Emotionality or Rationality of the Student Will Determine Which Phase Two Approach Is Best

An important contribution to the teacher's judgment regarding which approach is best for the student in phase two is the student's tendency to solve problems rationally or affectively.

Some students learn to engage in maladaptive behavior, because the rational processing of information is a definite influence in the formation of that behavior. With such a student, since rational influences play such a central role in the casuality of maladaptive behavior, a rational process can be applied for the resolution of the problem. With some students a clearly rational approach to the solution of a problem influences the student to change the maladaptive behavior.

Other students learn to engage in maladaptive behavior, because their affective functioning is the greater influence in the formation of that behavior. These students intellectually know the difference between right and wrong, but they are emotionally influenced to engage in maladaptive behavior. With such students, the influence of affect is so strong that the resolution of the student's problem lies in using an affective approach in phase two.

Therefore, in phase two, the teacher must recognize whether a rational or affective approach will best meet the needs of a particular student; and this judgment rests upon which was the greater influence in causing the student's problem and then utilizing a matching approach (rational or affective) which has potential for resolving the student's problem.

The Student's Progress in Phase Two is Proportionably Related to the Teacher's Success in Phase One

Phase two is not automatically productive. It is productive only in proportion to the teacher's effectiveness in phase one. If phase one was successful, then the stage is set for phase two to be effective. If phase one had little positive effect, then the stage is set for phase two to be ineffective.

An effective phase one is the catalyst for an effective phase two. Phase two is only as productive and useful to the student as was phase one; that is, there is a clear and influencing proportional relationship between phase one and phase two of counseling.

The Needs of the Student Must Always Remain Paramount in Phase Two

When determining a phase two approach, the teacher must always be certain that it will be congruent with the needs of the student. During phase two, the teacher is faced with the temptation of meeting the teacher's needs rather than those of the student. The teacher may possess a bias that only incorporates one way of working with students during phase two. If the teacher acts on this bias, the bias may be unrelated to the student's psychosocial needs.

The objectivity established in phase one must not be lost in phase two. This objectivity must be continued into phase two so that the teacher can keep the focus on the needs of the student rather than allowing the teacher's needs to intrude. Doing this requires that the teacher have a high level of self-discipline; doing this means that the teacher is able to focus on student needs and exclude personal needs from the helping process.

The Teacher's Phase Two Approach Must Be Based Upon An Accurate Reading of the Student's Needs in Phase One

Phase two will tend to be productive if the teacher's phase two approach is based upon an accurate assimilation of the student's psychosocial needs in phase one. Phase two becomes effective because the teacher has taken the time to absorb the student's psychosocial life-style in phase one. When the student has fully discussed personal psychosocial attitudes and behaviors in phase one and the teacher has absorbed their meaning, the teacher is able to identify the helping process which needs to be implemented in phase two. Such an accurate assimilation will occur in proportion to the student's willingness to self-disclose. The student will be willing to talk about psychosocial concerns if the teacher creates a relationship which is comfortable enough for the student to be open to such disclosures.

Regardless of Which Approach is Used in Phase Two, There Should Be Evidence That the Student's Behavior Has Improved

Having students feel good about themselves is a desirable goal of counseling. Feeling good about oneself is essentially having a congruence between what a person is and what that a person would like to be. But for the self to feel good, positive statements must be matched with positive behavior. To talk a good game is one thing; to play a good game is far more difficult. A student's improved self-concept must be actualized through behavior which represents an improved self-concept. Actions speak louder than words, and improved student actions (behaviors) are clear indicators of counseling's effectiveness.

Phase Two Can Include a Non-Counseling Approach to More Accurately Meets and Needs of the Student

Some counseling loyalists see benefits occurring only within the context of a person-to-person talk-centered counseling relationship. Some behavior-modification specialists see benefits occurring only outside of the counseling relationship in carefully planned behavioral experiences.

Which is generally the more effective approach is really not a valid issue. The basic issue is which is the better approach for *this* student with *this* identified set of needs. For one student, the talking process may be the best mode for influencing behavioral change. For another student, the talking process yields little. This student changes behavior only as a result of being involved in concrete experiences.

Knowing which approach is better for a particular student can only occur after the teacher has assimilated the student in phase one, but all teachers who counsel should realize that phase two cannot be planned in advance. What to do in phase two must be connected to the identified needs of a particular student, and we can only know those needs by our participation with the student in phase one. Phase one enables us to know what to do in phase two. For some students, phase two may not include the traditional person-to-person dialogue. It may include non-counseling experiences which are congruent with the psychosocial needs of a particular student.

The Teacher Must Be Prepared to Go Back to Phase One if Phase Two is Not Producing Results

If carefully constructed, phase two will generally meet the needs of a student. If the evidence of the student's behavior, however, indicates that phase two is not working, then a reassessment of the student's psychosocial needs is appropriate. This is best accomplished by going back to phase one. By doing this, the teacher is able to gain a more accurate understanding of the psychosocial needs which influence the student's behavior.

Teachers whose phase two approach does not produce results will often find that the necessary assimilation of the student, required in phase one, did not occur deeply or well. Therefore, instead of struggling through phase two with an approach that is ineffective, the teacher should return to phase one in order to develop a better assimilation of the student and to re-establish the helping relationship.

Anyone lost in the complexity of any behavior clarifies that behavior by returning to a much more simple and understandable form of the behavior. This simple principle of human experiencing is most appropriate when the teacher's phase two approach is not yielding results. By returning to an uncomplicated phase one, the teacher is able to reassess the psychosocial information needed to construct a more accurate phase two.

BASIC COUNSELING CONCEPTS

Phase I

All Students expect:

- to be given the opportunity to explore and clarify feelings and attitudes
- to be respected as a person
- to be treated with justice
- to have an equalized relationship with the teacher
- to be heard and understood
- to develop a trust relationship with the teacher
- to have the opportunity for self-actualization

Phase II

Many students:

- desire to solve or resolve their own problem
- know themselves well and are, therefore, in the best position to solve or resolve a problem
- possess the ability to develop self-determined solutions
- can achieve self-actualizing behavior
- can solve specific problems because of an improved self-confidence
- desire to be sensitive to the causes which prompt certain behaviors

Other students:

- desire teacher assistance and/or intervention in solving a problem
- possess limited self-knowledge
- find it difficult to develop self-determined solutions
- have difficulty in becoming self-actualizing
- have difficulty becoming self-confident
- desire to change a behavior without any concern for the cause of that behavior
- are inclined to be concrete

CONCLUSIONS: SOME PROPORTIONAL EFFECTS

- Counseling will be effective *in proportion to* the qualitative *assimilation* of the student's attitudes and behavior in phase one and the accurate *accommodation* of the student's psychosocial needs in phase two.

- Phase one will have *a proportional influence* on phase two; if phase one is successful, then phase two will be successful; if phase one is ineffective, then phase two will be ineffective.
- Phase two cannot stand alone and work well; it works well when it follows phase one; phase one makes phase two effective.
- The student's progress in counseling is *proportionately related* to the human qualities of the teacher; if the teacher possesses genuine human qualities, then the student will make progress; if the teacher does not possess these qualities, then the student will not make progress.
- Students will make progress in counseling *in proportion to* their trust for the teacher; students who have trust in the teacher will make progress; students who have little or no trust in the teacher will make little or no progress.
- The progress of a student in counseling is *proportionately related* to the voluntarism of the relationship; the student who voluntarily enters the counseling relationship will make progress; the student who is coerced into the relationship will make little or no progress.

LEARNING TO BECOME A TEACHER COUNSELOR: TEACHER EFFECTIVENESS TRAINING

Perhaps one of the two most systematic applications of the client-centered or person-centered philosophy and approach to teachers counseling in the classroom is embodied in Teacher Effectiveness Training developed by Thomas Gordon (1972) a former student and colleague of Carl Rogers. Gordon sees that technological advances in instructional methodologies and innovations in educational philosophy are beginning to demand a radically new role for teachers in their relationships with students. This role departs from the traditional one of authoritative information giver and instead requires the teacher to perform certain functions for which most teachers have not been trained or at least not adequately trained.

1. Facilitating self-directed learning
2. Conducting productive student-centered classroom discussion
3. Serving as an educational consultant to students
4. Faciliating student problem-finding
5. Fostering a classroom climate of intellectual freedom and creativity. Equally important, this new role departs from the traditional

one of the teacher as the classroom disciplinarian controlling student behavior by reprimands and threats of punishment. Instead, the new role of the teacher requires such new skills as:

(1) Fostering students' self-control and self-discipline to avoid both authorian or permissive approaches to discipline
(2) Developing self-responsibility and independence in students
(3) Fostering student participation in rule-setting
(4) Resolving classroom conflicts through mutual problem-solving. Finally, teachers need to learn effective new skills of communicating with students that have a high probability of:
    (1) Enhancing student's self-esteem
    (2) Reducing students' dependence
    (3) Helping students solve their own problems
    (4) Making students feel understood
    (5) Reducing the psychological distance between teacher and students
    (6) Reducing student hostility toward teachers
    (7) Influencing students to have consideration for the needs of teachers and other students
    (8) Producing a relationship of mutual respect between teacher and student

Teacher Effectiveness Training was designed by Gordon not only to teach client-centered principles and skills but to give additional training in the special problem solving skills required for teachers to become effective in this new role. Because TET provides a kind of training that many teachers did not receive in their formal academic training, it greatly increases their own professional potential for making a significant contribution to the improvement of the educational process and to teacher-child and parent-child relations. Some of the skills taught in TET which are of particular value are:

(1) Non-evaluative listening for helping students solve their own problems
(2) Reflecting feelings — active listening
(3) Sending "I" messages — communicating genuineness
(4) A method for involving a teacher and a student in the process of resolving their own conflicts
(5) A win-win method of getting a class to work out a "contract" with the teacher that defines rules of classroom behavior
(6) A framework for helping parents change their child-rearing practices

(7) Methods for conducting effective group counseling with troubled or under-achieving students.

Teacher Effectiveness Training is a good example of a teacher-counselor training approach which can be used in staff development programs. It is primarily an educational program which emphasizes skill development utilizing small group discussion, role playing, experiential learning, behavioral homework assignments, readings, and feedback as learning tools.

HUMAN RESOURCES DEVELOPMENT (HRD): TRAINING FOR ACQUISITION OF COUNSELING SKILLS

Another systematic program for training teachers as counselors is the Human Resources Development Model (HRD) which was originally conceived by Robert R. Carkhuff and his colleagues in the early 1960s. Subsequent development, application, and research have made it one of the most widely used training approaches in professional and para professional counselor education programs. The model uses training methods and materials shown to be most efficient in producing acquisition of helper skills, especially interpersonal counseling skills which have been identified as contributing to positive outcomes in helping relationships (Cash 1984). Carkhuff's model expanded Carl Roger's core conditions (empathic understanding, unconditional positive regard, and genuineness) to include many additional facilitative interpersonal skills.

A systematic human relations development program was begun by Truax and Carkhuff (1967). Working with Rogers at the University of Wisconsin they and others began to investigate the effect of the presence of the "common thread" in the therapist-client relationship. They discovered that certain conditions or dimensions offered by the therapist, when present at high levels, led to growth on the part of the client and, when absent or present only at low levels, led to deterioration of the client. The accumulated evidence of the validity of the "core" conditions, or dimensions, as they were to be called are found in several volumes, especially in Rogers et al. (1967), Truax and Carkhuff (1967), Carkhuff and Berenson (1967), Berenson and Carkhuff (1967), Carkhuff (1960a, 1969b), Carkhuff (1971b), and Berenson and Mitchell (1974).

As the research progressed, several new dimensions were discovered and scales for rating these dimensions were developed (Carkhuff 1969a,

1969b; Carkhuff and Berenson 1969b; Truax and Carkhuff 1967). Eventually Carkhuff (1969a, 1969b) refined, renamed, and standardized the scales of the core dimensions and added a rationale which seemed to complete the model for a helping relationship. Although further refinement of existing dimensions and scales and the search for new dimensions continues, there is now available a substantial body of research and knowledge to support a preferred mode of helping.

The original HRD core dimensions of *empathy, unconditional positive, regard,* and *genuineness* (often called congruence) came from Rogers (1957). As a result of subsequent research on helper skills and helping outcomes *concreteness, confrontation,* and *immediacy* were added to the intial list of core conditions (Carkhuff 1969a, 1969b). The addition of *problem solving* and *program development skills* (Carkhuff and Berenson, 1976) to the training system reflects how HRD, as an eclectic developmental model, has continued to add counseling skills to the helping process.

The Helping Process

Helpers begin to build their base with helpers by first responding with empathy, respect, and warmth. As the helper begins to develop a base with the helpee through empathy, respect, and warmth, the helpee self-explores in greater and greater depth. In fact, the clue to whether or not the helper is being successful in the early phase of helping is based on the degree to which the helpee uses helper responses to make deeper and more thorough self-explorations.

The dimensions of concreteness, genuineness, and self-disclosure are next carefully implemented. When helpers press for greater concreteness or specificity on the part of the helpees, they introduce a certain degree of threat. The same thing occurs when helpers become more genuine and set the stage — model — for the helpees to become more genuine. Helpers' self disclosure encourages greater intimacy in the relationship, which can lead increased threat to the helpees. In other words, these three dimensions increase the threat level for the helpee, and they are thus action-oriented as well as facilitative. In addition to the relationship between level of threat and the action phase, these three dimensions are also involved in the problem-solving or planning stages of the action phase.

The description is oversimplified, but this is generally the pattern of helping. An important understanding is that during this process the helper is really reinforcing certain behaviors and extinguishing others.

Showing empathy, respect, and warmth generally reinforces whatever helpees say or do, which increases the probability of self-exploration and problem exploration.

Responding with appropriate levels of concreteness, genuineness, and confrontation results in more selective reinforcement. Helpers are no longer speaking strictly from the helpees' point of view. They begin to focus on aspects of helpee behavior that they think will be more productive, they begin to relate more of their own feelings which reinforce in a certain direction, and they point out discrepancies in helpee behavior. These helper behaviors increase the probability that helpees will understand themselves and their problems.

If an adequate relationship has been established, high levels of confrontation clearly reinforce certain kinds of behavior and extinguish others. These helper responses increase the probability that helpees will act on their problems and try to find some direction to follow which may solve their problems.

The art of helping includes first knowing how to respond helpfully and then knowing when to seek higher levels on various dimensions or when to use interchangeable responses. Many beginnings helpers learn to show interchangeable empathy, respect, and warmth but never become capable of displayig other, more action-oriented dimensions. They often say, "I don't want to be responsible if she makes the wrong decisions so I always make sure it's her decision," or "I don't want her to become dependent on others to make her decisions." These are legitimate concerns but they must be kept in perspective.

Helpers who display only interchangeable levels of empathy, repsect, and warmth are not very selective in what they reinforce. This often results in helpees accepting their problems as a permanent part of themselves instead of solving them. If helpees are rewarded for discussing their problems over and over without moving toward some goal, they become desensitized to the problem and begin to think it's normal to have that problem.

The HRD model has made great contributions to the contemporary movement to demystify psychotherapy, especially in regard to processes operating in interpersonal communication. Its operational definitions of helping skills and its functional basis for explaining their use in the helping process provide a person with tangible skills and a cognitive strategy for guiding the use of those skills in human relationships. The HRD helper skills training program has shown great flexibility in its capacity to be applied to different populations. It has an impressive capability to be modified to effectively and efficiently train individuals or groups of people needing specific skills to cope with environmental or personal living demands. HRD interpersonal skills training has been widely applied in helping teachers to develop high levels of interpersonal (or counseling) skills. (Carkhuff, Berenson, and Pierce 1977, Aspy and Roebuck 1977, and Gazda 1977). The power of the HRD model in helping teachers to function at high levels of interpersonal functioning and consequently to improve student learning has been validated by Aspy and his colleagues (1977).

REFERENCES

Arbuckle, D. S. (1959). *Teacher counseling.* Cambridge, MA: Addison Wesley.
Aspy, D. N. and Hadlock, W. (1967). The effects of high and low functioning teachers upon student performance. In R. R. Carkhuff (Ed) *Beyond Counseling and Therapy.* New York: Holt Rinehard.
Aspy, D. & Roebuck F. (1977). *Kids don't learn from people they don't like.* Amherst, MA: Human Resources Development Press.
Barth, R. S. & Rathbone, C. H. (1971). *A bibliography of open education: Advisory for open education.* Newton, MA: Educational Development Center.
Berenson, B. B. and R. R. Carkhuff, (1967). *Sources of Gain in Counseling and Psychotherapy; Readings and Commentary.* New York: Holt, Rinehard & Winston.
Berenson, B. G. and K.M. Mitchell (1974). *Confrontation: For Better or Worse!* Human Resource Development Press.
Boy, A. V. & Pine, G. J. (1963). *Client-centered counseling in the secondary school.* Boston: Houghton Mifflin.
Boy, A. V. & Pine, G. J. (1976). Equalizing the counseling relationship. *Psychotherapy: Theory, Research, and Practice,* 1, 20-25.
Boy, A. V. & Pine, G. J. (1979). Human therapeutic experiences. *Counseling and Human Development,* 11, 2-8.
Boy, A. V. & Pine, G. J. (1982). *Client-centered counseling: A renewal.* Boston: Allyn.
Carkhuff, R. R. & Berenson, B. G. (1967). *Beyond counseling and therapy.* New York: Holt, Rinehart and Winston.
Carkhuff, R. R. (1969a) *Helping and Human Relations: A Primer for Lay and Professional Helpers.* Vol. 1: *Selection and Training.* New York: Holt, Rinehart & Winston.
Carkhuff, R. R. (1969b). *Helping and Human Relations: A Primer for Lay and Professional Helpers.* Vol. 2: *Practice and Research.* New York: Holt, Rinehart & Winston.
Carkhuff, R. R. (1971a). "Helping and human relations; A brief guide for training lay helpers." *Journal of Research and Development in Education* 4, no. 2, 17-27.
Carkhuff, R. R. (1971b). *The Development of Human Resources: Education, Psychology, and Social Change.* New York: Holt, Rinehart & Winston.
Carkhuff, R. R. (1972). *The Art of Helping.* Amherst, Mass.: Human Resources Development Press.

Carkhuff, R. R., Berenson, D. H. and Pierce, R. M. (1977). *The Skills of Teaching.* Amherst, Mass.: Human Resource Development Press.

Cash, R. W. (1984). The human resources development model. In D. Larson (Ed.) *Teaching Psychological Skills.* Monterey, California: Brooks Cole Publishing Co.

Copeland, E. J. (1977). Counseling black women with negative self concepts. *The Personnel and Guidance Journal,* 55, 397-400.

Corey, G. (1986). *Theory and practice of counseling and psychotherapy.* 3rd ed. Monterey, CA: Brooks-Cole.

Coulson, W. (1970). Inside a basic encounter group. *The Counseling Psychologist,* 2, 6-22.

Ellis, A. (1972). *Emotional education.* New York: Julian Press.

Flynn, E. & LaFaso, J. F. (1974). *Designs in affective education.* New York: Paulist.

Gazda, G. (et al.) (1977). *Human Relations Development: A Manual for Educators.* Boston, Mass.: Allyn and Bacon.

Gordon, Thomas (1972). *Teacher Effectiveness Training.* Pasadena, California: Effectiveness Training Associates.

Hart, J. T. (1970). The development of client-centered therapy. In J. T. Hart & Tomlinson, T. M. (Eds.), *New directions in client-centered therapy.* Boston: Houghton Mifflin, 3-22.

Hiebert, B. A., Martin, J. & Marx, R. W. (1981). Instructional counselling: The counsellor as teacher. *Canadian Counsellor,* 15, 107-114.

Hall, R. T. & Davis, J. U. (1975). *Moral education in theory and practice.* New York: Prometheus.

Jacobs, A. (April, 1975). "Research on methods of social intervention: The study of the exchange of personal information in brief personal growth groups." Paper presented at the invited Conference on Small Group Research, Indiana University, Bloomington.

Martin, J. & Hiebert, B. A. (1982). *Instructional Counselling.* Vancouver: Centre for the Study of Curriculum and Instruction, University of British Columbia.

Mosher, R. & Sprinthall, N. (1971). Psychological education: A means to promote personal development through adolescence. *The Counseling Psychologist,* 2, 3-82.

Patterson, C. H. (1973). *Theories of counseling and psychotherapy.* New York: Harper and Row.

Pine, G. J. & Boy, A. V. (1976). Teaching and valuing. *The Clearing House,* 49, 313-315.

Pine, G. J. & Boy, A. V. (1977a). A humanistic view of adolescence. *Counseling and Human Development,* 10, 4-12.

Pine, G. J. & Boy, A. V. (1977b). *Learner-centered teaching: A humanistic view.* Denver: Love.

Pine, G. J. & Boy, A. V. (1979a). Self-enrichment through teaching. *The Clearing House,* 53, 46-49.

Pine, G. J. & Boy, A. V. (1979b). The humanist as a teacher. *The Humanist Educator,* 17, 146-152.

Rogers, C. R. (1942). *Counseling and psychotherapy.* Boston: Houghton Mifflin.
Rogers, C. R. (1952). *Client-centered therapy.* Boston: Houghton Mifflin, 483-522.
Rogers, C. R. & Dymond, R. F. (1954). *Psychotherapy and personality change.* Chicago: University of Chicago Press.
Rogers, C. R. (1957). "The necessary and sufficient conditions of therapeutic personality change." *Journal of Consulting Psychology* 21, 95-103.
Rogers, C. R. (1961). *On becoming a person.* Boston: Houghton Mifflin.
Rogers, C. R. (1967). The conditions of change from a client-centered viewpoint. In B. Berenson & R. Carkhuff (Eds.), *Sources of gain in counseling and psychotherapy.* New York: Holt, Rinehart and Winston.
Rogers, C. R., Gendlin, E. T., Kiesler, D. J. and Truax, C. B. (1967). *The Therapeutic Relationship and its Impact: A study of Psychotherapy with Schizophrenics,* Madison: University of Wisconsin Press.
Rogers, C. R. (1969). *Freedom to learn.* Columbus, OH; Charles E. Merrill.
Rogers, C. R. (1970). *On encounter groups.* New York: Harper and Row.
Rogers, C. R. (1972). *Becoming partners: Marriage and its alternatives.* New York: Delacorte.
Rogers, C. R. & Wood, J. (1974). Client-centered theory: Carl Rogers. In A. Burton (Ed.), *Operational theories of personality.* New York: Brunner-Mazel.
Rogers, C. R. (1975). Empathic: An unappreciated way of being. *The Counseling Psychologist,* 5, 2-10.
Rogers, C. R., (1977). *On personal power.* New York: Delacorte.
Rogers, C. R. (1980). *A way of being.* Boston: Houghton Mifflin.
Rogers, C. R. (1983). *Freedom to learn in the 1980s.* Columbus, OH; Charles E. Merrill.
Truax, C. G. and Carkhuff, R. R. (1967). *Toward Effective Counseling and Psychotherapy: Training and Practice.* Chicago: Aldine.
Weinstein, G. and Fantini, M. (1970). *Toward humanistic education.* New York: Praeger.

CHAPTER IV

THE REFLECTIVE PROCESS: FOUNDATION FOR EFFECTIVE TEACHER COUNSELING

THE PREVIOUS CHAPTER introduced the reader to the theory and process of client-centered counseling. This chapter will present the most fundamental element of that process, reflection of feelings, and give it the detail necessary for its successful application in phase one of counseling. Phase one of counseling is basically built upon the process of reflecting the student's feelings. By doing this, the teacher assimilates the psychosocial needs of the student, builds an affective and facilitative relationship, and lays the foundation for judging which process will best meet the psychosocial needs of the student in phase two.

Reflection of feelings is a concept not well understood at the application level. Through this chapter we hope that teachers who counsel will be better inclined to apply it with skill and accuracy. If applied well, reflection of feelings will enable the teacher to fundamentally improve phase one of the counseling process. And as Hansen, Stevic, and Warner (1982) have indicated, reflection of feelings contributes to some basic requirements for effective counseling (p. 109).

THE ROOTS OF THE REFLECTIVE PROCESS

Reflection of feelings has been traditionally used by many counselors and psychotherapists in their work with clients. It was first identified as a powerful therapeutic process in 1942 in the landmark book by Carl R. Rogers, *Counseling and Psychotherapy* (Rogers, 1942). This book was the foundation for the development of other humanistic concepts of counseling and it still serves as a fundamental viewpoint for the successful application of counseling. Through the years the process of reflecting feelings has also been applied to improving interpersonal communication in teaching, administration, organizational behavior, marriage and its alternatives, parenting, race relations, the building of community, conflict resolution, social action, the physician-patient relationship, and interpersonal relations in general. Rogers has recently identified an expanded application: as a foundation communication process which can lead to international understanding, so vital to harmony and peace among nations (Rogers, 1982).

Rogers (1942), in his first major contribution to our understanding of reflection of feelings, let us know that the process is not easy: "Probably, the most difficult skill to acquire in counseling is the art of being alert to and responding to the feeling which is being expressed" (p. 133).

Rogers (1942) also helped us to understand that reflecting a feeling is not responding to the logical content of what a client is communicating: "If the counselor is to accept these feelings, he must be prepared to respond, not to an intellectual content of what the person is saying, but to the feeling which underlies it" (pp. 37-38).

In his second book, Rogers (1951) added to our understanding of the process of reflecting feelings by indicating that the teacher-counselor's function is to assume "the internal frame of reference of the client, to perceive the world as the client sees it, to perceive the client himself as he is seen by himself, to lay aside all perceptions from the external frame of reference while doing so, and to communicate something of this understanding to the client" (p. 29).

Rogers (1951) elaborated further when he said: "Essentially what the therapist attempts to do is to reconstruct the perceptual field of the individual, at the moment of expression, and to communicate this understanding with skill and sensitivity" (p. 289).

Rogers (1951) concluded that the teacher-counselor "tries to adopt the internal frame of reference of the other person, to perceive what the other person perceives, to understand what is in the central core of the speaker's conscious awareness—in a sense, to take the role of the other person" (p. 352).

In more recent publications, those who develop models for helping others also recognize the importance of reflection of feelings as a foundation for the helping process. George and Cristiani (1981) indicate that after the helper has accurately perceived the client's feelings, the helper then "feeds back to clients, as accurately as possible, the feelings they are expressing. The counselor hopes that the clients will be able to view these feelings more objectively" (p. 70).

Hansen, Stevic, and Warner (1982) concur with the preceding and reinforce the therapeutic importance of the helper's ability to reflect the client's feelings.

WHY REFLECT FEELINGS?

Brammer and Shostrom (1977) have identified the advantages accruing to the counseling process when the helper is able to successfully reflect the client's feelings. Their view is summarized as follows:

1. Reflection helps the individual to feel *deeply understood.*
2. The reflection technique helps to break the so-called neurotic cycle, often manifested in marital counseling and expressed by such phrases as "She won't understand me, and therefore I won't understand her."
3. Reflection impresses clients with the inference that *feelings are causes of behavior.*
4. Reflection causes the *locus of evaluation* to be in the client.
5. Proper reflection gives . . . the feeling that (the client) . . . has the *power of choice.*
6. Reflection *clarifies the client's thinking so that* . . . the situation (can be seen) more objectively.
7. It helps communicate to the client the idea that *the counselor does not regard him (or her) as unique and different.* (The counselor is not shocked.)
8. Reflection helps clients to *examine their deep motives* (pp. 189-191).

An inner core of feelings contributes to our self-concept which influences us to think and behave as we do. If our inner feelings about ourselves are positive, then our self-concept will be positive. We'll think well of ourselves and have confidence that we can improve the quality of our psychosocial life experiences. A positive self gives us a sense of personal power and decreases the possibility of being psychosocially victimized. On the other hand, a set of negative feelings about ourselves will produce a self-concept which feels powerless in its ability to control reactions to threatening psychosocial life experiences. We then perceive ourselves as victims who have no control over what happens to us.

Feelings have an enormous impact upon our thinking and behavior. They form the critical core which influences our thinking and behavior. Therefore, in any effective teacher counseling the student's inner world of feelings must be entered in order to understand what motivates the student's thinking and behavior.

CONDITIONS FOR REFLECTING FEELING

The process of reflecting feelings is both an attitude toward the student and a learnable skill. As an attitude it emanates from the teacher-counselor's identification with the human principles of client-centered counseling. Rogers (1975) has indicated that when the teacher-counselor is deeply committed to respecting the student as a person and believes in the student's capacity to improve and change, to move toward values which enhance one's personhood, manage behavior, make decisions, and solve problems, then the teacher-counselor forms a helping relationship characterized by an empathic understanding of the student's inner world of feelings. With an attitude of empathy as the foundation for the helping process, the teacher-counselor easily moves toward the skill of reflecting feelings, since the skill is a natural application of an empathic attitude. Once the reflective process is understood and learned, its application occurs in a natural, human, and facilitative manner; it flows easily. If the teacher-counselor is attitudinally empathic toward the psychosocial needs of students, then the ability to reflect feelings is not awkward. It is a way of entering the student's inner world of feelings; feelings that influence the behavior that others see and respond to. Being attitudinally empathic and caring makes reflecting feelings a natural process.

Another teacher-counselor without a commitment to the importance of empathy and caring can still use the reflective process. It can be used as a therapeutic technique or skill rather than as a natural application of one's empathic and caring attitude. As a technique, the reflective process will lose some of its helping potential, but it will still work. The student will have a better response to its empathic application, but the student will still respond well to its application as a technique. It will serve either helper well. It will not only facilitate the building of a counseling relationship, but the reflective process will also enable the teacher-counselor to learn about the student's inner world of motives, values, attitudes, and behaviors which have contributed to the development of a problem. Reflecting the student's feelings, then, produces two clear results. It enables the helping relationship to develop while at the same time enabling the teacher-counselor to learn about the student's life-style values.

In order for feelings to be reflected well, certain conditions must first be met. The effectiveness of the reflective process occurs in proportion to the existence of these conditions. If they exist well, then the teacher-counselor is able to apply the relflective process in a natural way. If these conditions exist minimally, then the reflective process loses its potential to be effective.

Be Convinced That the Student Has the Power to Change

Reflecting the feelings occurs easily and well when the teacher-counselor is convinced that the student has the capacity to change attitudes, values, thinking, and behavior. When the teacher-counselor is convinced of this, the reflective process is applied because of the teacher's conviction that it will produce positive results. The student will change. The student needs to feel the stimulus of the reflective process in order to talk about those feelings which are influencing behavior. Once the student realizes the contribution of these feelings to one's behavior, the student is in a position to do something about the behavior; and changing one's behavior will mean that the student needs to change the feelings which cause the behavior. Understanding and improving those feelings is the catalyst for understanding and improving one's behavior.

Be Convinced That Feelings Influence Thinking and Behavior

Once the teacher-counselor realizes the powerful influence of the student's feelings upon thinking and behavior, the teacher-counselor becomes committed to utilizing reflection of feelings as a process for helping the student get in touch with those feelings. Once the student becomes sensitive to how feelings influence thinking and behavior, the student can begin to change those feelings; and once those feelings change, the student's thinking and behavior will also change, much like a chain reaction.

In order for the teacher-counselor to be sensitive to feelings, two pitfalls must be avoided. The first is the temptation to be an analyst; the tendency to try to analyze the student's feelings and put them in some known diagnostic framework and explain the meaning of these feelings to the student. The second is the temptation to be solution oriented: to listen to and reflect the student's feelings for awhile and then revert to offering the student a solution to the problem. Both temptations are indicative of our natural desire to want to do something to help the student, but doing either or both will interfere with the student's movement toward the necessary understanding of how one's feelings are affecting one's thinking and behavior. This realization puts the student in control of doing something about these feelings rather than waiting for someone else to solve the student's problems. Self-resolution of a problem is deep and long-lasting. Other-than-self resolution is superficial and short-term.

Be Aware of the Veracity of the Student's Presenting Problem

Too many teacher-counselors hear the student's presenting problem and quickly begin to work on that problem and its solution. Even if a solution is developed that appears reasonable, the problem solved is often superficial. Students tend to begin a counseling relationship with superficial concerns. They try to present themselves as reasonable people who don't possess serious problems. They typically talk about a class "D" problem. The teacher-counselor who quickly responds and begins helping the student with the class "D" problem may appear to be efficient. In reality, however, this student has not been given the opportunity to move beyond a class "D" problem toward a class "A" problem. The teacher-counselor moved so quickly toward responding to the class "D" problem that the student didn't have the time to identify and talk about the existence of a class "A" problem.

Experienced teacher-counselors realize that what the student talks about in the early session of a counseling relationship is not what the student talks about in the middle or later counseling sessions. Students need a period of time to warm up, to feel comfortable with the counseling process. After they've warmed up, they feel inclined to talk about more serious class "A" problems. Other students don't realize that they have a class "A" problem until they're well into a counseling relationship. As they begin to peel back layers of feelings, they typically go from class "D" to "C" to "B" to "A" problems. It takes time for a student to get in touch with the deepest of experiences and feelings which affect current thinking and behavior, especially those experiences and feelings which are repressed.

Be Attitudinally Empathic

The teacher-counselor who is genuinely empathic is able to enter the deeper recesses of a student's inner world of feelings. Empathy is that quality which enables a teacher-counselor to feel, just as deeply as the student, the very same feelings that the student is feeling (Gordon, 1980). A teacher-counselor cannot do this as well when the reflective process is used as a technique. As a technique, there is some penetration of the student's inner world of feelings, but the penetration is superficial when compared to what the student experiences when working with a counselor who is attitudinally empathic (Rogers, 1975).

The attitudinally empathic teacher-counselor penetrates the student's feelings more deeply, because the reflective process is being used in a natural rather than a mechanical manner. What to say next to the student is easily known by this teacher-counselor. And what is reflectively said is congruent with what the student is feeling and prompts the student to examine those feelings with greater care.

Empathic understanding has been identified as a powerful helping attitude. Reflection of feelings is the teacher-counselor's vehicle for expressing empathic understanding. All teacher-counselors consider themselves to be empathic, to a degree. Feeling empathy is one thing; expressing empathy is another. Empathy expressed within the vigorous framework of the reflective process enables the teacher-counselor to be empathic from the beginning of the counseling relationship to its conclusion. Feeling empathic toward the student without a process model (reflecting feelings) for expressing that empathy leaves the teacher-counselor frustrated. The empathy is not expressed and its therapeutic potential lies dormant. Empathy toward the student needs a vehicle for its expression, and the most scientifically accurate and humanistic vehicle for its expression is the reflective process.

Possess an Affective Vocabulary

Many teacher-counselors who are attitudinally empathic and understand the reflective process still experience difficulty in expressing that empathy. This is a simple technical problem that can be overcome by expanding one's affective vocabulary.

Most people have reasonable cognitive vocabularies. We can easily discuss, clarify, and reach conclusions about a rational topic. Schools, families, and society have trained us to do this reasonably well. We do, however, have difficulty in expressing affect or feelings. Schools, families, and society have been deficient in expanding our affective vocabularies, perhaps not purposely deficient but deficient all the same. So much of life is concrete that we become conditioned to use words and phrases which represent that concrete reality. To many, the vagueness of feelings prompts us not to have much experience in using words which accurately describe feelings. We prefer to use concrete words, since they appear to describe a precise reality. We tend not to use abstract words, the words which convey feelings, simply because such words often sound vague.

The teacher-counselor who expects to reflect feelings well, however, must devote time and energy to expanding one's affective vocabulary, since the possession of such a vocabulary will facilitate the process of reflecting feelings. Danish, D'Augelli, and Hauer (1980) have produced a list of 377 words designed to help expand one's affective vocabulary (pp. 40-42). Some time spent with such a list will improve the teacher-counselor's ability to reflect feelings.

Be Patient with the Reflective Process

Some teacher-counselors have said, "I tried the reflective process and gave it up. It didn't work." The authors' observation is that the process will work if the teacher-counselor gives it the time to work. You can't expect to apply reflection of feelings for ten minutes and see magnificent results. You must patiently and steadily apply it over a series of meetings before the process begins to produce results. It takes time to apply the reflective process and it takes time for the student to begin to respond to the process and talk about feelings.

We live in a society in which "doing it quickly" is too often the goal. We are surrounded by fast-food enterprises, microwave ovens, jet travel, quick divorces, and computers that promise to process information more quickly than their competitors. If we apply this attitude of quickness to reflecting feelings, then the process will fail. Reflection of feelings requires the utmost of patience in steadily applying it and making it work. There are no short-cuts, gimmicks, or tricks which will speed up the process. It takes time to do it well.

The time required to reflect feelings well and produce results should not be surprising if one looks at the typical problems possessed by students. Those problems didn't develop yesterday or the day before. Student problems are basically interpersonal and have developed over a period of time. It seems logical, then, that time will be needed for the student to identify the cause of a problem and the best way to solve it. A student's problem that has developed over a period of two years will not be resolved by a teacher-counselor in one reflective counseling session.

THE PROCESS OF REFLECTING FEELINGS

Once the teacher-counselor has internalized the preceding conditions for reflection of feelings, the process can begin. Internalizing these conditions alerts the teacher-counselor to focus on the feelings of the student.

The process cannot be effectively implemented until the teacher-counselor is attitudinally ready to hear the feelings which accompany the words, but it is this special kind of listening which enables the reflective process to occur. Following are some important elements of that process.

Read the Student's Feelings Accurately

Beneath almost everything that a student says is a set of feelings. These feeling are not often well verbalized, but they exist. Regardless of what the student may choose to discuss, feelings accompany that discussion. Even what appears to be an innocuous statement regarding snowfall will, more often than not, also contain feelings about the snowfall. The student may either feel elated about the snowfall, because of the opportunity to "get away from it all and go skiing," or the student may be terrified about driving conditions on the road.

Almost everything we say has two dimensions: the content dimension and the feeling dimension. The content dimension consists of the facts contained in a student's statement. The student may say, "I'm five feet two inches tall, weigh 175 pounds, and live in a three-room apartment on Elm Street. If I could lose some weight I'd feel a lot better about myself." The facts contained in the student's statement are the student's height, weight, size of apartment, and its location. The feeling contained in the student's statement is the dissatisfaction regarding being overweight and the effect of that added weight upon the student's self-image. The reflective teacher-counselor pays no attention to the facts contained in the student's statement but pays full attention to the feeling contained in the statement. The student's feeling is read, absorbed, and internalized by the teacher-counselor and reflected back to the student with a statement approximating the following: "You don't feel good about your body image. You'd like to be able to lose some weight." Such a reflective statement by the teacher-counselor will prompt the student to continue talking about feelings. Such a continuation will give the teacher-counselor additional feelings to reflect and will prompt the student to explore the same feeling more deeply or other disturbing feelings. Each time that the student makes a statement containing a feeling, the teacher-counselor recognizes the existence of that feeling by reflecting it. Reflecting feelings can be viewed as a conditioning process whereby the student is encouraged to express feelings because of the stimulus provided by the reflective responses.

The reflective teacher-counselor must hear what the student is feeling rather than what the student is saying, and those feelings must first be identified before they can be reflected. An accurate reading of the student's feelings will enable the teacher-counselor to make accurate reflections.

Be Sensitive to Same, New, or Conflicting Feelings

The reflective teacher-counselor stays attentive to the student's feelings. Those feelings often remain the same, especially at the beginning stages of counseling, but as counseling progresses those feelings often undergo obvious or subtle changes. The teacher-counselor must be alert to these changes.

A wife in counseling may spend a number of meetings expressing feelings of disappointment about her marriage. She may spend much time unraveling the feelings which reinforce that disappointment. At one meeting she may focus on her husband's financial irresponsibility, at another on his sexual disinterest, and at another she may express disappointment about his lack of interest in being a good father. The feelings throughout these counseling sessions are constant: disappointment about her husband's attitudes and behavior. Toward the middle stages of counseling her feelings shift from disappointment to a new set of stronger feelings which revolve around anger toward her husband. The reflective counselor mut be alert to the emergence of these new and stronger feelings, read them, and reflect them back to the client. As the counseling relationship continues, the client begins to present conflicting feelings. Although she is angry about her husband's attitude and behavior, she also feels a conflict because of a simultaneous resurgence of the love she experienced at the beginning of her marriage. Such conflicting feelings must be recognized by the counselor and reflected back to the client. There has been a change in the client's feelings and the counselor sensitizes the client to this change throughout the reflective process.

The client's movement from feelings of disappointment, anger, and renewed love doesn't occur in one meeting. These changes in feelings become expressed over a series of meetings. The last feeling, that of renewed love, is reached after having first worked through the feelings of disappointment and anger.

The preceding example is not presented as being the normal developmental progression of feelings in counseling. It is merely presented as an example of how one client processes her feelings with a reflective counselor. A different client, with the same initial feelings and working with the same counselor, may move through an entirely different set of feelings about her marriage and husband and terminate counseling not with a renewed sense of love but with a clear determination to end the marriage.

Each student has a unique set of feelings and gets in touch with them in a very individualized way with a reflective teacher-counselor. The teacher-counselor must be sensitive to the fact that students do move from one set of feelings to another and must be prepared to respond to these changes throughout the reflective process.

Reflect Primarily, But Also Clarify

When the teacher-counselor has achieved a reflective tempo in response to the student's feelings, that tempo has to be maintained in order for the student to receive help. When the teacher-counselor is able to steadily reflect the student's feelings, the student will have a release from those feelings and become able to move toward rational thoughts regarding how to solve a problem. Along the way, however, the student sometimes stumbles, becomes confused, and gives the teacher-counselor feelings which are confusing, complex, and contradictory. Some inexperienced teacher-counselors who are overly committed to the reflective process feel that every student expression of feeling must be matched with an appropriate and accurate reflective response. Not all statements of feelings, however, are made with full clarity. Some feelings are couched in hesitation and uncertainty. Others are characterized by being ambiguous and contradictory. When the student is expressing feelings which fall into these categories, the experienced reflective teacher-counselor asks the student to clarify the intended feelings with statements like, "I don't quite understand that," "You're confusing me . . . please help me understand what you're feeling," "You're not quite certain how you feel and so am I," and "I'm confused . . . I don't know whether you feel good or bad about that."

If the student leads the teacher-counselor down a path of hesitant, uncertain, ambiguous and contradictory feelings, and the teacher-counselor follows, then we have two confused participants in the counseling process. When one hears confusing feelings, the teacher-counselor realigns, refocuses, and expedites the reflective process by requesting that the student clarify these feelings (Egan, 1975).

Be Sensitive to Student Corrections of Reflections

Reflection of feelings is virtually a fail-proof process. The teacher-counselor can afford to be occasionally inaccurate when reflecting, because the teacher-counselor's greatest ally for improving the accuracy of a reflection is the student.

After an affective communicating process has been established, the student begins to listen very carefully to what is being reflected. The student is essentially monitoring the teacher-counselor's reflections and judging their emphatic content and accuracy. When the student hears the teacher-counselor responding with an inaccurate reflection, the student usually responds with, "That isn't quite what I feel. What I'm feeling is . . . " Such student corrections serve the reflective process well. They enable the teacher-counselor to correct the accuracy of a reflective statement.

At the beginning of a counseling relationship, however, the student is unsophisticated regarding the reflective process and may not have the sensitivity to correct a process which the student has not yet sufficiently experienced. It is, therefore, crucial for the teacher-counselor to be highly accurate with reflective responses at the beginning of a relationship with a student. Once the student begins to understand what the teacher is trying to accomplish by using the reflective process, the student will make corrections when the teacher-counselor's reflections are inaccurate.

Be Disciplined in Applying Reflective Responses

In reflecting the student's feelings, the teacher-counselor assumes the internal frame of reference of the student and perceives experiences as the student perceives them.

When the teacher-counselor makes this identification with the feelings of the student, the teacher-counselor translates that identification into words that accurately represent the feelings of the student; and mirrors back to the student those feelings so that the student may take a look at what they mean.

When the teacher-counselor accurately identifies with the feelings of the student and wants the student to know this, the teacher-counselor prefixes the reflection of feeling with such phrases as:

- You are saying . . .
- You feel . . .
- If I understand you correctly . . .
- I'm not sure I follow you, but is this it . . .
- I gather that you mean . . .
- Let's see if I really understand that . . .

Some teacher-counselors so deeply identify with the feelings of a student that their reflections of feelings gradually move from saying, "You feel that . . . " to "*I* feel that . . . ." This kind of transition takes place when the teacher-counselor develops such a deep and empathic identification with the feelings of the student that it becomes more natural to use "I feel . . . ." rather than "You feel . . . " when responding. Using "I" rather than "You" is a quantum step forward for the teacher-counselor; but when the step is taken, it occurs in a natural manner when the teacher-counselor feels so closely drawn to the feelings of the student that the most natural response involves the use of "I." The following *teacher-counselor* reflections of feelings convey the depth of empathic identification that can occur when responding to the feelings of students by the use of "I":

- I never could speak to her. I was always afraid that I'd be criticized.
- It's hard to be me. I want to but I never seem to be able to say what's on my mind.
- I wish I could get mad, but somehow I just don't think that I would be heard.
- I feel myself moving toward becoming a more likeable person and it's exciting!
- I wish I could stop being my own worst enemy. Sometimes, I feel that if I could like me then things would begin to improve.
- I'm confused. I was never like this before . . . before I seemed to have an idea of what to do.
- If I could only do it, then maybe my nervousness wouldn't be so bad.
- There are times when I don't even understand myself . . . times when about all I know about me is my name.

Once again, the preceding statements are teacher-counselor responses to the feelings of students. They represent reflections of student feelings; they are responses that teacher-counselors can comfortably engage in after they have accurately read and responded to the feelings of students (Boy & Pine, 1982).

REFLECTING FEELINGS: EXPANDING ITS EFFECTIVENESS

Reflecting the student's feelings also has another potential—it can incorporate "additives," a procedure that has been explored by Carkhuff

(1973), Egan (1975), and Turock (1978) and has been found to be effective as an expander of the reflective process. That is, a pure reflection of the student's feelings can be expanded to include an additive that is confrontative, interpretive, or challenging. When well timed, such additives can serve to give the student an added dimension of self-awareness not typically included in a standard reflection of feeling. For example, a standard reflection by a teacher-counselor might be: "You feel discouraged and lonely during this period of life."

A teacher-counselor additive that is *confrontative* would be: "You feel discouraged and lonely during this period of your life *and have lost the courage to do something about it.*" An additive that is *interpretive* would be: "You feel discouraged and lonely during this period of your life *and would feel much better if you only knew that your parents cared for you.*" An additive that is *challenging* would be: "You feel discouraged and lonely during this period of your life *and you are content to stay this way.*"

Reflecting the student's feelings can be done in a basic way or with additives that can be tacked on to a basic reflection. An additive can be used on certain occasions when such an additive serves to give the student a new insight that could not be achieved if the teacher-counselor's response was confined to just a basic reflection (Boy & Pine, 1982).

To Continue or Limit the Reflective Process?

Many students achieve progress in solving their problems when the teacher-counselor does nothing else but empathically reflect their feelings. When the teacher-counselor only uses reflection of feelings throughout a counseling relationship, that process represents the application of the traditional and well-established client-centered approach to counseling. To be purely client-centered is to follow a counseling theory for which there is more than ample research evidence indicating its effectiveness. If the teacher-counselor, however, decides that with another student the reflection process has taken the student just so far and the student needs to go beyond that point, then the teacher-counselor can apply a different approach, because that different approach better serves the needs of the student. The following guidelines will enable the teacher-counselor to judge when to more beyond reflection of feelings in the counseling process. The teacher-counselor does this (Boy & Pine, 1982) when the student:

1. Has achieved an emotional catharsis and is no longer overwhelmed by incapacitating feelings.

2. Is more open and honest in assessing the self and the attitudes and behaviors which constitute the self.
3. Shows a movement from emotionally based communication to rationally based communication.
4. Is motivated and willing to energize the self toward solving or resolving a problem (p. 20).

This chapter represents our attempt to clarify the foundation process of reflecting feelings. Its sections have dealt with the roots of the reflective process, the rationale for reflecting feelings, the conditions necessary for the reflective process to occur, and the process itself.

The teacher-counselor's attitudinal commitment to, and accurate application of, the reflective process will enable that teacher-counselor to possess a helping skill that has enormous potential. When applied well, the reflective process will improve a teacher's ability to help students solve and resolve psychosocial problems on a deeper and more permanent basis. For the teacher-counselor who learns how to qualitatively apply the reflective process, the ultimate beneficiaries will be those students who profit from its application.

REFERENCES

Boy, A. V. & Pine, G. J. (1982). *Client-centered counseling: A renewal.* Boston: Allyn and Bacon.

Brammer, L. M. & Shostrom, E. L. (1977). *Therapeutic psychology.* 3rd ed. Englewood Cliffs, NJ: Prentice-Hall.

Carkhuff, R. R. (1973). *The art of problem solving.* Amherst, MA: Human Resources Development Press.

Danish, S. J., D'Augelli, A. R. & Hauer, A. L. (1980). *Helping skills: A basic training program.* New York: Human Sciences Press.

Egan, G. (1975). *The skilled helper.* Monterey, CA: Brooks-Cole.

George, R. L. & Cristiani, T. S. (1981). *Theory, methods, and process of counseling and psychotherapy.* Englewood Cliffs, NJ: Prentice-Hall.

Gordon, T. (1980). *Leader effectiveness training.* New York: Bantam Books.

Hansen, J. C., Stevic, R. R. & Warner, R. W., Jr. (1982). *Counseling: Theory and process.* 3rd ed. Boston: Allyn and Bacon.

Rogers, C. R. (1942). *Counseling and psychotherapy.* Boston: Houghton Mifflin.

Rogers, C. R. (1951). *Client-centered therapy.* Boston: Houghton Mifflin.

Rogers, C. R. (1975). Empathic: An unappreciated way of being. *The Counseling Psychlogist,* 5, 2-10.

Rogers, C. R. (1982). Nuclear war: A personal response. *Monitor,* 13, 6-7.

Turock, A. (1978). Effective challenging through additive empathy. *The Personnel and Guidance Journal,* 57, 144-149.

CHAPTER V

PRINCIPLES AND CONDITIONS OF LEARNING: THEIR APPLICATION TO PSYCHOSOCIAL AND ACADEMIC EDUCATION

PSYCHOSOCIAL development must be an integral part of what students experience while attending school. Students must cease to look upon school as an institution which solely promotes their academic development. When students perceive going to school as a meaningless experience that more meets the needs of teachers than those of students, we cannot blame them for being truant and eventually dropping out. This and similar perceptions of school spread quickly among a student population and the result is a constant struggle between students and teachers, with the students resisting what teachers are attempting to teach and teachers trying to convince an alienated audience that the learning experience is beneficial.

The advantage of integrating psychosocial development with a standard academic curriculum is that each will enrich and expand the other. When a student is able to participate in projects dealing with his or her psychosocial development, the student begins to feel that school is an interesting place to be. It's concerned with his or her development and survival as a psychosocial being. School becomes connected with the problems that people are dealing with in real life. The student also becomes attracted to the school's academic curriculum and stops fighting it. He or she realizes that it too contributes to one's development but in a different way. That student realizes that one's academic development is of equal importance if one is to participate in a more informed life today and in the tomorrows that lie ahead as an adult.

The student who is psychosocially stable has a greater interest in a school's opportunities for academic learning than its psychosocial experiences can still learn something from those experiences. None of us can claim to be psychosocially perfect. All of us have areas which can be improved in our psychosocial response patterns. Therefore, in a school which offers experiences in psychosocial development, the academically interested student can maintain a primary interest in academics and a secondary interest in his or her psychosocial development. The important point is that a good school (a school that is good for students) will make both psychosocial and academic experiences available to students and will let each student get involved in each of these areas according to the individual student's needs and interests. Students should have both psychosocial and academic learning experiences available in school, but the emphasis put on either would be according to each student's needs and preferences.

The learning process which the student experiences in learning about either psychosocial development or academics is essentially the same. In the past, we have had the misconception that academic learning is a gruelling experience that takes place with a tough teacher in a disciplined atmosphere. When such an atmosphere exists, the student doesn't learn about how the subject matter enriches the human condition or its connection to the realities of adult life or making a living. The student collects the facts necessary to pass a test and then begins collecting the new facts that will be necessary for passing the next test. To the authors, such a process is not learning, it is merely the collection and regurgitation of facts. Learning is a different experience. Learning is going beneath the surface of a subject, learning about its intentionality, learning about how it has and will contribute to the well-being of humanity, seeing the subject's ability to improve life, seeing the unity of knowledge rather than focusing on its diverse elements, sensing the relationship between this subject and other subjects studied, knowing how the subject can be concretely used now and in one's adult life, knowing the areas in which the subject is weak (those areas which need further research), knowing the subject's areas of strength and how these strengths can be utilized, and knowing that what we know about any subject is only a very small fraction of what there is to know.

This chapter emphasizes principles and conditions of learning that contribute to the student's psychosocial development, regardless of whether the student is engaged in a psychosocial or academic learning experience. The teacher who utilizes these principles and conditions does not turn them on when teaching about psychological development and turn them off when teaching an academic subject. The teacher applies these principles and conditions in both settings because of the realization that students will be more attracted to learning when these principles and conditions are present in either learning experience.

PRINCIPLES WHICH FACILITATE LEARNING

Learning in the process of changing behavior in positive directions. By behavior we mean attitudes, ideas, values, skills, and interests. Positive directions mean directions which enhance, develop, and expand the self, other persons, and the community.

The implicit goal of all learning is to enable individuals, groups of people, and communities to become more fully functioning, psychosocially stable, effective, and able to fulfill potentials (Blocher, 1977; Pine & Boy, 1979).

Learning is an experience which occurs within the learner and is activated by the learner. The process of learning is primarily controlled by the learner and not by the teacher. Changes in perception and behavior are more products of human meaning and perceiving than of any forces exerted upon the individual. Learning is not only a function of what a teacher does, says, or provides for a learner; more significantly, learning is connected to something which happens in the unique inner world of the learner. It flourishes in a situation in which teaching is seen as a facilitating process that assists learners to explore and discover the personal meaning of events for them (Rogers, 1979).

No one directly teaches anyone anything of significance. If teaching is defined as a process whereby the teacher clarifies an experience or a piece of knowledge, then little student learning occurs as a result of this process and the learning that does take place is usually inconsequential. People learn what they want to learn, they see what they want to see, and they hear what they want to hear. Learning cannot be imposed. When we attempt to impose ideas on people, they resist. When we create an atmosphere in which people are free to explore, nourish and develop ideas in dialogue and through interactions with other people, we educate them. Very little learning takes place without personal involvement and meaning on the part of the learner. Unless what is being taught has personal meaning for the individual, that individual will shut it out. People forget most of the content "taught" to them and retain only the content that they use in their work or the content that is relevant to them in their psychosocial development (Rogers, 1983).

Learning is the discovery of the personal meaning and relevance of ideas. People more readily internalize and implement concepts and ideas which are relevant to their needs and problems. Learning is a process which requires the exploration of ideas in relation to self so that people can determine what their needs are, what goals they would like to formulate, what issues they would like to discuss, what content they would like to learn, and how much energy they will devote to the learning process. What is relevant and meaningful is decided by the learner and must be discovered by the learner.

This means that the relevant curriculum, as a set of experiences, emerges from learners, while the curriculum that is prescribed by agents external to a group of learners is merely tolerated. The school is the microcosm of the larger society. Unfortunately, for a number of students it is a microcosm of inadequacy and of failure. As a social institution the school can contribute to the lowering of self-esteem, because it demands success-oriented behavior; but, often in its demands for such behavior, it paradoxically does not provide opportunities through the curriculum for the attainment of even a small increment of success for many members of its captive population. As an institution that perpetuates middle-class values, the school's curriculum ordinarily represents a prestigious and traditionally academic avenue for success achievement. For the people who cannot travel this avenue because the curriculum does not make any sense to them personally, school is an experience characterized by failure, shame, friction, and frustration.

If the formal curriculum of the school (psychosocial or academic) does not provide positive experiences, the subliminal curriculum often does. The subliminal curriculum of the school, like the hidden major portion of the iceberg, is a natural extension of the visible and formal curriculum of the school. It is within the life-style experiences of the school that meaningful learning does occur. Though hidden, it represents for many individuals more effective and lasting learning, because it mirrors vital concerns and values of relevancy to the students. It is a curriculum of their choosing that includes the subjects of love, work, play, morality, justice, and human relationships—subject matter which isn't dealt with adequately and honestly in the formal curriculum (Rogers, 1976). When recalling our school days, this is the curriculum we remember because of its profound effect on our psychosocial development, then and now.

Learning (behavioral change) is a consequence of experience. People become responsible when they assume responsibility; they become independent when they experience independent behavior; they become able when they experience success; they begin to feel important when they are important to somebody; they feel like someone when someone likes them. People do not change their behavior merely because someone tells them to do so or tells them how to change. For effective learning, giving information is not enough. People become responsible and independent not from having other people tell them that they should be responsible and independent but from having experienced authentic responsibility and independence (Williams & Long, 1979).

Learning is a cooperative and collaborative process. Cooperation fosters learning: "Two heads are better than one." People enjoy functioning independently, but they also enjoy functioning interdependently. The interactive process appears to "scratch and nick" people's curiosity, potential, and creativity. Cooperative approaches are enabling. Through such approaches, people learn to define goals, to plan, to interact, and to try group arrangements in problem-solving. Paradoxically, as people invest themselves in collaborative group approaches, they develop a firmer sense of their own identity. They begin to realize that they count, that they have something to give and to learn. Problems which are identified and delineated through cooperative interaction appear to challenge and to stretch people to produce creative solutions and to become more creative individuals (Rogers, 1979).

Learning is an evolutionary process. Behavior change requires time and patience. Learning is not a revolutionary process. When quick changes in behavior are demanded, we often resort to highly structured procedures through which we attempt to impose learning. Whether such learning is lasting and meaningful to the learner is doubtful. Implicit in the principles and conditions for learning presented in this chapter is an evolutionary model of learning. Learning that is characterized by free and open communication, active and personal involvement, freedom from threat, and trust in the self; and all of this is evolutionary in nature (Pine & Boy, 1977).

Learning is sometimes a painful process. Behavioral change often calls for giving up the old and comfortable ways of believing, thinking, and valuing. It is not easy to discard familiar ways of doing things and incorporate new behavior. It is often acutely uncomfortable to share one's self openly, to put one's ideas under the microscope of a group, and to genuinely confront other people. If growth is to occur, pain is often necessary. However, the pain of breaking away from the old and the comfortable is usually followed by appreciation and pleasure in the discovery of an evolving academic idea or a changing psychosocial self (Sweeney, 1975; Kearney, 1982).

One of the richest resources for learning is the learner. In an era when so much emphasis is being placed upon computers, instructional media, electronic gadgets, books, and speakers as resources for learning, we tend to overlook perhaps the richest resource of all: the learner. Each individual has an accumulation of experiences, ideas, feelings, and attitudes which comprise a rich vein of material for problem solving and learning. All too often this vein is barely tapped. Situations which enable people to become open to themselves, to draw upon their personal collection of data, and to share their data in cooperative interaction with others maximize both academic learning and psychosocial development (Rogers, 1977).

The process of learning is affective as well as cognitive. Learning is affected by the total state of the individual. People are feeling beings, as well as thinking beings, and when their feelings and thoughts are in harmony, learning is maximized. To create the optimal conditions for learning to occur, *people must come before purpose* (Gendlin & Beene, 1968). Regardless of the purpose of a group, it cannot be effectively accomplished when other things get in the way. If the purpose of the group is to design and carry out some task, it will not be optimally achieved if people in the group are arguing and working against each other. If the purpose of the group is to discuss current issues and problems in an academic subject with reason and honesty, then it will not be achieved if people are afraid to communicate openly. Barriers to communication exist in people, and before we can conduct the "official business" of academic learning, we need to work with the people problems that may exist in a group. It might be said that in any group, regardless of the people problems which exist, enough group intellectual capacity remains intact for members of the group to acquire information and skills. However, to maximize the acquisition and internalization of ideas, it is reasonable that the people problems need to be dealt with first (Rogers, 1979).

Learning fuses work and play. People have always enjoyed a job well done. Joy in accomplishment is deeply rooted in human nature. Yet, in the learning of values, one of the most confusing areas centers on the perceptions people have of work in the classroom. Several psychological studies indicate that well-integrated, emotionally healthy people seem to see little difference between work and play. For them, there is no dichotomy between work and play. It is interesting to note that young children are so eager for accomplishment that it is often impossible for many of them to draw a line between work and play. This is because their work is of their own choosing. It has not been forced upon them.

Do we really value work? We certainly stress the importance of work. However, there is some question in our society as to whether we truly value work. We often perceive it as a necessary evil. How familiar is the suggestion: "Hurry and finish your school work so you can go out and play" to the elementary school child? How often are work and play dichotomized in repeated statements by teachers so that when a child reaches adolescence the child has the feeling there is something negative about the word *work*?

We can help people to learn that play and work are on the same continuum by providing an atmosphere in which their learning experiences evolve in accordance with their needs, capacities, and interests. By doing this we make learning a satisfying experience. By developing a learning climate which encourages the full use of the unique abilities of students, we make work more meaningful. By the recognition which students achieve through cooperative interaction rather than competition, we heighten this sense of industry.

It is commonly thought that work is fatiguing, while play is refreshing. The fact, however, seems to be that what is fatiguing or refreshing is more related to one's *attitude* toward the task than the actual energy expended in accomplishing the task. Learning which accentuates the discovery of the personal meaning and relevance of ideas and experiences may be strenuous at times, but it is enjoyable. It epitomizes the synthesis of work and play (Lepper & Gerene, 1975).

Learning is a spiritual experience. Learning implicitly or explicitly is an experience that expresses values. The data an individual chooses to internalize are a function of an individual's values. The data an individual chooses to exchange and share are reflections of what one deeply cares about. The questions a person seeks to answer, the skills an individual desires to acquire, the values one weighs and ponders over, and the ideas that are developed, ultimately emanate from the deeply rooted first concerns inherent in one's nature: Who am I? What is my relationship to the world in which I live? What can I do that is worth doing? These are human and spitirual questions which lie at the base of all learning. These are questions which are shared by all persons as part of their spiritual inclinations. Learning which deals explicitly and openly with these questions represents the highest and most relevant form of learning (Boy & Pine, 1971).

The learner is a free and responsible agent. The person is a choosing agent unable to avoid making choices throughout life. The person is a free agent in the sense that one is absolutely free to establish goals. There are not goals which one cannot choose. The beginning point in both creating values and learning is the setting of goals. The learner is a responsible agent who is personally accountable for the values inherent in the goals one chooses (Morris, 1966).

The learner defines the self through the choices made plus the actions taken. Thought without action is meaningless. The learner is actualized through action. Learning is choosing and acting. Learning is the actualizing (putting into action) of one's intellectual and psychosocial potential.

At every moment the person is free — free of extenal forces and free of what the person has been. An individual's past life is history; it no longer exists *now* in the present. A learner is influenced by external agents or by one's past life only when the learner chooses to be influenced by these forces.

Accompanying the person's freedom is the awesome burden of responsibility. Each learner is responsible for what the self is and does. In choosing and acting, the person chooses and acts within a social context (having responsibility toward others), cannot avoid the weight of this freedom, and cannot give away this freedom and responsibility to the state, to parents, to teachers, to weaknesses, to one's past or environmental conditions and influences (Patterson, 1973).

The processes of problem solving and learning are highly unique and individual. Each person has a unique style of learning and solving problems. Some personal styles of learning and problem solving are highly effective, other styles are not so effective, and still others may be ineffective. We need to assist people to define, and to make explicit to themselves, the approaches they ordinarily use so that they can become more effective in problem solving and learning. As people become more aware of how they learn and solve problems and become exposed to alternative models used by other people, they can refine and modify their personal styles so that these can be employed more effectively (Hansen & Maynard, 1973).

Teaching is learning. Since learning is defined in this chapter as the process of changing behavior in positive directions, it follows that teaching is learning. Teaching, however, in a traditional sense refers to a didactic procedure relying on an external stimulus-internal response notion of motivation. This is a view of learners as organisms to be made into something. This view suggests that learners cannot be trusted to decide what is good and relevant for themselves, someone else (the curriculum maker) must decide; then some other people (teachers) must determine what forces should be exerted to keep learners moving through this "good experience." In such a situation, students are objects (organisms to be made into something) but not necessarily learners. It is no wonder that school dropout rates have become so alarming.

An enhancing learning situation is characterized by a curriculum that is defined by the learners' choices of good and relevant experiences, and by the presence of a teacher who is a learner. Learners are free and responsible persons who bring to any interaction and relationship an accumulation of experiences, ideas, feelings, attitudes, and perspectives. Learning occurs when free and responsible people (students and teachers) are open to themselves, draw upon their personal collection of data and share their data in cooperative interaction. As a learner, the person designated "teacher" shares data when they are needed by others and in turn draws upon the data that others provide for the teacher's own growth and development. Training is the direct dissemination of ideas, facts, and information in a structural relationship which permits little or no feedback from learners and which occurs for the purpose of altering behavior to accomplish an objective formulated by agents or agencies external to the learning group. Unfortunately, this is a definition which all too accurately describes much of the behavior known as teaching (Kraft, 1975; Brophy & Evertson, 1976) and is one of the reasons why the teaching profession does not command the respect of a community.

CONDITIONS WHICH FACILITATE LEARNING

Learning is facilitated in an atmosphere which encourages people to be active. The learning process thrives when there is less teacher domination and talk and more faith that students can find alternatives and solutions. Listening to people and allowing them to make use of the teacher and the group as a resource facilitates the active exploration of ideas and solutions to problems. People are not passive receptacles into which we can pour the "right" values, the "right" answers, and the "right" ways of thinking. People are active and creative beings who need the opportunity to become involved—to participate. They recognize that when they are part of what is occurring—when they are personally involved—their learning is facilitated. Learning is not poured into people; learning emerges from people (Purkey & Novak, 1984).

Learning is facilitated in an atmosphere which promotes and facilitates the individual's discovery of the personal meaning of ideas. This means that the teacher, rather than directing or manipulating people, helps them to discover the personal meaning of knowledge. The teacher creates a situation in which people are freely able to express their needs rather than having their needs dictated to them. Learning becomes an activity in which the needs of the individual and the group are considered in deciding what issues will be explored and how they will be explored.

No matter how permissive or unstructured a learning activity may be, there exist implicit goals in the activity itself—a teacher is never goalless. Learning occurs when the goals of the teacher accommodate, facilitate, and encourage the individual's discovery of person goals and personal meaning in events. The art of helping people to change their behavior requires the development of goals which provide sufficient latitude for people to explore and internalize behavior which is satisfying and growth-producing to themselves and has implications regarding their relationships with others (Rogers 1976; Combs, 1982). Regardless of what is learned, it usually has psychosocial consequences.

Learning is facilitated in an atmosphere which emphasizes the uniquely personal and subjective nature of learning. In such a situation, each individual has the feeling that personal ideas, feelings, and perspectives have value and significance. People need to develop an awareness that all that is to be learned is not outside nor external to themselves. They develop such an awareness when they feel their contributions and their value as people are genuinely respected and appreciated (Rogers, 1976).

Learning is facilitated in an atmosphere in which difference is good and desirable. Situations which emphasize the "one right answer," the "magical solution," or the "one good way," to act or to think or to behave, narrow and limit exploration and inhibit discovery. If people are to look at themselves, at others, and at ideas openly and reasonably, then they must have the opportunity to express their viewpoints, no matter how different they may be. This calls for a learning atmosphere in which different ideas can be *accepted* (but not necessarily agreed with). Differences in ideas must be accepted if differences in people are to be accepted (Rogers, 1976).

Learning is facilitated in an atmosphere which consistently respects one's right to make mistakes. Where mistakes are not permitted, then the freedom and the willingness of people to take chances and make choices are severely limited. Growth and change are facilitated when error is accepted as a natural part of the learning process. The learning process requires the challenge of new and different experiences, the trying of the unknown, and therefore necessarily must involve making mistakes. In order for people to learn, they need the opportunity to explore new situations and ideas without being penalized or punished for mistakes which are a necessary part of the learning process. The teacher who feels and acts on the need to be always right creates a limiting and threatening condition of learning (Pine & Boy, 1976).

Learning is facilitated in an atmosphere which tolerates ambiguity. In a rigid and defensive atmosphere, people feel they cannot take the time to look at different solutions, they feel uncomfortable without answers, and they have more concern for "right" answers than good answers. The open exploration of solutions calls for time to explore many alternatives and time to proceed without the pressure of needing immediate answers (Pine & Boy, 1976). The immediate answers are often the least desirable.

Learning is facilitated in an atmosphere in which evaluation is a cooperative process wih an emphasis on self-evaluation. If learning is a personal process, then people need the opportunity to formulate the criteria to measure their progress. Criteria established by the teacher are mostly artificial and irrelevant to persons in group. Traditionally, the behavioral change and growth that occurs in learning have been measured by the degree to which people can regurgitate what others have tried to spoon-feed to them. It is obvious that anyone can play the game of "giving the teacher what the teacher wants." A more viable and meaningful evaluation occurs when people are free to examine themselves and determine the amount of learning that has occured and the degree to which the amount conforms to one's personal goals. Self-evaluation (and peer feedback) enable people to judge how much they have learned (Patterson, 1973; Combs, 1982).

Learning is facilitated in an atmosphere which encourages an open self rather than a closed self. Problem solving and learning require that personal feelings, attitudes, ideas, questions and concerns be openly brought to light and examined. To the degree that an idea, a thought, a feeling or an attitude (related to the topic at hand) is held back and not openly expressed—to that degree are the processes of learning and discovery inhibited. People need to feel that they can try something (fail if necessary) without being humiliated, embarrassed or diminished as persons. Openness of self occurs in an atmosphere free from psychosocial threat. People can invest themselves openly in the collaborative and interactive process of learning when they know that no matter what they say or express, it will not result in punishment or penalties which have psychosocial consequences (Rogers, 1976).

Learning is facilitated in an atmosphere in which people are encouraged to trust in themselves as well as in external sources. They become less dependent upon authority when they can open up the self and when they feel that who they are is a valuable resource for learning. It is important that people feel that they have something to contribute to the learning experience rather than feeling that all learning means the acquisition of facts and information from some external agent for use sometime in the future. People learn when they begin to see *themselves* as the wellsprings of ideas and alternatives to problems. Learning is facilitated when people begin to draw ideas from both themselves and others rather than relying solely on others, especially the teacher (Pine & Boy, 1977).

Learning is facilitated in an atmosphere in which people feel they are respected. In a group in which value is placed upon the individuality of the members and upon the relationships that exist within the group, people learn that someone cares for them. A genuine expression of care *on the part of the teacher* and a warm emotional climate generate an atmosphere of safety in which people can explore ideas and genuinely encounter other people (and learn) without any threat. Confrontations and differences of opinion become constructive forces in a group in which people experience that they are respected as persons. A safe atmosphere need not exclude personal confrontations which can be effective catalysts for learning (Rogers, 1976).

Learning is facilitated in an atmosphere in which people feel they are accepted. People are free to change when they feel that change isn't being imposed upon them. It is paradoxical, but the more we try to change people, the more resistant they become to change. A person must *be* before the person can *become*. Accepting a person means that we accept that person as he or she *is*. When we do, the person is free to take a look at the self, personal values, and to change. A person must *be* before the person can *become*. When a person does not have to defend personal values, he or she can examine them. An insistence on change contains an implicit note of rejection. In effect, we say to people, "I can't accept you as you are; you must change." People need to feel they have an option: to change or not to change. They develop this feeling when they experience that they are accepted for who they are. When people or their values are attacked, it is natural that they defend themselves. People who are busy defending themselves or their values are not free to learn (Purkey & Novak, 1984).

Learning is facilitated in an atmosphere which permits confrontation. With free and open communication, with a non-threatening psychosocial climate, the unique self of each person has an opportunity to be. In such free and open situations it is inevitable that person will confront persons and ideas will challenge ideas. Confrontations can contribute to learning. They provide opportunities for people to have their ideas and themselves viewed and tested from the vantage point of other people or the group. No person learns fully about the self in isolation from others. A person's behavior change and ideas are refined and modified on the basis of the feedback one gets from other people. Confrontation is a proving ground which enables ideas to be synthesized, new ideas to emerge and people to change (Kearney, 1982).

The most effective teacher is the teacher who creates the conditions by which the teacher's need to inform is minimized. The teacher who creates learning conditions which facilitate both academic and psychosocial development gradually moves away from being a dispenser of information. Such a teacher becomes a resource person and learner who enables persons in the group to emerge as vital human resources and active learners. The facilitating conditions which the teacher tries to foster lead to free and open communication, confrontation, acceptance, respect, freedom from threat, the right to make mistakes, self-revelation, cooperation and collaboration, active and personal involvement, shared evaluation, and responsible behavior. Successful teaching produces an individual who no longer needs to be taught by someone else. Instead, there emerges a person who has the confidence to depend upon one's own intellectual and psychosocial resources as the best catalyst for learning (Morris, 1966).

The teacher creates the climate for learning by becoming a facilitator who views *the self* as a learner and authentically behaves as learner. Such a teacher is an inquiring and valuing person who conveys spontaneity, curiosity, warmth and empathy; who listens and attends to others; who conveys acceptance and respect; who understands affective as well as cognitive meanings; and who confronts in a genuine and caring way. Such a person creates an atmosphere in which these qualities can be experienced by members of the learning group. To the degree that the teacher becomes a facilitator and learner — to that degree will academic and psychosocial learning become enhanced (Boy & Pine, 1982).

REFERENCES

Blocher, D. H. (1977). The counselor's impact on learning environments. *The Personnel and Guidance Journal,* 55, 352-355.

Boy, A. V. & Pine, G. J. (1971). *Expanding the self: Personal growth for teachers.* Dubuque, IA: William C. Brown.

Boy, A. V. & Pine, G. J. (1982). *Client-centered counseling: A renewal.* Boston: Allyn and Bacon.

Brophy, J. E. & Evertson, C. M. (1976). *Learning from teaching: A developmental perspective.* Boston: Allyn and Bacon.

Combs, A. W. (1982). *A personal approach to teaching: Beliefs that make a difference.* Boston: Allyn and Bacon.

Gendlin, E. T. & Beebe, J. (1968). Experimental groups. In G. Gazda (Ed.), *Innovations to group psychotherapy.* Springfield, IL: Charles C Thomas.

Hansen, J. C. & Maynard, P. E. (1973). *Youth: Self-concept and behavior.* Columbus, OH: Charles E. Merrill.

Kearney, A. (1982). *Decision making, attitudes, feelings: Intermediate level.* Appleton, WI: ME-ME.

Kraft, A. (1975). *The living classroom: Putting humanistic education into practice.* New York: Harper and Row.

Lepper, M.R. & Green, D. (1975). Turning play into work: Effects of adult surveillance and extrinsic rewards on children's intrinsic motivation. *Journal of Personality and Social Psychology,* 31, 479-486.

Morris, V. (1966). *Existentialism in education.* New York: Harper & Row.

Patterson, C. H. (1973). *Humanistic education.* Englewood Cliffs, NJ: General Learning Press.

Pine, G. J. & Boy, A. V. (1976). Teaching and valuing. *The Clearing House,* 49, 313-315.

Pine, G. J. & Boy, A. V. (1977). *Learner-centered teaching: A humanistic view.* Denver, CO: Love.

Pine, G. J. & Boy, A. F. (1979). Self enrichment through teaching. *The Clearing House,* 52, 46-49.

Purkey, W. W. & Novak, J. M. (1984). *Inviting school success: A self-concept approach to teaching and learning.* 2nd ed. Belmont, CA: Wadsworth.

Rogers, C. R. (1976). The interpersonal relationship in the facilitation of learning. In R. R. Leeper (Ed.), *Humanizing education: The person in the process.* Washington, DC: Association for Supervision and Curriculum Development.

Rogers, C. R. (1977). *On personal power.* New York: Dell.

Rogers, C. R. (1979). The foundation of the person-centered approach, *Education,* 100, 98-107.

Rogers, C. R. (1983). *Freedom to learn in the 1980s.* Columbus, OH: Charles E. Merrill.

Sweeney, T. J. (1975). *Adlerian counseling.* Boston: Houghton Mifflin.

Williams, R. L. & Long, J. D. (1979). *Toward a self-managed life-style.* Boston: Houghton Mifflin.

CHAPTER VI

THE PSYCHOSOCIALLY SENSITIVE TEACHER

WHAT IS the psychosocial educator like? From our own observations and those of others, we identify the following as being typical of the psychosocial educator:

1. The psychosocial educator has self-respect and a positive self-concept.
2. The psychosocial educator is congruent. The dichotomies between real self and role self, between the selfish and the unselfish, between the conscious and the unconscious, between the inner self and the outer, between the affective and the cognitive, become integrated in the psychosocially stable teacher. The psychosocially stable teacher is honest with the self and with others.
3. The psychosocial educator thinks well of others. Liking and accepting the self, this teacher is able to like and accept others. While such a teacher can and does act independently, there is also the realization that one's psychosocial stability is interdependent with the psychosocial stability of others. The psychosocially stable teacher engages in and likes cooperative relationships and functions harmoniously in such relationships.
4. The psychosocial educator develops, holds, and lives human values and these values are related to the well-being and enhancement of others. There is the tendency to be drawn to values which enhance the self, others, and the human community.
5. The psychosocial educator sees the self in the process of becoming; sees life as a continuous process of becoming rather than a static state of being; knows that dealing with problems is a characteristic of living; and not only accepts change but makes change.

6. The psychosocial educator sees the value of mistakes. Such a person is not afraid to move forward and is willing to test the unknown and tread new paths. The psychosocial educator makes experience an asset and profits from mistakes, thereby continually refining and modifying the self and improving its humanness.
7. The psychosocial educator trusts personal feelings and intuition, and trusts experiencing and the evidence of the senses. Internal reactions and feelings serve as a rich resource for behaving and for problem solving.
8. The psychosocial educator is open to experience, open to the stimuli of persons and an environment, and open to the data and points of view expressed by others in that environment. The psychosocial educator is open to what is going on now, both internally and externally.
9. The psychosocial educator is initiatory, and more creative than reactive. While such a person can flow smoothly with an environment, there is also the tendency to be an initiator who exercises control over one's environment. Such a teacher does not wait for others to do something that needs to be done.
10. The psychosocial educator is natural and spontaneous and expresses these qualities in positive and enhancing ways. This person enjoys life, is sensitive to the needs of others, and lives optimistically and energetically.

The psychosocial educator is not perfect. Conflict, anxiety, guilt, and hurt are experienced. However, there is lack of identification with neurotic classifications of problems and more of an identification with communication breakdowns between and among people and how they can be repaired and improved. This teacher feels troubled when reality indicates that one should feel troubled. Ordinarily, this teacher does not create problems, but when reality creates problems, he or she is able to respond.

Because the psychosocial educator genuinely trusts the self, there is a desire to be in touch with the feelings which influence behavior. At times, this teacher is confrontive and may express anger. When anger is felt and expressed, it always is couched in human values. The anger is expressed at the behavior of another rather than at the person as a person. The person is always respected as a person. Such a teacher's anger is not destructive, because when it is expressed there is follow up in order to preserve the relationship and to make sure that the anger has served as a constructive medium of interpersonal communication but has not diminished the relationship itself.

THE SELF-ACTUALIZING PSYCHOSOCIAL EDUCATOR

The psychosocial educator develops a positive, humanizing, and nourishing classroom climate. Such a climate emanates from which the teacher is as a person. This person's teaching style reflects psychosocial stability and is characterized by a deep respect for the learner, effective communication, empathic acceptance of the student; concentration on the needs, problems, and feelings of students; and liberality.

The Psychosocial Educator Respects Students

Effective teaching comes from a philosophy in which respect for the learner is paramount. This means respecting the learner's individuality, complexity, uniqueness, capacity for making choices, humanness, and the right to govern one's own life and select personal goals. Respect for the learner is based upon the teacher's recognition of the dignity of the learner as a member of the human species. Dignity, as defined in most dictionaries, means "intrinsic value." When we say we act in recognition of the dignity of the individual, we are saying that each person has value — value that is not determined by what the individual has accomplished, or what clothes one wears, where one lives, how one looks, or how one speaks. The value of each student lies simply in the fact that he or she is a human being occupying the same space on earth as us and at the same time.

It is easier for the teacher who respects the self to respect students. The teacher who does not have self-esteem cannot view others as having esteem. To the degree that a person believes in one's personal dignity will that person believe in the dignity of another. Erich Fromm (1956) put it accurately when he wrote:

> The logical fallacy in the notion that love for others and love for oneself are mutually exclusive should be stressed. If it is a virtue to love my neighbor as a human being, it must be a virtue — and not a vice — to love myself, since I am a human being too. There is no concept of man in which I myself am not included. A doctrine which proclaims such an exclusion proves itself to be intrinsically contradictory. The idea expressed in the Biblical "Love thy neighbor as thyself!" implies that respect for one's own integrity and uniqueness, love for and understanding of one's own self, cannot be separated from respect and

love and understanding for another individual. The love for my own self is inseparably connected with the love for any other being. (P. 49.)

Because of the psychosocial reciprocity of the teacher-student relationship, when the teacher deeply values the student, a corresponding appreciation of the teacher's worth develops in the student. The more the student sees the self as a person of dignity, the more the student begins to respect the dignity of the teacher. The teacher's respect for the student influences the student's respect for the teacher.

The Psychosocial Educator Develops Effective Communication in the Classroom

Effective communication occurs when the teacher receives what students want to communicate and the students receive what the teacher wants to communicate. Communication between teacher and students is expressed via affective, cognitive, verbal, and non-verbal modes. Effective teaching requires open modes of communication, and this is facilitated by a non-threatening learning situation that fosters teachers and student resonance to each other's intention and goals.

To be resonant to another, a teacher must be free from those misinterpretations of experiences which distort perceptions. The teacher needs to develop "emotional antennae" that are keenly sensitive to the non-verbal and subtle cues conveyed through *tone* of voice, posture, bodily movement, a way of breathing, physical mannerisms, expression of the eyes—in other words, the subterranean signals that constitute the subliminal "language" of communication. Teacher sensitivity to the complementary combination of verbal and non-verbal, cognitive and affective codifications opens up possibilities of communication which otherwise would be closed. Such sensitivity enables the teacher to directly receive and transmit feelings in a clear and honest way. Perhaps the notion of *directly experiencing* is best captured in the words of Emerson, "What you are speaks so loudly that I can't hear what you say." Although productive communication does demand that the teacher be sensitive to what the student says and how it is said, it further asks the teacher to experience what the teacher is and what the teacher is experiencing (Stanford & Roark, 1974).

Tuning in to the feelings of the learner means that the teacher must be free from the tendency to misinterpret or obstruct feelings. The psychosocially stable teacher is maximally open to experience. The teacher's perceptions are capable of change and adjustment, and it is not necessary to distort perceptions to fit a personal bias. Openness to experience depends upon the teacher's freedom from psychosocial threat. When that threat is absent, the teacher becomes free to respond to the humanness coming from others. The more positive the human qualities of the teacher, the more positively the teacher relates to students. The more the teacher accepts his or her human qualities, the more the teacher can accept these qualities in students. The learner who is accepted and who experiences a relationship in which openness is prized becomes more open to personal experiences.

An especially important component of effective psychosocial communication is the ability of the teacher to listen. The kind of listening we refer to here is non-evaluative. To listen, the teacher must immerse the self in the learner's flow of experience (Kagan, 1976). Listening to the learner is not like listening to a news broadcast or a lecture, where we listen with one ear, while preparing our opinion about what is being said. Listening to the learner is not "polite" or "social" listening in which the teacher waits for the learner to finish talking in order to get the teacher's own point across. Listening does not mean the kind of listening where the teacher merely tolerates what the learner is saying. Listening to the learner is not an analytical process in which the content of the learner's communication is broken down into parts so that the parts can be examined for their accuracy. Listening to the learner means having an affective and cognitive congruence with what the learner is feeling and saying. It is a process requiring the teacher to be psychosocially stable so that the listening process will not be distorted. Hermann Hesse (1951), in the story *Siddhartha,* eloquently describes the kind of listening we are describing when Hesse writes about one of the lessons Siddhartha learns from the river: "But he learned from it continually. Above all, he learned from it how to listen, to listen with a still heart, with a waiting open soul, without passion, without desire, without judgment, without opinions" (p. 109). And Siddhartha experiences genuine listening as he speaks with his friend, Vasudeva: "As he went on speaking and Vasudeva listened to him with a serene face, Siddhartha was more keenly aware that ever of Vasudeva's attentiveness. He felt his troubles, his anxieties, and his secrete hopes flow across to him and then return again. Disclosing this world to the listener was the same as bathing it in the river until it became cool and one with the river" (p. 109).

The learner needs the psychosocial attention of the teacher, and when the learner experiences deep listening the learner recognizes that the teacher is attentive, cares, and is interested. Quality listening encourages self-discovery and facilitates the development of empathy—another important element in effective communication. Empathy and sensitive listening are entwined. Empathy is the placing of one human spirit within another so that there is emotional congruence between teacher and student. The teacher empathizes when the teacher assumes, insofar as is possible, the internal frame of reference of the learner, perceives the world as the learner perceives it, lays aside all perceptions from an external frame of reference and communicates something of this understanding to the learner (Rogers, 1979). Empathy occurs only when the teacher listens.

Empathy is experiencing the learner's reality even though that reality may not be congruent with "objective" reality. This is difficult to do, since most of us have learned to look at others according to external and "objective" criteria. But looking at another person in terms of our own viewpoint (bias) is one of the biggest barriers to effective communication. Productive communication cannot occur unless the teacher understands the learner from the learner's viewpoint. Viewing the learner from an external frame of reference may help the teacher to *know about* the learner, but this does not mean the teacher *knows* the learner. To know and understand, one must be able to empathize, enter the student's set of perceptions and understand why the student feels and responds as he or she does.

The Psychosocial Educator Accepts Students

Accepting a person means allowing that person the right to *be* so that that person may *become.* When a person doesn't have to defend values, when that person can *be,* that person is free to change. The student who is free to be unique, to be different, is free to take an honest look at personal values. Acceptance of the student means giving the student the opportunity of holding and expressing personal meanings without ridicule, attack, or moralization. It is the right to see things in an individualized way (Rogers, 1983).

When the classroom atmosphere is psychosocially safe, the student feels free to express his or her psychosocial values. When the student experiences the human qualities of a teacher, the student feels safe to explore personal meanings. The teacher who does not accept students makes it impossible for them to accept themselves. Students feel accepted only when they experience acceptance. If a student does not feel that "It's all right to be myself here," does not feel that difference is valued, the student becomes defensive. The defensive student feels compelled to defend personal values and consequently narrows perceptions because of the threat represented by a teacher's moralization or condemnation. On the other hand, the student who is accepted, who feels, "It's all right to be me, I can say what I like, I can be negative, I can be positive, I can be confused, I can talk, I can be silent, no one is going to judge me or preach to me, I can be what I feel," will feel inclined to freely and openly relate to the teacher.

The psychosocially secure teacher does not approve or disapprove of the feelings being expressed by students. There are no reservations, conditions, evaluations, and judgments of the student's feelings but rather a positive regard for the student as an individual. The student is valued regardless of the feelings expressed. Anger, envy, or self-condemnation are accepted as representing how the student feels about something. True teachers acceptance is unaffected by the student's expression of negative feelings. It is not acceptance up to this or that point and no further. It does not depend upon the student's acting or talking a certain way, upon the student's socioeconomic background, religion, or IQ. It is not dependent upon the student's meeting certain moral or ethical criteria. It is complete. It is a necessary element for effective psychosocial education.

The Psychosocial Educator Concentrates on the Needs, Problems, and Feelings of Students

The more the teacher focuses on the needs, problems, and feelings of students, the more the teacher emphasizes the existential character of learning. This means communicating to students that it is their needs and their concerns which are important, that their feelings and their experiences are of value and relevance. It means giving students the feeling that they can trust their experiences and their meanings. The teacher who freely and without reservation can say, in effect, "It is you who are important, it is your experiences that count and not someone else's, it is your being that is significant, it is your internal 'advice' that is relevant," is the teacher who can create a facilitative psychosocial atmosphere. In a psychosocially supportive classroom the student begins to feel that some of the most meaningful learning is the learning that comes from within each of us. When the student experiences the faith and trust of the teacher, the student begins to realize tha one's inner voice can lead to the most satisfying and appropriate behavior, and that this personally satisfying and appropriate behavior becomes so because it is in balance with the well-being and rights of others (Long, 1978).

The Psychoscial Educator Possesses Liberality

Perhaps one of the most distinctive and salient qualities of the psychosocial educator is liberality. Liberality is a quality in the learning atmosphere that sums up the effect of the teacher's acceptance, empathy, respect, and understanding for the student. The teacher does not create an atmosphere of liberality by telling students they are free to express themselves. Students feel free to explore their capacity for self-directed growth when they experience liberality (Gutmann, 1985).

To express liberality requires emotional security and self-acceptance on the part of the teacher. The teacher's beliefs and values will be often tested by students who hold different views. But the psychosocially stable teacher has no need to defend beliefs and values when they come under attack. If the student is to grow into an understanding of personal experiences, the student must feel free enough to talk about those experiences wihout being afraid of what the teacher will say or think. The emergence of the authentic self, the evolvement of self-understanding, and the exploration of the student's internal world will come about when the student feels free to hold and talk about personal values. Liberality, then, is a quality present in effective psychosocial education (Rogers, 1983).

THE EFFECTS OF PSYCHOSOCIAL LEARNING EXPERIENCES

The teacher who creates a quality teaching relationship with youngsters will find that psychosocial growth occurs among students as a reaction to the learning atmosphere. As a result of the student's experience with psychosocially sensitive learning experiences:

The Student Assumes Responsibility. The student becomes involved in learning and assumes responsibility for his or her academic and psychosocial development. Since the teacher has freed the student to learn, the student responds by learning.

The Student is Accepted. The student feels respected as a person who is able to make worthy contributions. The positiveness of the teacher's attitude enables the student to feel comfortable and non-defensive in the learning atmosphere. This comfort facilitates the student's psychosocial development (Rogers, 1979).

The Student is Motivated. As a result of experiencing a teacher's psychosocial maturity, the student is influenced to learn both psychosocial and acadmeic subject matter. The student begins to value the importance of both psychosocial and academic development and acquires a desire to learn those things which are relevant to each.

The Student is Actively Involved in the Process of Growth. Academic and psychosocial development occur, because both have attracted the attention of students and have prompted their participation. The student will become involved when a learning experience is related to intellectual curiosity or psychosocial needs. Relevant learning experiences are those which attract the student's participation (Blocher, 1977).

The Student Interacts on a Human Level. As a response to a psychosocially mature teacher, the student does not assume facades but reacts to learning experiences in a very human way which includes the participation of emotions. Anyone who has deeply learned anything has learned it because emotional reactions were part of the learning process. What was learned was emotionally significant; the learner felt its importance in a visceral manner (Weinhold, & Elliott, 1979).

The Student Exists in a Safe Atmosphere. The student must feel free from threat or coercion if the student is to be secure enough to respond to academic or psychosocial teaching. No one has ever been coerced into learning or changing behavior. Such changes have occurred because one has felt safe enough to explore issues. When the teacher provides a psychosocially safe atmosphere, the student feels motivated to participate in the learning process (Rogers, 1983).

The Student is Understood. The psychosocially mature teacher is committed to penetrating and understanding the student's viewpoint. The teacher's respect for the student finds its expression in an understanding attitude that enables the student to be hesitant or confident, aware or insensitive, courageous or fearful. A psychosocially mature teacher wants to understand the different perceptions and values held by students. When the student feels understood, the student is encouraged to fulfill his or her academic or psychosocial needs (Curwin, 1976).

The Student is Self-Disciplined. The student finds the inner desire to engage in responsible behavior. Teachers enable this to occur by providing a learning atmosphere in which the student has to rely upon the self for control rather than upon others. Teachers furnish the student with the opportunity for self-management by developing a learning atmosphere in which the student looks to the authority of the self to guide personal behavior (Kindsvatter, 1982).

The Student Verbalizes with Ease. When the student associates with a psychosocially mature teacher, the student learns to communicate either academic facts or feelings comfortably and honestly. The student has no need to be defensive when the student senses that it is acceptable to be open and honest with the teacher. Such comfort enables the student to honestly respond to learning experiences. The student's ideas and questions are not couched in evasive language designed to guard viewpoints and feelings rather than reveal them. The student is able to discuss issues of relevance rather than what the student feels the teacher wants to hear (Graves, 1983).

The Student Achieves Insight. As a result of the relationship with a psychosocially mature teacher, the student is able to learn academic facts as well as learning about the psychosocial aspects of one's behavior. The student is able to learn, because the classroom atmosphere provides an opportunity to discover the fundamentals of both subject matter and psychosocial development. The student achieves an understanding of the uniqueness of one's life and experiences. More light is shed on facts to be learned and feelings which need to be understood. This process occurs because the teacher provides an atmosphere in which the student's insight is far more relevant than it would be if the student were solely provided with the teacher's insight (Boy & Pine, 1977).

The Student Is More Aware of Appropriate Attitudes. Because of the qualitative nature of a student's relationship with a psychosocially mature teacher, the student does not have to be told what attitudes are appropriate or inappropriate. As a human being, the student is aware of which attitudes help or hinder one's intellectual or psychosocial functioning. The student becomes sensitive to personally satisfying attitudes, because the student has had an opportunity to ponder those attitudes which either enhance or inhibit one's psychosocial development. The student is not only more aware of personally appropriate attitudes, the student discovers attitudes which enhance his or her relations with others. The student looks beyond the self rather than just depending on the self. The importance of the feelings of others are more openly sensed and respected (Purkey & Novak, 1984).

The Student is Valuing. The student becomes involved in the identification, development, and evaluation of values, placing them in a hierarchy that is beneficial to one's psychosocial stability. Because the student has the chance to think about and evaluate values, the student rejects values which produce self-defeating behavior and moves toward those which produce self-enhancing behavior. This evaluation of values occurs because the student exists in a learning atmosphere in which values are confronted and the student is, in turn, confronted by those values. It is only when a student is openly able to consider and reject certain negative and self-defeating values that more sustaining and positive values can be identified to take their place. Effective psychosocial teaching enables the student to become value conscious and evaluate which values support or diminish one's psychosocial stability and that of others (Simon, 1972).

The Student Responds to Genuineness. The student senses the genuine quality of the teacher and responds by being genuine. The student can easily sense a lack of genuineness. If the teacher has positive regard and respect for youngsters, this attitude finds its expression in a genuineness that the student senses. When the student has internalized the genuine quality of the teacher, the student genuinely involves the self as a response to that quality. The student trusts the relationship and responds to it by becoming more deeply involved in the learning process. Such genuineness must be present in the teacher if the student is to respond. Any attempts to feign genuineness will be easily sensed and rejected by students (Rogers, 1983).

The Student Evaluates the Interaction with the Teacher. Such evaluations are talked about among students and contribute to the teacher's reputation among students. A powerful force enhancing the work of the psychosocial teacher is the degree of respect coming from students. When students respect the teacher, both academic and psychosocial development are enhanced (Boy & Pine, 1982).

In summary, we believe that students respond primarily to the teacher as a person and that optimal academic learning and psychosocial development occur because of the role-model influence of psychosocially mature teachers.

The challenge for psychosocial educators is twofold: (1) to see and create the opportunities which will stretch and expand themselves as psychosocial persons and (2) to create conditions in classrooms which will contribute to both the student's academic and psychosocial development.

PROCESSING PSYCHOSOCIAL INFORMATION WITH STUDENT GROUPS

Today's teacher is often called upon to provide student groups with psychosocial information. The outside-of-school lives of students is often in such turmoil that teachers become activated to help by providing students with a variety of psychosocial information. This information is designed to enable students to make better decisions about life situations which have the potential is being psychosocially debilitating or destructive.

Psychosocial information is that which contributes to improving the psychological maturity and stability of students. Information typically used to accomplish this is that dealing with alcohol and substance abuse, human sexuality, marriage, parenting, divorce, sexual abuse, death and dying, family violence, suicide, nutrition, and coping with stress, anxiety, and frustration. The teacher must be sensitive not only to the information being presented but to the emotional reactions of students to that information. Discussing the attractions and consequences of alcohol and drug use is quite different from discussing the qualities of a poet's rhyme scheme or the logic of a geometric theorem.

Before turning to the processing of psychosocial information with students, let us first consider some assumptions regarding information in general.

ASSUMPTIONS REGARDING INFORMATION

Information is accurate. We assume that information is accurate. Some information is. The answer at the end of a mathematical equation is usually accurate, but its accuracy depends upon the process used to determine the answer. The labels which indicate the contents of processed food must be accurate according to law, but recent headlines tell us that some of this food is inaccurately labeled.

Information is objective. We assume that information is free from bias; that it is a balanced and accurate presentation of all the facts. When the information reaches us, we want to rely on its objectivity. The objectivity of information, however, can be questioned, especially when one examines, for example, the information provided by pro-life groups and pro-choice groups over the issue of abortion.

Information produces insight. Those who dispense information want to affect the thinking of others by increasing their insight regarding a topic. Those who furnish information assume that it will make us keenly aware of the issues surrounding a topic and we'll develop an insight that we didn't previously possess. Apparently, those arrested for driving while intoxicated have paid no attention to the voluminous information regarding the legal consequences of such behavior.

Information changes behavior. Because it is assumed that information produces insight, it is also assumed that insight will produce a change in behavior as an outcome of that insight; that pre-information ignorance will be replaced by post-information informed action. The assumption that we all need in order to change our behavior in the voting booth is information that will influence us to vote for one political candidate rather than another. Those who study voting behavior have long realized that voters cast their ballots because of emotional reactions to an issue rather than a rational appraisal of the information accompanying an issue.

FACTORS AFFECTING A STUDENT GROUP'S PROCESSING OF PSYCHOSOCIAL INFORMATION

Although the accuracy and objectivity of general information can be challenged and the ability of that information to produce insight and change behavior is often questionable, let us assume that the psychosocial information being used with a student group does possess all of the desired characteristics. It is accurate, objective, and has the potential to produce insights that will influence their behavior.

There are, however, other factors which will affect a group's acceptance and use of information. These other factors are outside the information itself and are more associated with the group's psychosocial makeup and its effect upon the acceptance and use of information.

The student group's feelings. Feelings will often interfere with a group's acceptance and use of psychosocial information. The information may be accurate and objective, but the group fails to achieve the desired insight, because obstructive feelings coming from some group members prevent the information from entering the group's thinking process. Feelings interfere with thinking, since feelings intrude on the thinking process and its ability to reach logical conclusions. If group members were always rational, then here would be no problem. We would merely feed information into rational group members who would process that information toward a logical conclusion. Our minds do not function this smoothly, however. Our ability to think is not that easily mobilized. Our minds are affected by feelings which interfere with our thought processes (Rogers, 1980).

A teacher who wants a student group to process psychosocial information accurately must first be sensitive to obstructive feelings within group members and how these feelings interfere with the rational processing of that information.

The student group's self-concept. One's self-concept serves as a guardian of which information will be allowed into the mind for consideration. Information which is not a threat to one's self-concept will be allowed to enter, while threatening information will be rejected (Boy & Pine, 1982).

A teacher desiring to have a group process psychosocial information accurately must be sensitive to the group's self-concept and how it will affect the acceptance and use of that information. When threatening information is introduced to a group, its threat level can be gauged by observing the negative reactions of group members. When the threat level is present, the processing of information will be better served when the group puts the information aside and instead engages in a process of examining the group's self-concept. Such a process will enable a group to more accurately know how the processing of information is influenced by a group's self-concept. Information is more effectively processed when that information coincides with a group's self-concept. Other information which may be threatening to the group's self-concept may be introduced in later group meetings when the group's self-concept has been more clearly identified and established by group members.

The problem being considered. There are some problems which are clearly rational and can be rationally solved by a group. When the problem being considered is rational and group members are functioning rationally, then a rational conclusions is achievable. One can determine a group's rationality by listening for the number and tone of obstructive feelings that come from group members. When there is an absence of obstructive feelings, a group is able to process information accurately. The problem being considered is rational and the mind is, therefore, clear enough to process information. When a group's consideration of a problem is, however, filled with obstructive feelings, then objective information will not deflect a group away from these feelings. In an affective problem presentation in a group, one must be prepared to listen and respond to the obstructive feelings of the group, since the group's ability to process psychosocial information is influenced by these feelings (Boy, & Pine, 1982).

The student group's perceptions. Information that is completely objective and accurate probably doesn't exist. Information is usually tilted one way or another. Six persons may look at one piece of information and perceive that information in six different ways.

Groups also have perceptions which influence how they will react to information (Belkin, 1980). The perception of one student group may prompt that group to reject information about the benefits of avoiding alcohol and drugs. Another group's perception may cause that group to be receptive to the same information. All information is filtered through our perceptions, and a lifetime of experiences help to shape those perceptions. Perceptions are complex and are individualized psychosocial reactions to life experiences. Therefore, there may be as many different percepions as there are groups processing information.

The student group's values. Another filter through which information must pass is the group's system of values. Perceptions can sometimes be unclear to a group, because they've been formed over a long period of time as a result of many complex and sometimes contradictory experiences. Values are more clear and precise. We know how we stand on a number of issues. Value-laden issues are those dealing with religious beliefs, marriage, divorce, abortion, mercy killing, and disarmament. Our values influence how we feel, think, and behave.

Our values clearly influence how we will respond to certain information (Simon, 1972). Information which coincides with our values in accepted, while information which is contrary to those values is rejected. When a group responds to information, the group's response will often represent the group's values. Those values are always present and will have an influence on a group's acceptance or rejection of certain information.

FACTORS AFFECTING A TEACHER'S USE OF PSYCHOSOCIAL INFORMATION

It is assumed that a teacher who gives a group information does not contaminate its presentaiton. The teacher, however, is subject to the normal frailties of being human. When a teacher interprets and presents information to a group, that information is often colored by any one or a combination of the following factors.

The teacher's feelings. As long as the teacher does not have feelings about the psychosocial information being presented, then that information will tend to be objectively presented. Most psychosocial information presented, however, is accompanied by a teacher's subjective feelings about the information. On the issue of death and dying, one teacher may possess feelings about the topic which are completely different from those of another teacher. Both teachers may feel that they are discussing the topic objectively. One teacher's discussion, however, will include fears about death and dying, while another's discussion will include an acceptance of the process.

We have many feelings about many things. One teacher may support the purpose of an abortion group and promote that purpose as information is presented to students. Another teacher may not support the purpose of the same group and is likely not to support that purpose as information is presented. Both teachers are dealing with the same information, but the feelings of the first influence a positive presentation, while the feelings of the second influence a negative presentation.

The teacher's self-concept. The teacher's self-concept will influence the manner in which information is presented to a group. One teacher's self-concept may revolve around controlling the group. This teacher's self-concept produces a managerial relationship in which information is often presented in an autocratic manner. Another teacher's self-concept may resolve around facilitating the process whereby a group can accurately judge information. This teacher encourages the group to be objective in its acceptance or rejection of psychosocial information.

The student group's problem. One teacher may see information as the best solution to help a group solve a problem, regardless of the group's problem. This teacher pays little attention to the group's obstructive feelings, attitudes, and values, because the teacher's commitment to an informational solution prompts the teacher to be insensitive to how these factors obstruct the processing of information. Another teacher may sense that a group's obstructive feelings, attitudes, and values must first be addressed before the group can process information. Such a teacher attends to the group's feelings, attitudes, and values because of their influence on the processing of information.

Some human problems have a body of information regarding how those problems have been solved. Some teachers feel that presenting that information will automatically help groups to achieve insight and change behavior. Such teachers are insensitive to those group feelings, attitudes, and values which will block the acceptance of that information even if that information is solid gold and stamped with a seal of authority.

The teacher's perceptions. How a teacher perceives the self, the communication process, and the role of the teacher will influence how information is used with groups (Arbuckle, 1975). Such perceptions may come from the teacher's life experiences, beliefs, family influences, or the program which prepared the person to become a teacher. All, or a combination of these influences, help to form a teacher perceptions which often become part of the communication process and influence how information is used with a group and the authority put on that information.

When a teacher perceives the self as being omniscient, the communication process is teacher centered, the role of the teacher is excessively controlling, and what is considered to be the best solution comes from the teacher. Such a teacher relies heavily on the use of only certain information approved by the teacher. When another teacher perceives the self as facilitating the processing of information by a group, this teacher encourages a group to freely consider both the effective and rational components of a topic under discussion. There are no teacher-imposed limits regarding what is discussed and how it is discussed.

The teacher's values. A teacher's personal values will influence how the teacher behaves toward a group while processing psychosocial information. Our values serve as the fuel for our behavior. They cannot be avoided because of the dominant influence they have on all dimensions of our lives (Boy & Pine, 1982). The teacher who values the accurate processing of psychosocial information will exhibit human attitudes toward groups which will free them to examine both the emotional and rational factors which contribute to the quality of a group's discussion and the degree of clarity achieved on a topic.

GUIDELINES FOR PROCESSING PSYCHOSOCIAL INFORMATION IN GROUPS

Let us assume that the factors affecting the use of psychosocial information with student groups have been overcome or at least neutralized; the information possesses enough qualities of objectivity to be used, the group is reasonably receptive to the introduction of information, and the teacher is reasonably free from bias about certain information and able to present it objectively. The concluding section of this chapter presents guidelines designed to assist the teacher to more effectively introduce and discuss psychosocial information with student groups (Boy, 1986):

- Respond to the human qualities of the group before attempting to introduce and discuss psychosocial information. Be attentive to the group's feelings, attitudes, values, and self-concept and the degree to which each will block the group's acceptance and use of information. When interfering affective factors are present in a group, the teacher should first consider using a communication process designed to neutralize these factors so that they do not interfere with the group's discussion.

- A proven communication approach which will help the teacher to overcome interfering affective factors in a group is the process of *reflecting a group's feelings*. This process is detailed in Chapter IV. When the teacher first attends to the group's feelings, attitudes, values, and self-concept by utilizing the reflective process, the result is that the group feels that the teacher has acknowledged the human qualities of group members, has been attentive to the group's viewpoint, and the group is drawn to feel comfortable with the teacher and the information under consideration. After the human qualities of a group have been recognized by the teacher, the group becomes more receptive and responsive to a topic under consideration.
- Teachers must carefully examine psychosocial information that is used with groups. It cannot be assumed that all psychosocial information is objective. Teachers who use printed psychosocial information with groups should heed the words of Pietrofesa et al. (1978): "A greater degree of validity need not be attributed to information simply because it is printed" (p. 334).
- Psychosocial information must be related to clearly identified student needs. Student needs can be more accurately determined when the teacher first attends to the group's self-concept by utilizing the reflective process. Without an understanding of the group's self-concept, the teacher may be prone to an inaccurate identification of the group's psychosocial needs and a corresponding inaccurate understanding of the group's information needs.
- Psychosocial information must be connected to the group's perceptions (Pietrofesa, et al., 1978). Information which is not accepted and used is usually not congruent with a group's perceptions. Information which the group accepts, internalizes, and processes is usually congruent with the group's perceptions. Understanding the group's perceptions is critical in determining which type of psychosocial information has the best chance of being accurately discussed by a group.
- Psychosocial information introduced to a group must be properly timed. Information which is properly timed will be discussed by a group, while improperly timed information will receive little or no

response. A group's attitude must be open and receptive to certain psychosocial information. Using information when a group's attitude is not open to that information will insure its rejection. Proper timing occurs when the teacher precedes the introduction of information by becoming aware of a group's psychosocial values and attitudes.

- A group's emotional reaction to psychosocial information must first be discussed before the information can be rationally discussed. The teacher should focus on the affective meaning of information to a group rather than focusing on the information itself or its meaning to the teacher. As a group discusses the personal meaning of information, the teacher should be attentive to the group's emotional reactions and deepen and sharpen those reactions so that they will not interfere with the rational discussion and processing of information.
- Psychosocial information presented to a group should contain objective facts rather than generalities, gratuitous assertions, or self-serving statements. Teachers must be alert to information which may have the characteristics of propaganda.
- Psychosocial information should be viewed as a resource for a group rather than as a device whereby a teacher manipulates a group. The teacher's objective attitude toward information will influence a group to be more receptive when discussing that information.
- The teacher should focus early contacts with a group on the relationship between them rather than on the information being processed. Group members should experience the teacher as someone who values group members as human beings. When a group experiences such respect, they become more able to deal with the content of psychosocial information.
- The teacher should provide a group with opportunities to secure supplemental psychosocial information outside the classroom. When such opportunities are provided, the group deepens and widens the processing of psychosocial information as well as its quality and accuracy.
- A group's ability to effectively process psychosocial information will be increased when a teacher first deals with those factors which obstruct a group's receptivity to that information: the group's feelings, attitudes, values and self-concept.

COOPERATIVE LEARNING

Most of the teaching and learning in our society occurs in groups. Yet despite the ubiquity and pervasiveness of teaching and learning in groups, educators receive minimal training and preparation on how to coordinate and lead groups in ways to maximize students' learning. Simply asking students to sit around a table to carry on a productive or meaningful discussion is all too often ineffective in promoting cognitive and affective learning. Although people spend a significant portion of their lives talking with one another, they have not developed the abilities, skills, and attitudes required for group discussion to acquire new information, knowledge, skills, and understandings. To address the need for productive learning in groups Johnson and Johnson (1987a, 1987b) have developed a process of cooperative learning which reflects the application of the research and theory of group dynamics and group counseling. Their work has been implemented in schools across the country and demonstrates the power of groups in maximizing intellectual and psychosocial learning (Sharan, et al., 1984; Slavin, 1983).

A cooperative learning group is one whose purpose is to ensure that group members learn specific subject matter, information, knowledge, and skills, and procedures. Learning is the primary purpose of the group. Johnson and Johnson (1987a:360) indicate that in order to be effective a cooperative learning group must have the following elements:

1. a clear, cooperative goal structure
2. accurate two-way communication among members
3. widespread participation and leadership among group members
4. the use of consensus to arrive at answers, solutions, and decisions
5. power and influence based on expertise and access to information and social skills, not on authority
6. the frequent occurrence of controversy
7. the open confrontation and negotiation of conflicts of interest among members and between the group members ad the coordinator
8. high cohesiveness
9. high trust among members
10. a climate of acceptance and support among members and between the group members and the coordinator
11. group norms promoting individual responsibility and accountability, helping and sharing, and achievement

12. generally high group and interpersonal skills among members.

Cooperative learning groups typically move through seven stages (Johnson & Johnson, 1987a:362-365).

Stage One: Defining and Structuring Procedures and Becoming Oriented

When a learning group begins, students are usually concerned about what is expected of them and what the goals of the session are. Group members want to know what is going to happen; what is expected of them; whether or not they will be accepted, influential, and liked; how the group is going to function; and who the other group members are. When a learning group first meets, the coordinator defines the procedures to be used, assigns participants to groups, communicates the task, establishes the cooperative interdependence among members, and generally organizes the group and announces the beginning of the group's work.

Stage Two: Conforming to Procedures and Getting Acquainted

As students follow the prescribed procedures and interact around the task, they become acquainted with one another and familiarize themselves with the procedures until they can follow them easily. They learn the strengths and weaknesses of the group members. During this stage the group members are dependent on the coordinator for direction and clarification of the goals and procedures of the group. The coordinator stresses the following group norms: (1) taking responsibility for one's own learning and the learning of the other members of the group, (2) providing help and assistance to other members, (3) responding to other members in an accepting, supportive, and trustworthy way, (4) making decisions through consensus, and (5) confronting and solving problems in group functioning.

Stage Three: Recognizing Mutuality and Building Trust

The third stage of group development is marked by students (1) recognizing their cooperative interdependence, and (2) building trust among themselves. A sense of mutuality is built as group members recognize that they are in fact interdependent and that they are in a sink-or-swim-together situation. Students begin to take responsibility for each other's learning and appropriate behavior. They accept and internalize the reality that, if they wish to do well, they have to ensure that all other group members learn the assigned material, complete the assigned work, and participate actively in discussions.

Stage Four: Rebelling and Differentiating

The fourth stage of group development is marked by group members (1) rebelling against the coordinator and the procedures, and (2) differentiating themselves from each other through disagreements and conflicts. On the road to maturity a group will go through a period (sometimes short, sometimes long) of challenging the authority of the coordinator. It is an ordinary occurrence and should be expected. This swing toward independence contrasts sharply with the dependence demonstrated by students during Stage 2. Many group members may have the attitude that learning is a passive process in which they can slip by without doing much work. Participation in a cooperative learning group requires students to take responsibility for their own learning and the learning of the other members of their group, and to participate actively in the group's work.

Stage Five: Committing to and Taking Ownership for the Goals, Procedures, and Other Members

During this stage, dependence on the coordinator and conformity to the prescribed procedures are replaced by dependence on the other members of the group and personal commitment to the collaborative nature of the experience. The "changing hands" from coordinator's group to our group that began in the previous stage is finalized in this stage. The group becomes "ours" rather than "hers". Group norms become internalized and group members enforce the norms on themselves; the coordinator no longer has to enforce the norms and encourage group members to cooperate with each other.

Stage Six: Functioning Maturely and Productively

As members' commitment to one another and to the cooperative accomplishment of the group's goals increases, the group achieves maturity, autonomy, and productivity. A definite sense of group identity emerges as the group becomes a mature working unit possessing the skills and attitudes necessary for effective collaboration in maximizing all members' learning. Group members can work together to achieve a variety of learning tasks and can deal with controversy and conflicts of interest in constructive ways. The group's attention alternates between task and maintenance concerns. Group members clearly collaborate to achieve the group's goals while ensuring that their relationships with each other are maintained at a high quality level.

Stage Seven: Terminating

The life of every group is finite. The learning group eventually ends and the members go their separate ways. The more mature and cohesive the learning group, and the stronger the emotional bonds that have been formed among group members, the more potentially upsetting the termination period is. The ending of the group may be painful for members and the coordinator alike. Nevertheless, group members deal with the problems of separating so that they can leave the group experience behind them and move on to new experiences.

Not all stages last the same amount of time. Many groups move very quickly through the first five stages, spend considerable time functioning maturely, and then terminate quickly.

The role of the teacher in coordinating the group is to (1) introduce, define, and structure the learning group; (2) clarify procedures, reinforce members for conforming to the procedures, and help members become acquainted; (3) emphasize and highlight the cooperative interdependence among group members and encourage their engaging in both trusting and trustworthy behaviors; (4) accept the rebellion by and differentiation among group members as a normal process and use confrontation and constructive negotiation to help members establish their independence from each other and the prescribed procedures; (5) facilitate the members' committing themselves to and taking ownership for the group's goals, procedures, and other members; (6) be a consultant to the group providing needed material and informational resources for the group to function effectively; and (7) signal termination and help the members move on to future groups.

Coordinating and leading a cooperative learning group requires considerable knowledge and skill. Teachers interested in using this powerful approach to maximize the learning of their students must know how to structure the learning group, set goals, determine the appropriate size of the group, arrange space, materials, and use room design, assign roles and responsibilities, articualte cooperative goals structure and tasks, observe and monitor the behavior of the group members, intervene to teach needed group skills, evaluate the quality and quantity of group productivity, assess how well the group is functioning, establish norms of participation, model good communication skills, promote interaction within the group, and summarize and clarify members' contributions.

Johnson and Johnson have described the cooperative learning group process in several publications (1987a, 1987b, 1987c). There are two handbooks containing cooperatively structured lessons for classes from preschool through adult education (Chasnoff, 1979; Lyons 1980), a movie demonstrating the use of cooperative learning groups (Johnson and Johnson 1980), and a newsletter for educators wishing to exchange ideas with others interested in using cooperative learning procedures (*Report on Cooperative Learning*). In summary, cooperative learning groups are a research based and effective pedagogical approach which epitomizes the integration of intellectual and psychosocial development. It's potential for maximizing learning makes us feel more optimistic about schools fulfilling the mission of educating the whole person.

REFERENCES

Arbuckle, D. S. (1975). *Counseling and psychotherapy: An existetial-humanistic view*. Boston: Allyn and Bacon.

Belkin, G. S. (1980). *Introduction to counseling*. Dubuque, IA: Wm. C. Brown.

Blocher, D. H. (1977). The counselor's impact on learning environments. *The Personnel and Guidance Journal*, 55, 352-355.

Boy, A. V., & Pine, G. J. (1982). *Client-centered counseling: A renewal*. Boston: Allyn and Bacon.

Boy, A. V. (1986). Guidelines for using information in counseling. *Journal of Counseling and Human Services Professions*, 1, 149-151.

Chasnoff, R. (Ed.) (1979). *Structuring Cooperative Learning: The 1979 Handbook*. New Brighton, MN. Interaction Book Co.

Curwin, R. (1976). *Discovering your teaching self: Humanistic approaches to effective teaching*. Englewood Cliffs, NJ: Prentice-Hall.

Fromm, E. (1956). *The art of loving*. New York: Harper and Row.

Graves, D. H. (1983). *Writing: Teachers and children at work*. Exeter, NH: Heinemann Educational Books.

Gutmann, A. (1985). Democratic schools and moral education. *Notre Dame Journal of Law, Ethics & Public Policy*, 1, 461-494.

Hesse, H. (1954). *Siddhartha*. Trans. by Hilda Rosner. New York: Vintage Books (Imprint of Random House).

Johnson, D. W. and Johnson, R. T. (1987a). *Joining Together: Group Theory and Group Skills* (3rd edition). Englewood Cliffs, NJ: Prentice Hall.

Johnson, D. W. and Johnson, R. T. (1987b). *Learning Together and Alone: Cooperative, Competitive, and Individualistic Learning* (2nd edition). Englewood Cliffs, NJ: Prentice Hall.

Johnson, D. W. and Johnson, R. T. (1987c). *A Meta Analysis of Cooperative Competitive and Individualistic Goal Structures.* New York: Lawrence Erlbaum.

Kagan, N. (1976). *Influencing human interaction.* Washington, DC: American Personnel and Guidance Association.

Kindsvatter, R. (1982). The dilemmas of discipline. *Educational Leadership,* 40, 512-514.

Long, L. (1978). *Listening-responding: Human relations training for teachers.* Monterey, CA: Brooks-Cole.

Lyons, V. (1980). *Structuring Cooperative Learning: The 1980 Handbook* New Brighton, MN. Interaction Book Company.

Pietrofesa, J. J., Hoffman, A., Splete, H. H. & Pinto, D. (1978). *Counseling: Theory, research and practice.* Chicago: Rand McNally.

Pine, G. J. & Boy, A. V. (1977). A humanistic view of adolescence. *Counseling and Human Development,* 4, 4-12.

Purkey, W. W. & Novak, J. M. (1984). *Inviting school success: A self concept approach to teaching and learning.* Belmont, CA: Wadsworth.

Rogers, C. R. (1983). *Freedom to learn in the 80s.* Columbus, OH: Charles E. Merrill.

Rogers, C. R. (1980). *A way of being.* Boston: Houghton Mifflin.

Sharan, S., Kussell, P., Hertz-Lazarowitz, R., Bejarano, Y., Raviv, S., and Sharan, Y. (1984). *Cooperative Learning in the Classroom: Research in Desegregated Schools.* Hillsboro, N.J.: Erbaum.

Simon, S. B. (1972). *Values clarification.* New York: Hart.

Slavin, R.E. (1983). *Cooperative Learning.* New York: Longman.

Stanford, G. & Roark, A. E. (1974). *Human interaction in education.* Boston: Allyn and Bacon.

Weinhold, B. K. & Elliott, L. C. (1979). *Transpersonal communication.* Englewood Cliffs, NJ: Prentice-Hall.

CHAPTER VII

TEACHING FOR PSYCHOSOCIAL DEVELOPMENT

MUCH HAS BEEN written about the important role of the teacher in the formation of human behavior. One doesn't have to look far to uncover reams of testimony supporting the strategic and influential role that teaching plays in the development of civilizations and societies. What has been said for hundreds of years by numerous writers is true today: *Teaching is important, it is valuable, it matters,* and *it is needed.* When the teacher is creative, imaginative, and invests in developing a positive and facilitative learning environment, the teacher will have his or her psychosocial well-being enhanced (Pine & Boy, 1976).

Teachers have considerable autonomy in the classroom. The autonomy to create, to change, and to foster psychosocial growth is an outcome of the teacher's psychosocial stability which finds its expression in the teaching process. It is easy to blame the lack of a teacher's creativity and resourcefulness onto other factors. Teachers can blame the negative aspects on their work on the interferences that come from parents, administrators, and school boards. They are easy scapegoats. The reality, however, is that 90 percent of the teacher's work occurs with little or no interference from others. Freedom and autonomy in the classroom are sacred values in teaching. However, it is what is done with that freedom and autonomy which counts (Good, Biddle, & Brophy, 1975).

Everything a teacher does, says, or teaches has or could have significant impact on the psychosocial growth of pupils. How the teacher teaches helps learners to discover their resources and limitations. The teacher is the central figure in innumerable situations which can help the learner to realize and accept the self or which may bring humiliation, shame, rejection, and self-disparagement. There are countless ways in which the imaginative and fully committed teacher can promote the psychosocial growth of pupils and also contribute to the teacher's own psychosocial growth.

While it may sound like an overstatement, there is perhaps no more rewarding, satisfying, and fulfilling experience than the awareness that what one has done as a teacher has significantly contributed to the academic *and* psychosocial development of students. There is a personal satisfaction which is difficult to articulate that comes from observing students growing and developing as positive ad highly functioning rational and psychosocially stable human beings (Moustakas, 1966).

TEACHING AND THE SELF: A SYMBIOSIS

In every act of teaching the teacher defines the self as a psychosocial person. A person's view of teaching is a reflection of one's psychosocial values and stability. There is a reciprocal relationship between teaching and one's psychosocial well-being. The person who is deeply attuned to the teaching process knows that it is a vehicle for expressing and fostering those psychosocial beliefs which nurture the growth of others (Aspy & Buhler, 1975; Noad, 1979).

There is a symbiotic relationship between a person's psychosocial values and work (Stefflre, 1968). If this symbiotic relationship is to be psychosocially enriching for the teacher, then the teaching process must provide opportunities for the teacher to express positive psychosocial values. There are few careers which offer so much opportunity for the expression of one's psychosocial beliefs.

TEACHING: A PERSONAL EXPRESSION OF PSYCHOSOCIAL VALUES

The teacher who is psychosocially stable will make a significant contribution to the psychosocial development of students. The teacher's role as a teacher is greatly influenced by the teacher's psychosocial values. The psychosocially stable teacher has self-respect. One cannot respect others unless one first has self-respect. From a psychosocial foundation of respecting the self it becomes natural to project this attitude of respect to students. Students know when they are in the presence of a teacher who respects them. This respect is known to students not by what the teacher says or does but by the human and caring attitude beneath what the teacher says and does (Curtis & Altman, 1977; Wolf & Schultz, 1981).

TEACHERS NEED ENRICHING PSYCHOSOCIAL EXPERIENCES

Facilitative teaching requires deep respect for the worth of the individual, empathic understanding, realness, concreteness, and a personel investment in the process. These qualities are reflections of a teacher's psychosocial stability. In order for teachers to optimally develop these qualities, they themselves need positive psychosocial experiences. *People become what they experience and teachers are no exception.* Unfortunately, the debilitating psychosocial atmosphere in which teachers often work, and the lack of trust and stereotyped expectations they experience, tend to diminish them as persons. Too often, the teacher's genuineness becomes hidden and repressed by a professional facade of rationalism and stoicism. The teacher sometimes has a stereotyped unflattering image which the public has created, which has been perpetuated by the mass media and which in turn has been internalized by some teachers. The teacher's psychosocial stability will require that the teacher discard a professional mask and become real. Herbert Kohl (1970:70) suggests one approach for doing this:

> For ten minutes (a day) cease to be a teacher and be an adult with young people, a resource available if needed and possibly a friend, but not a director, a judge or executioner. Also, try to make it possible for the ten minutes to grow to fifteen, twenty, so long as it makes sense to you and your pupils. It is not unlikely that these ten minutes may become the most important of the day, and after a while, may even become the school day.

TEACHERS CAN CREATE ENRICHING PSYCHOSOCIAL EXPERIENCES

Such a suggestion implicitly states that teachers can do more than react to experiences, they can *create* experiences which will nourish them as persons. Teachers need to find ways to reveal themselves as persons. This is not easy to do, since most of us have been inculcated since childhood with the attitude of not showing how we really feel. Many of us have learned to hide our feelings, because we fear being rejected or hurt. Self-disclosure does involve a risk but so does psychosocial growth. Finding out who we are and being who we are can be an anxiety-provoking process. But for the teacher who is willing to risk and to make the necessary investment to close the gap between the role self and the real self, the risk of taking off one's professional mask is more than compensated for by the richness and fulfillment which comes with the liberation of the "essential" or psychosocial self. Disclosing one's self to others provides a therapeutic release, enables one to develop strong affiliations with others, and contributes to our psychosocial stability (Weinhold & Elliott, 1979).

FRIENDSHIP AS AN ENRICHING PSYCHOSOCIAL EXPERIENCE

Authenticity, genuineness, and self-revelation are necessary qualities for psychosocial development. If the real self of the teacher is visible only outside the school, then the chances of positive psychosocial experiences developing in the classroom are remote. Despite the continuous contact with students, teaching can be a lonely profession (Silberman, 1970). Teachers need a chance to discuss their problems with each other, they need opportunities to share their successes, and they need time to blow off steam. Friendships offer teachers, as with anyone else, one of the most rewarding opportunities for self-discovery. Friendships require give and take—they are reciprocally therapeutic relationships which provide opportunities for exploration and mutual learning and can result in self-awareness and a modification of behavior. People, in defining close friendships, put an emphasis on self-disclosure. Each of us carefully nominates a few companions to fulfill the intimate role of being unofficial therapists. Teachers need "unofficial therapy" which enables them to search for a deeper understanding of themselves. If teachers are to influence the psychosocial climate of the classroom, then they must have psychosocial experiences which enable them to be real and genuine. If teachers cannot be themselves, then they, in turn, will be unable to have a positive influence on the psychosocial development of students. One of the most important experiences for teachers, then, is to develop a few honest and close friendships so that they can have access to "unofficial therapy" (Boy & Pine, 1974; Boy & Pine, 1982).

PSYCHOSOCIAL DEVELOPMENT THROUGH RELATIONSHIPS WITH OTHERS

Through relationships with colleagues and students, the teacher can learn more deeply about the self as a person. Historically, Jersild (1952) pointed out that the significance of relationships with others provides a simple but profoundly important aid to self-examination. He says: "If one would know what he thinks about himself and how he feels about himself, let his glance turn to others, for the kinds of thoughts and feelings he has with regard to others are likely in one way or another to reflect his attitudes toward himself" (p. 46).

Through their relationships with each other, teachers can explore their own capacities for psychosocial growth. Rather than competing with each other, teachers need to engage in cooperative relationships. This calls for giving, and receiving. Kildahl (1970) indicates that there is little alienation among people who join and work together for a common and concrete human goal. He feels that one of the ways in which people derive a sense of meaning—a sense that their life counts for something—is to give help to others. The implication for teachers seems to be quite clear. Mere verbalizations about teamwork are not enough. Beginning and experienced teachers, young and old, need not only to exchange ideas but also to share materials and aid each other through helpful behavior (Paquette, 1987; Slavin, 1987).

Teachers can learn to be more real as they interact with each other in helpful ways which are *non-exploitive*. This means that an experienced teacher offers assistance to a newcomer, not for the purpose of winning the newcomer over and inducting the newcomer into an existing "teaching" value system, but because the experienced teacher genuinely cares to help the newcomer. It also means that a young teacher doesn't attempt to convert a more experienced teacher to a new approach but is willing to share skills, techniques, and ideas when they are requested. Helping relationships have to be built on empathy, mutual trust listening, compassion, and honesty (Hamachek, 1978). If teachers cannot create supportive psychosocial experiences among themselves, if they cannot be real with each other, then surely it will be difficult for them to be real in the classroom and create the necessary atmosphere for the psychosocial development of students (Smith, 1987).

Learning to become a better teacher requires collegial relationships and a collaborative support environment where not knowing something becomes a resource for learning. Learning to share and sharing to learn are critical to the personal and professional development of teachers. It's time to knock down the walls that separate teachers from teachers and build learning partnerships where teachers become more aware of their common resources and problems. (Brandt, 1987, Hammond and Foster, 1987; Neubert and Bratton, 1987, and Wildman and Niles, 1987.)

RECREATION AS PSYCHOSOCIAL EXPERIENCE

In 1892, William James in *Talks to Teachers* speaking on the *Gospel of Relaxation* (1958) said, "Just as a bicycle chain may be too tight so may one's carefulness and conscientiousness be so tense as to hinder the running of one's mind" (p. 132). James's ideas on relaxation are as appropriate for teachers today as they were in his day. While the work of the teacher should be taken seriously, there is the possibility and danger that the teacher will take oneself too seriously. A balance needs to be struck in teaching so that the teacher can integrate play with work. The teacher who knows how to play will seldom become discouraged or bored with teaching. Recreational experiences offer change, a chance to look at life and one's work from a different and relaxed perspective. Recreatioal activities are necessary elements for self-renewal and an enriched teaching life (Boy & Pine, 1971).

The psychosocially stable teacher lives life—engages life by participating in or creating experiences "just for fun." Such a teacher uses play as a means of adding breadth and variety to experiences Recreation is a necessary experience for developing one's psychosocial stability but cannot compensate for the drudgery of work in which a person has no real interest or commitment. Because of one's commitment and deep involvement in teaching, the psychosocially stable teacher does not think of recreational experiences as merely something to counterbalance the displeasure one finds in teaching. For the psychosocially stable teacher, teaching offers the opportunity to integrate work and play.

The pychosocially stable teacher loves teaching but realizes that one's psychosocial stability cannot be maintained solely through teaching. This teacher looks forward to those diversions which provide opportunities for an unpredictable and fresh dialogue among the teacher's potentialities for sensing, wondering, loving, and laughing. Whether painting, boating, watching a ball game, dancing, singing, or hiking, the teacher lets the self go to drink in the beauty and vitality of the moment.

One can prescribe no list of magical recreational experiences which promote the psychosocial development of the teacher. Teaching with commitment can be demanding and enervating as well a rewarding and the rewards of teaching will diminish if one's commitment is not balanced by an involvement in recreational experiences. Just as it is important for children to play, it is important for teachers (and all adults) to play. Teachers who limit their lives to what is occurring in the classroom will find their psychosocial stability diminished. Life primarily confined to teaching begets narrowness in perceptions, feelings, perspectives and living. Recreational experiences can require commitment and a large expenditure of time and effort. But what makes any experience refreshing and recreational rather than fatiguing is one's attitude toward what is being done.

Psychosocially stable people find no dichotomy between work and play. An observer might see the psychosocially stable person's work in teaching as not work at all and might observe the same teacher as seemingly working very hard while engaged in recreational pursuits. There is no contradiction. The psychosocially stable person's teaching is characterized by joy as well as commitment and this person's recreation by commitment as well as joy. For the psychosocially stable teacher, there is a reciprocal interplay between teaching and play. Both complement each other and serve as a springboard for a creative and vital personal and professional life.

Recreational experiences offer the teacher an interlude, a break in the pattern of one's professional life that often reveals the secure web that has been woven around the self. The position of the teacher tends to evolve into a secure social and academic role and if one is not careful, teaching can cause one to overestimate the wisdom of one's own words. One of the occupational hazards of teaching is the development of the "god" complex. This can be avoided through recreational activities which bring the teacher into contact with a variety of people and experiences that not only "scratch and nick" one's thinking but also generate a balanced view of teaching and its relationship to life. Some of the experiences teachers need to obviate the potentially debilitating aspects of teaching are: developing relationships with those in other occupations where the teacher's kind of language is not pertinent, engaging in adult activities entirely unrelated to teaching, seeking companionship among those who are authentic enough to confront and challenge the teacher's "authority," developing a sense of humor so that teachers can laugh at themselves, seeing a play, taking a trip, becoming more real, and developing a non-exploitive commitment to the work of teaching.

It is particularly important that a teacher cultivate a sense of humor. Laughing at oneself and the absurdities of life helps the teacher to avoid making mountains out of molehills and creating problems. The joy one experiences through laughter offers a therapeutic release and the laughter which emanates from the willingness to recognize one's pretensions and frailties is a contribution to one's psychosocial stability.

Without the opportunities to re-create ourselves as persons, our teaching loses its vitality and freshness and our reservoir of psychosocially nourishing experiences becomes depleted. Recreation replenishes the teacher's psychosocial storehouse and adds new dimensions to one's teaching.

Teachers to be facilitative across time on a daily basis must be physically fit. Aspy and Roebuck (1977), in a study involving 300 teachers and 6000 students, found a decrease in levels of teacher-offered interpersonal conditions across a two year span. The general pattern was for the highest level to occur at the beginning of the year, to decline until Christmas, recover slightly after Christmas holiday, and to decrease until the end of the year, at which time the lowest level was recorded. The second study of one year duration involving a somewhat smaller population reported similar findings. The data suggested there was a fatigue effect and inferred a relationship between levels of interpersonal functioning and physical fitness. Williams and Colingsworth (1974) found that entering levels of physical fitness were some of the best predictors of the degree to which interpersonal skills learned in a workshop would be used in the classroom.

In several other studies Aspy and Roebuck (1976) found that: the teacher's level of physical fitness was significantly correlated with the frequency with which eye contact was made with students and with the number of times the teacher smiled when teaching; and, physical fitness was a better predictor of practicum performance by student teachers than grade point average. In reviewing the literature on the relationship between physical fitness and interpersonal functioning, Aspy and Roebuck (1983) concluded that physical fitness training translates directly into increased effectiveness, physical fitness is a parameter of professional development, and physical fitness training methodologies should be incorporated into preservice and inservice teacher education as well as the daily lives of teachers.

ADMINISTRATORS NEED TO PROVIDE ENRICHING PSYCHOSOCIAL EXPERIENCES

All that has been said about teaching can be said of school administration and teacher education. Administrators who trust, like, accept, understand, and empathize with their teachers help teachers to *experience* being trusted, likeable, accepted and understood. Teachers like any other group of people need to experience these attitudes in order for them to be real. Perhaps the most significant contribution an administrator can make to facilitate the academic and psychosocial development of students is to create a school climate in which the academic and psychosocial development of teachers can be nourished (Pine & Boy, 1979).

Frymeir (1987) in a provocative article "Bureaucracy and Neutering of Teachers" argues compellingly that we must stop undercutting teachers by creating conditions of work that blunt their enthusiasm and strifle their creativity. He says:

> During the 1960s an essay titled "The Student As Nigger" received wide coveage in the underground newspapers. Its thesis was that school people deliberately discriminate against students. It would be grossly inaccurate to say that most or even many people in the higher echelons of educational bureaucracies see "the teacher as nigger." But there is evidence that some teachers feel they are viewed in this fashion (p. 14).

The teacher is central to school improvement and the development of students. We must empower teachers to help them develop an internalized locus of control (Frymeir 1987:14). Teachers, principals, superintendents, school board members, and state legislators must realize and appreciate that empowering teachers will marshall the motivations and unleash the talents of those who work directly with children day after day. This means that teachers must have a significant voice and influence in hiring other teachers, choosing department heads, supervisors, principals, selecting instructional materials, planning in-service training programs, developing curriculum, and planning school programs. To empower teachers is to give them an internalized locus of control. People who have an internalized locus of control feel on top of things, feel they can make a difference, feel that what they do is important, have a sense of being in control of their own lives and of the events and things around them, are self confident and secure, and are willing to work hard, to learn, and to change. The more we honor and value teachers by empowering them as professionals the more we will improve our schools and help all our children achieve their potential.

The importance of one's psychosocial development should be included in those programs preparing persons to become teachers. Persons learning to become teachers will learn something about psychosocial stability through their interactions with professors and supervisors. The professor or supervisor who is growing and learning, who trusts students and is real with them, who listens to students and confronts them in facilitative ways, "teaches" the importance of psychosocial stability.

It is not enough to talk about the importance of psychosocial enhancement. Teachers need to *experience* individualization, acceptance, understanding, trust, authenticity, and being liked. In order for teachers to develop psychosocial awareness, they need to have positive psychosocial experiences. It is much easier for us to learn something if we experience it. The more teachers have these experiences and can provide these experiences for pupils, the more they, in turn, improve their own psychosocial development (Combs, 1982).

PSYCHOSOCIAL EXPERIENCES IN THE CLASSROOM

The more the teacher seeks, creates, and is offered experiences which contribute to the teacher's psychosocial development, the more the teacher will utilize psychosocial experiences in the classroom. Operating from a base of personal security, realness, and awareness, the teacher provides pupils with a growth-facilitating psychosocial classroom environment. Over two decades ago some fundamental principles for fostering the psychosocial development of students were identified by the American Association for Supervision and Curriculum Development in their *Individualizing Instruction* publication (1964):

1. Observing and listening to learners with care and concern.
2. Achieving openness in pupil-teacher relationships, to permit improved responses and interaction.
3. Helping learners toward the objective of personal relevance.
4. Recognizing and accepting different ways of responding, according to learners' individualized styles and needs.

5. Stimulating creation and recreation of self-image that encourages further development.
6. Questioning, probing and responding in ways that lead learners to assume responsibility.
7. Standing aside judiciously to let the learner discover and exercise personal resources.
8. Making development of the learner the chief goal in teaching subject matter.
9. Achieving free and affective responses and seeing their relationship to intellectual development.
10. Achieving free and constructive communication with learners.
11. Helping learners sense the living dynamics of humanity's creations, as revealed by history and the current scene.
12. Clearing the way, by whatever means, for stretching learners' minds and abilities in creative, self-fulfilling endeavors (pp. 161-162).

The more the teacher invests in this kind of teaching, the more teaching contributes to the student's psychosocial development. The more creativity and compassion the teacher puts into teaching, the more teaching defines the teacher as a creative and compassionate person. The more the teacher humanizes teaching, the more teaching humanizes the teacher. The more the teacher cares for students, the more they will care for the teacher. The more the teacher frees students to grow, the more the teacher grows. Psychosocial development occurs in proportion to the degree to which we find psychosocially stable teachers in our classrooms (Holmes, Holmes, & Field, 1974; Kraft, 1975; Combs, 1982).

A poem by Dorothy Law Nolte (1972) captures the gains for the pupil who is exposed to the psychosocially stable teacher:

If a child lives with criticism,
  He learns to condemn.
If a child lives with hostility,
  He learns to fight.
If a child lives with ridicule,
  He learns to be shy.
If a child lives with shame,
  He learns to be guilty.
If a child lives with tolerance,
  He learns to be patient.
If a child lives with encouragement,
  He learns confidence.

If a child lives with praise,
   He learns to appreciate.
If a child lives with fairness,
   He learns justice.
If a child lives with security,
   He learns to have faith.
If a child lives with approval,
   He learns to like himself.
If a child lives with acceptance and friendship,
   He learns to find love in the world.

RETAIN A POSITIVE ATTITUDE

To the pessimist, the proverbial half-filled glass of water is half empty. To the optimist, this same glass of water is half full. Each of us has a choice to perceive life, and our professional existence, from either a perspective of pessimism or one of optimism. A teacher, dedicated to the process of uplifting and enriching the human condition, has no recourse but to be, internally and operationally, hopeful and optimistic in the attitude which generates the teacher's personal and professional behavior.

This optimism is not based on an unrealistic act of burying one's head in the sand. It is an optimism based upon a realization that the real enemy of hope is our personal and professional negativism. If we feel that personal and professional developments are out of our control, that our attitudes and behaviors are determined by forces beyond our control, then the easiest thing to do is to sit back and allow these forces to grind us into oblivion. But when we are in control of the attitudes and behaviors, we can move them in positive directions which benefit students, ourselves, and the schools which employ us.

The roots of personal pessimism are within ourselves; conversely, the roots of personal optimism are within ourselves. We face an existential choice of furthering and developing our pessimistic or optimistic inclinations. If we choose to reinforce our pessimistic tendencies, we then do ourselves, our profession, and students a disservice. If we, instead, choose to nourish our tendencies toward optimism, we have energized ourselves toward a goal which will enable us to endure, manage, and change the circumstances which surround our personal and professional existence. The choice is ours; historically, it has always been ours and in our future it will always remain ours.

Worthwhile professional goals give clarity and meaning to our professional roles and behaviors. A periodic examination of these goals will produce a *gravitas* in our work.

The following guidelines regarding the teaching/learning process are meant to help us in that periodic examination of goals:

1. Listen to the feelings of students regardless of what subject we're teaching.
2. Respond to the feelings of students regardless of what subject we're teaching.
3. Realize that the student's individuality must be synchronized with the student's learning group.
4. Try to decrease the amount of our teacher talk and increase the amount of pupil talk.
5. Provide learning activities which stimulate student participation.
6. Be sensitive to the psychosocial concerns of the age group we're teaching.
7. Realize that students cannot devote all of their homework time to our subject or course.
8. Develop a genuinely human way of communicating with pupils, colleagues, administrators, parents, friends, and relatives.
9. Realize that as we provide a free and open learning environment we have a responsibility to make sure that students are making progress in their academic and/or psychosocial development.
10. Let justice prevail in our classrooms.
11. Realize that our own psychosocial stability is a positive influence on the psychosocial development of students.
12. Learn to separate the substantive elements of teaching and learning from the temporary and superficial elements.
13. Realize that the expression of our human attitudes of caring and respect will engender positive student attitudes toward us and the learning process.
14. Although those around us may not follow the highest of professional standards, our own professional commitment will not be compromised.
15. Realize that many students may be exposed to destructive psychosocial home environments which inhibit their ability to learn while in school.
16. Realize when our behavior is not objective and when it is defensive and self-serving.

17. Always try to conceptualize teaching and learning as simply as possible.
18. Realize that we are free agents when making professional choices and decisions.
19. Realize that the material gains we gave up to be teachers have been replaced with the satisfaction that our lives are given to the service of others.
20. Realize that nothing is perfect and if we insist on perfection we'll wind up being frustrated.
21. Take the responsibility for what's occurring in our classrooms and avoid the temptation to blame others.
22. Realize that some students do not see school as the most important experience of their lives.
23. Stay receptive to the feedback we receive regarding how our teaching can be improved.
24. Realize that educational technology cannot replace the human teacher in influencing the student's psychosocial development.
25. Realize that teaching provides us with an opportunity to express the human components of our self-concepts.
26. Realize that effective teaching is the process of helping students to identify ideals and determining the process for working toward those ideals.
27. Realize that the one who teaches the best is the one who teaches the least.
28. Stay informed regarding new developments which influence the process of teaching and learning.
29. Be an especially gentle and empathic listener to those whose conversations are filled with negative self-defeating feelings.
30. Be satisfied that our lives are being well spent in this most honorable of professions.

THE RIGHTS OF THE TEACHER

The constitutional or legal rights of teachers have been reasonably established and concern themselves with the following freedoms: academic, speech and association outside the classroom, religion, private life, mode of dress and grooming, and freedom from discrimination in the areas of gender, race, and age (Rubin, 1971). This section will not address itself to these freedoms, since they are known and established. It will instead concern itself with those more subtle and operational rights which affect a teacher's morale and commitment to continue a career in teaching.

In a society in which the rights of various persons are being recognized and respected, those of the teacher need to receive the same attention and respect if those who employ teachers expect them to maintain an enduring commitment to teaching as a career. The rights identified in this section have the potential of renewing a teacher's commitment to the profession, as well as serving as indicators of the concerns of teachers for those who have policy and administrative responsibility for improving the climate in which teachers work.

The Right to a Professional Role

Teachers often have their teaching responsibilities diluted by their involvement in a myriad of non-teaching assignments. These intrusive activities usually have nothing to do with improving the quality of instruction but are more related to improving the organizational and administrative structure of the school. Teachers are expected to spend some portion of each day performing these activities and do not have the option of declining participation in their execution. In some schools, the teacher's involvement in these activities often occupies more time than that available to teach. The justification for the teacher's involvement is non-teaching responsibilities usually comes from administrators; if teachers had their choice, they would not be involved in these activities.

Teachers understand that schools need to process forms, tabulate, evaluate, conduct surveys, gain permissions, and develop and submit reports. The basic issue, however, revolves around the amount of time that the teacher is involved. When these activities take an unreasonable portion of the teacher's time so that there is little time left to teach, then the value and necessity of these activities needs to be questioned. Sometimes, it appears to teachers that school administrators spend the major portion of each working day designing new non-teaching responsibilities for teachers.

The teacher's proper professional role should focus on teaching as the primary responsibility. Responsibilities which decrease the teacher's available time for teaching should be evaluated in terms of their contribution to improving the quality of instruction. Those responsibilities which contribute to improving that quality should be continued, while those which make little or no contribution should be eliminated. Teachers have a right to a professional role and schools which recognize and foster that right will do much to attract and retain competent teachers (Schwab & Iwanicki, 1982; Sparks, 1983).

The Right to Be Fairly Evaluated

Teachers have a right to fairness when their work is evaluated. They do not seek to avoid being evaluated; they simply want the evaluative process to be fair and free from bias.

Some schools create evaluative problems for teachers when they: (1) institute arbitrary evaluative criteria and impose these criteria on teachers; (2) employ criteria used to evaluate other professionals as "suitable" for evaluating teachers without recognizing role differences between teachers and other professionals; (3) utilize a haphazard, disorganized, and unclear approach to evaluation; and (4) do not implement the evaluative process in a democratic manner (Pine & Boy, 1975).

Teachers consider an evaluative process to be fair when it includes the teacher in determining the goals, criteria, and process of evaluation. When the teacher is involved in determining the goals of evaluation, those goals will include priorities important to improving the quality of instruction; when the teacher is involved in determining the criteria of evaluation, the teacher has the opportunity to include criteria which are appropriate for evaluating the teacher's performance of responsibilities; and when the teacher is involved in determining the steps in the evaluative process itself, the teacher has the opportunity to contribute to the objectivity and fairness of that process (Pine & Boy, 1975).

The teacher's right to be fairly evaluated must include the teacher's input into that process. When the teacher participates, there is greater assurance that the teacher will accept the evaluative process as an endeavor marked by fairness.

The Right to a School Climate Free From Politics

In some schools some decisions are made not because they enhance the teaching process or contribute to the educational development of students; they are usually made because of political favoritism or expediency. Political favoritism occurs for certain staff not because the staff member is exceptionally competent but because the staff member has maneuvered into a position whereby favors are gained. Politically expedient decisions are those designed to curry favor with individuals and groups, both in the school and outside the school, who in some way affect the school. Teachers in such a work environment usually become disenchanted, because the school's noble educational mission becomes submerged in a sea of pervasive political influences.

Teachers want to be employed in a setting which has a clear commitment to improving student learning; a setting in which that commitment is never blunted by decisions tainted with political favoritism or expedience. That really isn't very much to ask, but, unfortunately, some schools don't know how to behave unless they behave politically. They seek advantages not based upon the quality of teaching or learning but seek advantages which are linked to political considerations.

The professional teacher has a deep and abiding commitment to meet the learning needs of students through the teaching process. It is an honest commitment which can be nourished in proportion to a school's ability to create a politically-free work climate. When this occurs, the teacher's work is performed qualitatively and the school's positive reputation far exceeds one gained by political favoritism or expediency.

The Right to Fair Administrative Practices

Teachers do not expect administrators to be perfect. They recognize that administrators are faced with pressures and responsibilities that are often unknown by staff members. Teachers also know that one's decision to enter administration is a free choice which is accompanied by a salary differential. Teachers merely want administrators to live up to their responsibilities and perform those responsibilities with fairness. They want administrators to perform routine functions in an organized manner and want responsibilities affecting the school, staff, students, and parents to be characterized by fairness (Pine & Boy, 1979).

The best way for administrators to become more fair in their execution of responsibilities is to include teachers in the decision-making process. Including teachers will certainly take more time, but the issue of fairness will be better served when the time required is taken. Teachers will feel that a sharing of the decision-making process is an indicator of the administrator's respect for the opinions of teachers and that they have a stake in the outcomes of decisions made cooperatively. Creating such an administrative climate will cause teachers to perceive administrative practices as being fair and will be a welcomed contribution for improving and maintaining teacher morale.

The teacher's right to fair administrative practices will be enhanced by administrators who have a deep commitment to the importance of participatory democracy and the outcomes it can achieve.

The Right to Equalized Staff Relationships

Equalized relationships between and among staff members tends to be productive, while unequalized relationships tend to be non-productive. An equalized relationship is one in which staff members possess equivalent authority when dealing with each other or arriving at professional decisions. They deal with each other more openly when considering a decision, and each other's input into the decision is mutually respected. When the relationship is equalized between marriage partners, labor and management, and between and among nations, all parties tend to engage each other more cooperatively and with a sense of mutual trust. When such relationships are unequalized, the level of cooperation and trust tends to be diminished and the outcomes of that relationship tend to be non-productive (Pine & Boy, 1977, pp. 129-130).

In certain administrative situations, some staff members have more authority over the work behavior of others. If they exercise that authority without a sensitivity to the feelings and opinions of professional colleagues, then unnecessary barriers are created. When the authority is exercised in an atmosphere characterized by mutual trust and respect, then all parties involved profit, since whatever is communicated is assimilated and is a contribution to a shared decision. Shared decisions tend to be more enlightened, implementable, and pursued with more involvement and commitment.

Teachers who have equalized relationships with other staff members are free to communicate and contribute, since there are no repercussions for viewpoints expressed. Teachers have a right to equalized staff relationships and the beneficiaries of such relationships will be the school and the students served by that school. Teachers tend to be more creative, energetic, and productive as an outcome of equalized staff relationships.

The Right to Implement a Teaching Model

A teacher's implementation of a certain teaching model is a serious professional decision and is not made lightly. It is not based upon a teacher's whims or needs. It is anchored to the learning needs of students and is based upon the teacher's recognition that a bona fide teaching model must meet the following criteria, in that it possesses: (1) a viewpoint about the nature of human nature and its appropriate expression, (2) beliefs regarding how students learn and change behavior, (3) a commitment to certain teaching and learning goals, (4) a description of the teacher's behavior in the teaching-learning process, and (5) research evidence supporting the teaching model's effectiveness. A useful teaching model enables the teacher to find relatedness among diverse observations and experiences, compels us to consider teaching and learning factors that were previously overlooked, provides guidelines for monitoring our teaching behavior, tells us what to look for in the learning behavior of students, helps us to identify a process for improving that learning behavior, and helps us to make modifications in the teaching process so that it will better meet the learning needs of students (Boy & Pine, 1984).

A teacher's commitment to a certain teaching model, because of its documented effectiveness, must be matched by a school's respect for the teacher's right to apply that teaching model. Schools must realize that there are several professionally respected teaching models, and when they insist on the application of only one model, they are in conflict with research evidence supporting other theories, subvert the teacher's morale, and deny student access to teaching models which may be more effective in meeting their learning needs.

The acquisition and retention of the previously identified rights is a matter of assuming control over one's professional life rather than leaving that control in the hands of others. When teachers assume this control, then movement toward the implementation of these rights will be a natural outcome. In their reviews and recommendations regarding the process of reducing teacher stress, Pines (1980), Gmelch (1983) and Riccio (1983) all conclude that stress can be dramatically reduced when teachers take control over the events which occur in their work environments. All too often, rights are not freely given. They are earned by teachers who have learned to control the events occurring in their professional lives. These are the teachers whose commitment to teaching has an enduring quality.

REFERENCES

Aspy, D. N. & Buhler, J. H. (1975). The effect of teachers' inferred self-concept upon student achievement. *Journal of Educational Research*, 47, 386-389.

Aspy, D. N. & Roebuck, F. N. (1976). *A Lever Long Enough*. Dallas: National Consortium for Humanizing Education.

Aspy, D. N. & Roebuck, F. N. (1977). *Kids Don't Learn from People They Don't Like*. Amherst: HRD Press.

Aspy, D. N. & Roebuck, F. N. (1983). Physical fitness in counseling and teaching. *The Journal of Humanistic Education and Development*—21, 3, 115-123.

Boy, A. V. & Pine, G. J. (1971). *Expanding the self: Personal growth for teachers.* Dubuque, IA: Wm. C. Brown.

Boy, A. V. & Pine, G. J. (1974). Human understanding of human experiences. *Religious Humanism,* 8, 123-129.

Boy, A. V. & Pine, G. J. (1982). *Client-centered counseling: A renewal.* Boston: Allyn and Bacon.

Boy, A. V. & Pine, G. J. (1984). Student-centered counselor education. *California Association for Counseling and Development Journal.* 5, 21-27.

Brandt, R. S. (1987). Learning with and from one another. *Educational Leadership,* 44, 5, 3.

Combs, A. W. (1972). Some basic concepts for teacher education. *The Journal of Teacher Education,* 23, 2856-290.

Combs, A. W. (1982). *A personal approach to teaching: Beliefs that make a difference.* Boston: Allyn and Bacon.

Curtis, J. & Altman, H. (1977). The relationship between teachers' self concept and self concepts of students. *Child Study Journal,* 7, 17-26.

Frymeir, J. (1987). Bureaucracy and the neutering of teachers. *Phi Delta Kappan,* 69, 1, 9-14.

Gmelch, W. H. (1983). Stress for success. How to optimize your performance. *Theory into Practice,* 22, 7-14.

Good, T. L., Biddle, B. J. & Brophy, J. E. (1975). *Teachers make a difference.* New York: Rinehart and Winston.

Hamachek, D. E. (1978). *Encounters with the self.* 2nd ed. New York: Holt, Rinehart & Winston.

Hammond, J. & Foster, K. (1987). Creating a professional learning partnership. *Educational Leadership.* 44, 5, 42-44.

Holmes, N., Holmes, D. & Field, J. (1974). *The therapeutic classroom.* New York: Aronson.

Individualizing Instruction. (1964). Washington, DC: Association for Supervision and Curriculum Development.

James, W. (1958). *Talks to teachers.* New York: Norton.

Jersild, A. T. (1952). *In search of self.* New York: Teachers College Press, Columbia University.

Kildahl, J. P. (1970). Twelve ways to survive the rat race. *Boston Globe Magazine,* June 14, 28-34.

Kohl, H. R. (1970). *Open classroom.* New York: Vintage Books (Imprint of Random House).

Kraft, A. (1975). *The living classroom: Putting humanistic education into practice.* New York: Harper and Row.

Moustakas, C. E. (1966). *The authentic teacher: Sensitivity and awareness in the classroom.* Cambridge, MA: Howard A. Doyle.

Neubert, G. A. & Bratton, E. C. (1987). Team coaching: Staff development side by side. *Educational Leadership,* 44, 5, 29-33.

Noad, B. M. (1979). Influence of self concept and educational attitudes on elementary student teacher performance. *Educational Research Quarterly,* 1, 69-75.

Nolte, D. L. (1972). Children learn what they live. In J. D. Krumboltz, *Changing children's behavior.* Englewood Cliffs, NJ: Prentice-Hall.

Paquette, M. (1987). Voluntary collegial support groups for teachers. *Educational Leadership,* 45, 3, 36-39.

Pine, G. J. & Boy, A. V. (1975). Necessary conditions for evaluating teachers. *The Bulletin,* 59, 18-23.

Pine, G. J. & Boy, A. V. (1976). Teaching and valuing. *The Clearing House,* 313-315.

Pine, G. J. & Boy, A. V. (1977). *Learner-centered teaching: A humanistic view.* Denver: Love.

Pine, G. J. & Boy, A. V. (1979). Theory as a guide to administrative behavior. *NASSP Bulletin,* 63, 32-38.

Pines, M. (1980). Psychological hardiness: The role of challenge in health. *Psychology Today,* 14, 34.

Riccio, A. (1983). On coping with the stress of teaching. *Theory into Practice,* 22, 43-47.

Rubin, D. (1971). *The rights of teachers: The basic ACLU guide to a teacher's constitutional rights.* New York: Doubleday.

Schwab, R. L. & Iwanicki, E. F. (1982). Perceived role conflict, role ambiguity, and teacher burnout. *Educational Administration Quarterly,* 18, 60-74.

Silberman, C. E. (1970). Murder in the classroom. *The Atlantic Monthly,* 225, 82-97.

Slavin, R. (1987). Cooperative learning and the cooperative school. *Educational Leadership,* 45, 3, 7-13.

Smith, S. (1987). The collaborative school takes shape. *Educational Leadership,* 45, 3, 4-6.

Sparks, D. (1983). Practical solutions for teacher stress. *Theory into Practice,* 22, 33-42.

Stefflre, B. (1966). Vocational development: Ten propositions in search of a theory. *Personnel and Guidance Journal,* 44, 611.

Weinhold, B. K. & Elliott, L. C. (1979). *Transpersonal communication.* Englewood Cliffs, NJ: Prentice-Hall.

Wildman, T. M. & Niles, J. A. (1987). Essentials of professional growth. *Educational Leadership,* 44, 5, 4-11.

Williams, H. & Collingswood, T. (1974). Differential physical fitness levels and interpersonal skill acquisition. Dallas: *NCHE Monograph Series on Fitness,* Vol. 1-9.

Wolf, J. G. & Schultz, E. W. (1981). Teacher self-concept and perceived interpersonal competence. *The Humanist Educator,* 19, 65-72.

CHAPTER VIII

FOSTERING PSYCHOSOCIAL DEVELOPMENT THROUGH CAREER AWARENESS

THERE IS A symbiotic relationship between a person's self and the person's work. A person achieves this symbiotic union either by changing a self-concept to fit a work role or by changing the work role to fit the self concept or a little of both of these (Tiedeman & O'Hara, 1963). This viewpoint has significant implications for emphasizing career awareness as an integral part of the student's psychosocial development. In the next several pages we develop the theme of the symbiosis between work and the development of the self-concept and the reciprocal and integrating relationship that exists between work and the self-concept. This builds the rationale for viewing career awareness as a critically important contributor to the student's psychosocial development. Work is an expression of one's psychosocial values and some work represents a person's psychosocial maturity (Pate, 1980).

CAREER AWARENESS AND PSYCHOSOCIAL DEVELOPMENT

Career awareness has content and goals that go beyond occupational information or requiring that a student select a particular adult occupation while still in school. Career awareness has two purposes: (1) to help students understand that one's life work is an expression of one's self-concept and (2) one's work has an effect on developing and maintaining one's self-concept.

Through group experiences the teacher can facilitate self-understanding, promote positive self-concepts, develop interpersonal skills, and clarify values (Hazel, 1976), which are all important in the process of developing career awareness. Career awareness, then, is an outcome of the student's participation in psychosocial experiences in school. Career awareness helps the student to realize how one's psychosocial values can be enhanced or limited by a career.

The meaning of work in the life of the person has been the subject of thoughtful inquiry and speculation by many writers. The thrust of their writings, particularly those dealing with career development, occupational choice, and the role of work in human existence emphasize the "psychological and philosophical" person rather than "economic" person. Wrenn (1964) defines work as an "activity calling for the expenditure of effort toward some definite achievement or outcome. Paid or not, hard or easy, it is always effort toward a specified end" (p. 27). Accepting this definition moves one from looking at work as only an economic activity. Indeed, a random glance at Western literature and tradition indicates a long-held view that work holds more than economic value as the following statements attest:

> In all labor, there is profit.
> Proverbs XIV:23 — *Old Testament*

> Things won are done, joy's soul lies in the doing.
> Shakespeare — *Trolius and Cressida*

> Our deeds determine us, as much as we determine our deeds.
> George Eliot — *Adam Beede*

> I never intend a day to pass without asserting my identity; my work records my existence.
> David Smith in *David Smith*

> Always you have been told that work is a curse and labor a misfortune.
> But I say to you that when you work you fulfill a part of earth's fondest dream, assigned to you when that dream was born,
> And keeping yourself with labour you are in truth loving life; And to love life through labour is to be intimate with life's inmost secret.
> Kahil Gibran — *The Prophet*

Wilensky (1964) comments that historically persons "have attached meanings to their work as wondrously varied as the meanings they have attached to sex and play" (p. 126). Among the various meanings assigned to the role of work in human existence is the concept of work as therapy (Boy & Pine, 1971). Taube, Burns, and Kessler (1984) indicate that work has a profound influence on the mental health of the individual. Freud once remarked that all human problems revolve around love and work. It might also be said that all human problems can be dealt with through love and work.

The contribution of work to one's psychosocial stability is identified by Lathrop (1977), who says:

> A job is not just a job. Half of your waking hours are devoted to it. Its quality ramifies through all other aspects of your life. It determines your productivity and how far you will go in achieving full self-realization. It governs your happiness, the happiness of your family, where you live, and how well. The quality of the job you land now will inevitably affect the quality of your next one. (p. 10.)

The preceding viewpoint is confirmed by Morrow (1981):

> Work is the most thorough and profound organizing principle in American life. All work expresses the laborer in the deeper sense; all life must be worked at, protected, planted, replanted, fashioned, cooked for, coaxed, diapered, formed, sustained. Work is the way we tend the world, the way that people connect. It is the most vigorous and vivid sign of life in individuals and in civilizations. (p. 94.)

Playwright Arthur Miller, in his award-winning *Death of a Salesman* (1949), poignantly captures how work is an expression of who we are when one of his characters, Biff, says:

> I ran down eleven flights with a pen in my hand today. And suddenly I stopped, you hear me? I stopped in the middle of that office building, do you hear this? I stopped in the middle of that building and I saw— the sky. I saw the things that I love in this world. The work and the food and time to sit and smoke. And I looked at the pen and said to myself, what the hell am I grabbing this for? Why an I trying to become what I don't want to be? What am I doing in an office, making a contemptuous, begging fool of myself, when all I want is out there, waiting for me the minute I say I know who I am! (p. 132.)

CAREER DEVELOPMENT: POINTS OF VIEW

Psychoanalysts: The psychoanalysts have viewed work as a form of sublimation which allows us to channel instinctual drives in socially acceptable directions. According to this viewpoint, the surgeon is a sublimated sadist, the psychiatrist and the gynecologist are sublimated voyeurs, the actor is a sublimated exhibitionist, and so on. One psychoanalyst, Hendrick, 1943), translated the pleasure principle into a "work principle." He sees work as being motivated primarily by the need for efficient use of the muscular and intellectual tools. His work principle states that people seek and find primary pleasure in the efficient use of minds and hands and tools to control or alter an environment. Hendrick's work principle also suggests that work may satisfy other needs such as aggression, sex, and self-preservation.

Trait and Factor: The principal spokesperson for this approach has been Williamson (1950), who developed six steps to use when assisting students in their career awareness and development:

Analysis: Collection of data about the individual. Relies primarily on psychological tests for this data.

Synthesis: The data collected is evaluated in order to identify the individual's strengths, weaknesses, needs, and problems.

Diagnosis: The individual's central problem and its causes are identified.

Prognosis: The probable outcomes of options available are identified.

Assistance: The individual is helped to understand the relationship between one's self-knowledge and the requirements of different occupations.

Follow Up: The relevance of decisions made are examined. Further assistance is given, if needed (pp. 101-126).

Ginsberg: Ginsberg (1952) identified a series of stages through which the individual moves in the process of career development. In each of these stages, to varying degrees, the individual is affected by psychosocial needs, values, education, realities, and achievements:

Fantasy Period: Begins in early period of childhood and continues to about age eleven. Children visualize themselves as unrestricted regarding what they can accomplish.

Tentative Period: From about ages eleven to seventeen. Influenced by values, interests and abilities without a full consideration of reality factors. A substage is the transition period, at about age seventeen when the indiviudual realizes that current decisions will have an effect on one's future.

Realistic Period: Compromises are often made during this period among one's interests, abilities, education and job requirements, and self-concept. Occurs between age seventeen and young adulthood. Substages during this period are those of exploration (opportunities and options are investigated), crystallization (a choice is made and compromises are often included in the choice), and specification (one becomes specific and takes steps to implement the decision).

Ginsberg (1972) later included more flexibility in the process of one's career development and incorporated the following into his viewpoint: the process of career development is lifelong and more open ended; irreversibility of one's optimization of opportunities can be a stronger force than compromise; environmental constraints are better identified and considered; one's values play a more important role in the attainment of career satisfaction.

Roe: Perhaps the most comprehensive perspective on the value of work in satisfying psychosocial needs has been formulated by Anne Roe (1956), who relates the role of occupations in the individual's life to Maslow's (1954) hierarchy of needs. Roe believes that the meaning of work for the individual cannot be more than superficially studied without some idea of what sorts of things are significant for the individual and why. Accordingly, she selected Maslow's theory of personality as an instrument for focusing on the dynamic and emotional aspects of the meaning of work in the life of the individual.

For Maslow, human behavior is a consequence of a person's efforts to meet needs, to express the self, to make some rhyme and reason out of the world, and to achieve personal goals. Although the situation and the environmental context within which the individual exists may give one what one needs or be a hinderance, their influence is partially defined by the person's psychosocial purposes. The actions taken to satisfy career needs are initiated by psychosocial influences within the individual.

Maslow holds that motives and needs within the individual are organized into a hierarchy of prepotency. Under deprivation, the prepotent needs are more urgent and insistent than higher order needs. Until the prepotent needs are gratified, the higher-order needs will not emerge as consistent motivators of behavior. That is, as basic needs (food, clothing, shelter, safety) are met, the individual becomes free to seek higher psychosocial needs. According to this theory, then, the most direct way to develop a life at a higher psychosocial need level is through adequates gratification of the lower needs first. A summary of these needs is arranged and listed in their usual order of potency as follows.

1. *The physiological needs* are the most potent of all needs, and when these needs cannot be met, the person tends to become dominated by them and other needs diminish or fade away. The physiological needs include the needs for food, water, air, sex, sleep, etc. (i.e. the needs which work for our biological self-maintenance).
2. *The safety needs* are more often gratified than not in our society. They include the need for order, routine, the families, the known, and the need for security.
3. *The needs for belongingness and love* involve not only receiving but also giving love. They are reflected in the need people have for a place in their own groups and for affectionate relationships with other people.
4. *The esteem needs* are the needs for importance, self-respect, self-esteem, independence, and the respect and esteem of others.
5. *The need for information* is represented in our curiosity and inquisitiveness about human nature and behavior and one's environment.
6. *The need for understanding* is the desire to have some understanding of the world around us and of ourselves. It is reflected in the attempts of persons to interpret the world in terms of a philosophical or religious belief.
7. *The need for beauty* is expressed in the desire for beautiful surroundings and aesthetic communications.
8. *The need for self-actualization* is the desire to realize one's maximum potential. All that one *can* be one *must* be if one is to be happy. The more one is fitted to do, the more one must do. It is not only enjoyable to use our capacities, but it is also necessary for the person who is self-actualizing.

In relation to Maslow's hierachy of needs, Roe points out that in our society there is no single activity which is potentially so capable of providing some satisfaction to the person at all levels as is the person's occupation. An individual's job provides the money that can be exchanged for food and drink. It enables one to secure housing, clothing, and medical care and through pensions and savings provide for long-range safety needs. The need to be a member of a group and to belong and be loved can be gratified in part by a job. The work with a congenial group and to be needed and welcomed by the group are meaningful and significant elements in a satisfactory job.

Satisfaction of the need for esteem from self and others is derived in large part from an individual's occupation. In our culture, having a job in itself carries esteem. One of the most frequent observations made in psychological and sociological studies is that social and economic status depend more upon one's occupation than upon anything else.

Roe notes that little is known about the remaining groups of higher level needs (needs for information, understanding, beauty and self-actualization) to more than speculate about their relation to occupations. There does appear to be some evidence to indicate that these needs are expressed and satisfied most fully in the learned occupations. On the other hand, the work of Maslow provides ample illustrations of how the need for self-actualization is also gratified outside occupations as we know them.

What Roe's studies affirm is that there is more to work than making a living. Work as a source of need gratification is extremely important in our culture. Its importance may be attributable to just the fact that it meets so many needs so well. The value of work lies in its enormous potential for facilitating one's psychosocial development.

Super: One of the most well-known theories of career development characterized occupational behavior as a lifelong process which implements a person's self-concept. Super (1957) integrates psychosocial development with career development.

In the following summary of Super's position (1957), one can find a number of explicit and implicit psychosocial elements:

1. People differ in their abilities, interests, and personalities.
2. They are qualified, by virtue of those characteristics, each for a number of occupations.
3. Each of these occupations requires a characteristic pattern of abilities, interests, and personality traits, with tolerances wide enough, however, to allow both some variety of occupations for each individual and some variety of individuals in each occupation.
4. Vocational preferences and competencies, the situations in which people live and work, and hence their self-concepts, change somewhat with time and experience, making choice and adjustment a continuous process.
5. This process may be summed up in a series of life stages characterized as those of growth, exploration, establishment,

maintenance, and decline, and these stages may be, in turn, subdivided into (a) the fantasy, tentative, and realistic phases of the exploratory stage and (b) the trial and stable phase of the establishment stage.

6. The nature of the career pattern (that is, the occupational level attained and the sequence, frequency and durations of trial and stable jobs) is determined by the individual's parents, socioeconomic level, mental ability, personality characteristics, and by the opportunities to which the individual is exposed.

7. Development through the life stages can be guided, partly by facilitating the process of maturation of abilities and interests and partly by aiding in reality testing and in the development of the self-concept.

8. The process of compromise between individual and social factors, between self-concept and reality, is one of role playing whether the role is played in fantasy, in the counseling interview, or in real-life activities such as school classes, part-time work and entry jobs.

9. The process of career development is essentially that of developing and implementing a self-concept; it is a compromise process in which the self-concept is a product of the interaction of inherited attitudes, neural and endocrine makeup, opportunity to play various roles, and evaluations of the extent to which the results of role playing meet with the approval of superiors and fellows.

10. Work and life satisfactions depend upon the extent to which the individual finds adequate outlets for abilities, interests, personality traits, and values—they depend upon a person's establishment in a type of work, a work situation, and a way of life in which the person can play the kind of role which growth and exploratory experiences have led the person to consider congenial and appropriate.

The distinctive feature of Super's theory lies in its focus on career development as essentially a process of identifying and implementing a self-concept. In choosing one's work and through one's work behavior, a person defines the self. The person is actually saying, "What sort of person do I think I am? How do I want others to see me? What kind of person would I like to be? What are my values and needs? What can I do to reconcile my self—ideal with my real self? What outlets are there for me with my needs, values and interests, and aptitudes?" As one can readily see, these are some of the significant life questions confronting each of us. Answering these questions will often depend upon one's psychosocial maturity and stability.

Tiedeman and O'Hara: One's ego and its impact upon career development and maturity is the central concept contained in this viewpoint. Tiedeman and O'Hara (1963) indicate that ego identity defines the career development process: "Ego identity is the accumulating meaning one forges about himself as he wrestles with his relationship with society. Ego identity is a psychosocial phenomenon. It is the crystallizing of premises of existence which one forges both where one can and where one may in order to establish one's place in the world. Career development includes the development of an orientation toward work which evolves within the psychosocial process of forming an ego identity" (p. 4).

Tiedeman and O'Hara identify two major phases in which one's ego identity is the focus of career development (1963). The first phase is preoccupational, is characterized by anticipation, and consists of four steps:

Exploration: Various goals are considered and the imagination is used to try out roles.
Crystallization: Thoughts become stabilized and the individual prepares to move in a specific direction. Values and possible ego rewards are considered.
Choice: The person makes a specific decision, with ego identity playing a prominent role in the decision-making process.
Clarification: The choice is followed by further analysis. Doubts and uncertainties are reviewed and resolved.

The second phase is characterized by on-the-job implementation and adjustment and consists of three steps:

Induction: The person enters a job, seeks approval and recognition, and often sublimates the self to the new group or organization.
Reformation: One's ego becomes more comfortable and the person begins to assert one's needs and values in the work situation.
Integration: A balance is achieved between one's ego needs and the requirements of a job or work group (pp. 38-45).

Menninger: The therapeutic value of work has been explored and considered primarily in terms of the psychosocial needs that are satisfied by work. Menninger (1964) suggested that work at the conscious and unconscious levels enables the person: to find an acceptable outlet for aggressive drives; to win approval from superiors, peers, and significant other persons; to develop satisfying social relationships; to feel involved in a part of the world beyond the family complex; and to find a mission in life.

Hoppock: Hoppock (1967) developed a theory of occupational choice around the relationship between work and needs. He hypothesizes:

1. Occupations are chosen to meet needs.
2. The occupation that we choose is the one that we believe will best meet the needs that most concern us.
3. Needs may be intellectually perceived, or they may be only vaguely felt as attractions that draw us in certain directions. In either case, they may influence choices.
4. Vocational development begins when we first become aware that an occupation can help us to meet our needs.
5. Vocational development progresses and occupational choice improves as we become better able to anticipate how well a prospective occupation will meet our needs. Our capacity to anticipate depends upon our knowledge of ourselves, our knowledge of occupations, and our ability to make a connection between both.
6. Information about ourselves affects occupational choice by helping us to recognize what we want and by helping us to anticipate whether or not we will be successful in what the contemplated occupation is as compared with another.
7. Information about occupations affects occupational choice by helping us to anticipate how well satisfied we may hope to be in one occupation as compared with another.
8. Job satisfaction depends upon the extent to which the job that we hold meets the needs that we feel it should meet. The degree of satisfaction is determined by the ratio between what we have and what we want.
9. Job satisfaction can result from a job which meets our needs today or from a job which promises to meet them in the future.
10. Occupational choice is always subject to change when we believe that a change will better meet our needs.

Holland: According to Holland (1973), certain personality types are developed as a result of the interaction between factors of heredity and environment. These personality types are often linked to certain careers in which one's personality can be expressed. The personality types identified by Holland are:

Realistic: May prefer technical and skilled occupations. Prefers manipulation of objects, machines, tools, and animals.
Investigative: May prefer a career in the sciences. Analytic, curious, methodical, and reserved.
Artistic: May prefer a career in painting, writing, acting, and sculpture. Expressive, original, independent, and possesses artistic abilities.
Social: May prefer a career in teaching, counseling, and social work. Cooperative, friendly, persuasive, and values social relations.
Enterprising: May prefer a career with an organization oriented toward economic gains. Ambitious, dominant, optimistic, and social.
Conventional: May prefer a career in banking, accounting, or bookkeeping. Efficient, orderly, practical, and in control of self.

Holland goes on to identify work environments in which the preceding personality types would feel comfortable, productive, and able to fulfill themselves. The work environments identified are labeled the same as the personality types: realistic, investigative, artistic, social, enterprising, and conventional. According to Holland, one's personality type should be matched with a work environment in which that personality can be expressed.

Tuckman: Tuckman (1974) develops an eight-stage career development model which is sequential and based upon a foundation of self-awareness, career awareness, and the career decision-making processes.

Stage 1: Kindergarten and grade one (unilateral dependence). There is a reliance by the child on external controls. The child's career awareness is stimulated by observation and tools found in the home.
Stage 2: Grades one and two (some assertion of self). Child achieves some autonomy and realizes that people work.
Stage 3: Grades two and three (conditional dependence). The process of decision making is given attention (i.e., choosing friends). Self-awareness focuses on the areas of motives, needs, and relations with others.

Stage 4: Grade four (interdependence). Self-awareness focuses on the place of work in society, the skills needed in work, and some attention to decision making.

Stage 5: Grades five and six (external support). Child seeks approval as an indication of success. Increased focus on interests and goals, job requirements, and the decision-making process.

Stage 6: Grades seven and eight (self-determination). The self asserts itself. Career values and occupational fields become identified and investigated and the decision-making process becomes more refined.

Stage 7: Grades nine and ten (mutuality). Peer relations and values become more important. Motives, attitudes, values, and stereotypes, and their relationship to careers, become more seriously considered.

Stage 8: Grades eleven and twelve (autonomy). Self-awareness is achieved and exploratory work opportunities become experienced. Range of choice becomes narrowed and person becomes more specific regarding which careers enable the self to be expressed.

Tolbert: Tolbert (1980) presents an eclectic viewpoint regarding career development. He incorporates the major constructs contained in other viewpoints. Tolbert indicates that career development:

- Reflects cultural and political attitudes and values.
- Is individualized. Each individual is unique in potential, commitment, level of activity, and preference for type of activity.
- Is a major part of one's entire developmental process, extends throughout life, and is one of the principal organizing themes of life.
- Is largely determined by psychosocial experiences, with models furnishing a major influence.
- Has the self-concept as the major motivating force in career development.
- Is similar to other types of maturity and indicates the degree to which the person is mastering the career development tasks appropriate to one's age.
- Involves a lifelong series of choices, some minor and some major.
- Generally is characterized by the following stages: awareness, exploration, choice and preparation, establishment, and re-assessment.

- Is a central aspect of one's life-style and exerts a major influence on other aspects of that life-style.
- Is influenced by the person's accurate perceptions of influences within an environment and the person's ego strength in relation to that environment.
- Occurs normally when the individual perceives the self as being respected by family, friends, and those at work; the tasks performed at work are attractive and satisfying, the time demands of work are reasonable, and an occupation's salary enables a preferred life-style to be maintained.
- Produces a particularly difficult experience during retirement when one's career was central to one's self-concept and life-style prior to retirement.

THE TEACHER AND CAREER AWARENESS

It is inevitable that each child attending school today will be working at one or another job. A variety of people, events, and circumstances will affect the students' job choices. Some of the people who can be of immeasurable help in this process of choosing are classroom teachers.

What is the role of the teacher in relation to career awareness? The teacher is in a strategic position to facilitate career awareness by providing exploratory learning situations through which pupils can become more familiar with the opportunities which lie ahead in relation to particular subject-matter areas (Isaacson, 1977). The dissemination of occupational information in the various content areas should be an integral part of the student's experience while in school. Teachers could make it their business to have, along with a command of knowledge in curriculum areas, a knowledge of occupational information as it relates to the different parts of the curriculum (Splete & Sklare, 1977).

There are many ways to integrate occupational information with the curriculum. The teacher may begin the year's work by discussing the various opportunities of work in a field, or students may report occasionally on related occupations. For example, in health, the teacher, when presenting material on various diseases, can very nicely work in some information on the medical family of jobs that would be both interesting and pertinent to the study at hand. Likewise, in science the teacher, when dealing with mechanics, for instance, can certainly make students aware of some of the various occupations related to this area of study. The teacher could cover both professional and skilled or semi-skilled opportunities. Engineers, mechanics, designers, draftsmen, technicians, installation and maintenance personnel and the like could all be brought into this area of study.

Another way the teacher might handle the occupational aspect of specific content would be through the use of a bulletin board. Usually, there are several display areas in a classroom and one could be used solely for showing occupational information particular to either the specific topic being studied or the field generally. For example, at the beginning of the school year an interesting display might be prepared, entitled "Careers in Science." This would be of a general nature, covering all areas of science. If the teacher were covering one major area of science, a display entitled "Careers in Biology" or "Opportunities in Chemistry" or "Physics as a Career" might be arranged. As the instruction began to deal with specific topics, the teacher might bring the occupational bulletin board up to date by presenting job opportunities dealing with each one: "Opportunities in Medicine" or "Nuclear Physics as a Career" or "Making a Living Through Electricity." Whatever the specific topic might be, the teacher could provide information concerning all levels of jobs in that area.

This is an activity that the pupils themselves can manage. It might add a new dimension to the learning taking place if the pupils were aware of the occupational importance of the material they were studying.

Elementary teachers have many opportunities to develop career awareness through the various curriculum areas as the following indicates.

The language arts curriculum. The role that the elementary teacher may play in the dissemination of career information through language arts is widely varied. Not only may the teacher provide pupils with information regarding the obviously related fields such as journalism and free-lance writing but also may discuss such activities as writing for television, writing advertising copy, editing and reading for publishing companies, public speaking in all its various forms, and all endeavors related to these fields.

The elementary school teacher has a deep concern that students learn arts. These include all activities having to do with reading, writing, speaking, and listening. It does not require much time with the *Dictionary of Occupational Titles* to see that these four (reading, writing, speaking, and listening) are important in almost all occupations.

There are many jobs which require reading as a skill in order to perform any number of other specific jobs, but a limited number require reading as a basic skill or end in itself; among them are proofreading, editorial reading both for newspapers and for publishers, and analytic reading for some legal jobs.

The writing area offers so many possibilities for employment. All one has to do is think of the vast amount of written information that one comes in contact with every day: magazines, newspapers, ads, leaflets, signs, technical publications, newsletters, trade journals, etc. The list is almost endless and this writing is all done by professional writers. On the elementary school level, just a basic awareness of this huge area is perhaps sufficient, but on the middle school level it may be more beneficial to elaborate on the occupations which are specifically concerned with written communication.

Speaking is the basic means of human communication, and at first one may not realize the many ways in which people earn a living simply by speaking. There are radio and television announcers, actors, lecturers, demonstrators, information givers—even telephone operators depend in part upon their speaking abilities. The vital role that this aspect of language arts plays in virtually all careers should be stressed to pupils.

There are perhaps fewer careers which are specifically dependent upon the ability to listen than the ones previously cited, but a few come to mind immediately: there are drama reviewers and critics, music critics, piano tuners, etc. The fields of teaching, counseling, psychology, and psychiatry certainly utilize the ability to listen. As with speaking, however, the major emphasis, particularly in the lower grades, might well be more on the ability to listen accurately as a basic communication essential. Identifying which careers require accurate listening would engage the attention of pupils.

The social studies curriculum. The social studies curriculum offers a very natural framework for the use and dissemination of career information. By definition, social studies must directly try to relate a real world outside the classroom to a group of students who have individual interests, needs, personalities, and abilities. The social studies class can serve as a clearinghouse for career information. At one time or another, the social studies teacher will present, directly or indirectly, all manner of people and what they did, are doing, or are trying to do. One of the basic questions for the student in social studies could be: "What kind of person do I want to become?" This question gives the student the opportunity to integrate psychosocial values with one's career aspirations.

A number of career awareness units can be validly and appropriately included in a social studies curriculum (e.g. the history and development of the labor movement, credit and consumer finance, the structure of civil service, the world of work, community social structure, community living, the economy of the community, civil rights, and the women's movement).

The mathematics and science curriculum. The world in which we live is scientifically oriented. The demand for scientists and mathematicians increases annually. New scientific discoveries, the use of intricate and complex mathematical equipment, automation, and technolocial change are opening more and more career opportunities for students who are studying science and mathematics. By making students aware of the opportunities that exist for employment in the fields of math and science, the teacher can contribute substantially to their career development. The list of occupations directly related to the areas of mathematics and science is long. One publication lists over seventy jobs in the health field which are directly linked with mathematics, biology, chemistry, and physics. There is a voluminous amount of free occupational literature published each year which provides detailed information on the work of the statistician, accountant, actuary, biologist, geologist, chemist, oceanographer, physicist, atomic scientist, geophysicist, astronomer, meteorologist, metallurgist, auditor, catographer, and numerous others. Such information could be distributed in class, used for bulletin board displays, or even incorporated into units on "Careers in Science" or "Careers in Mathematics."

ACTIVITIES FOR DEVELOPING CAREER AWARENESS

Field trips. Can broaden the perceptions of young people regarding work. When trips are related to curriculum areas of study, youngsters have a twofold gain: They can see a real purpose in studying certain content areas in school as a result of seeing workers who must use these skills and knowledge on the job; and by exposing themselves to the working conditions under which workers must function, youngsters can determine whether or not they would want to pursue careers under such conditions. Orientation before the field trip is undertaken is important. Follow-up activities could include: scrapbooks featuring impressive information learned from the trip; role playing where students assume the role of the workers; discussions as a group followed by individual written summations, reports, and art murals. Letters written to workers who particularly interested the students would be an effective means of extending the field trip.

Careers of the month club. Using a different elementary curriculum area each month in the elementary grades, activities can be used within the standard instructional program to instill concepts about the world of work and occupations. Concepts which can be developed include "Work has dignity," "People work for various rewards or satisfaction," "Some workers produce goods," "Some workers produce services," "Careers grouped by job families," etc. (Ridener, 1973).

The career pyramid. (Rost, 1973) The Career Pyramid is an activity designed to provide students with the opportunity to realize and understand the interdependence of careers. Any job-related local event might be used to initiate the activity. One possibility would be to select a picture in a newspaper that depicts some event such as the construction of a new building in the community. On the board, make this event the top of the pyramid. Then engage the students in a discussion aimed at determining as many jobs as possible involved in such things as the development of the plans for the building, construction of the building, and operation and maintenance of the building. In order to provide some initial structure for this activity, broad categories such as planning, construction, etc., are provided so that students can organize their own thoughts. Once these categories are established, the activity can proceed, either with a large group or small groups. In the case of small groups, each group might be responsible for one of the general categories (e.g. maintenance). After each group has completed its task, the entire pyramid can be placed on a bulletin board for everyone's benefit.

Career corner. A special place just for career information. A large pegboard with manila packets containing information about various careers serves well in an activity area. The student is free to pursue the information packets and write a synopsis of what was learned on an index card. The card can then be catalogued in a special job bank folder for future reference. As material is added to the folder, the student can see where one's interests are centered.

Various film loops, filmstrips, and audiotapes or videotapes are also kept in the Career Corner for the student to use during free time. Audiotaped or videotaped information can be made by students if they interview people in the community about particular careers (Handel, 1973).

Seminars. A morning set aside for students to meet with various working members of the community provides an opportunity to view several career areas. The guests bring various objects of their trade for students to handle, and a set period of time is established for students to speak with the guests. At the end of 30 minutes, the children move to another room where they will meet another guest. At the end of the morning, everyone is brought together to discuss the value of the seminar experience (Handle, 1973).

The hat exhibit (Forsythe, 1972). The purpose of this activity is to focus on the world of work and to encourage students to think about many different areas of work. Who wears which hat on the job is the question. Students and teacher request headgear worn on the job from people in the community. The fire chief, the mail carrier, the baker, the telephone repairperson, the chef, etc., can contribute hats or caps. Pegboards and hat stands can be used to display the hats. Career information telling about the jobs represented by the hats can be made available to students.

Interviewing workers or parents (Otte, 1972). Students enjoy talking with adults. In order to add structure and make an interview more meaningful, the teacher can devise an interview guide with students. The teacher can give the students the objectives and ask them to devise a structured interview guide. This activity can be related to communication skills by having the student present an oral or written report.

Using resource persons (Otte, 1972). Many types of workers are represented among the parents of students in the school. Often, a parent or any interested adult will visit the school to discuss one's work in relation to a student activity. Preparing children to ask questions based upon the interview guide adds meaning to such a visit. School personnel may also participate.

Vocations week (Zeller, 1975). In such a program a school can have a one-week focus on the scope and variety of careers available to students. Highlights of such a week can be the availability of persons in the community who represent various occupations; occupational booths in which career information is made available; and an open theater in which films, filmstrips, and videotapes depicting various occupations are shown.

Real world participation (Splete & Hill, 1981). Students often participate in good government days by assuming the seats and roles of community and state officials. In this project, 29 sixth grade students spent an afternoon assuming the working roles of employees in the various stores at the Meadowbrook Shopping Mall in Rochester, Michigan. Students were able to directly experience the business world and gain an appreciation of what is involved in running a successful business. Follow-up activities enabled the students to continue their exploration of the work experience and its relationship to personal psychosocial values.

Workbooks. Many workbooks are available which enable students to develop an awareness of careers and their relationships to personal needs, interests, and abilities. One such workbook has been developed by Gill (1984). It is titled *Walkabout* and contains many activities and awareness units designed to help students in both their personal and career development. Gill (1984) indicates the *Walkabout* is the:

- process of becoming
- ability to look at the future
- exploration of your aspiration
- awareness of your vocation
- step-by-step process for career pathfinders
- method of getting your act together
- process of self-awareness
- method for growth as a total person
- paradigm for change in career development
- proactive approach to planning
- process that allows individuals to produce results
- process that requries you to act to make a difference
- evaluation of commitment to personal growth (p. 4).

In conclusion, a student's psychosocial development is enhanced when the student becomes sensitive to how a career is a vehicle for expressing the psychosocial values contained in one's self-concept, and when the student also learns how a career can contribute to one's psychosocial stability or mental health.

REFERENCES

Boy, A. V. & Pine, G. J. (1971). *Expanding the self: Personal growth for teachers.* Dubuque, IA: William C. Brown.

Forsythe, L. B. (1972). The hat exhibit. *Elementary School Guidance and Counseling,* 7, 52.

Gill, G.D. (1984). *Walkabout.* Sutton Mills, NH: Profile Development Associates.

Ginzberg, E. (1952). Toward a theory of occupational choice. *The Personnel and Guidance Journal,* 30, 491-494.

Ginzberg, E. (1972). Toward a theory of occupational choice: A restatement. *Vocational Guidance Quarterly,* 20, 169-172.

Handel, L. (1973). Three tips on career guidance activities. *Elementary School Guidance Counseling,* 8, 290-291.

Hazel, E. R. (1976). Group counseling for occupational choice. *The Personnel and Guidance Journal,* 54, 437-438.

Hendrick, I. (1943). Work and the pleasure principle. *Psychoanalytical Quarterly,* 12, 311-329.

Holland, J. L. (1973). *Making vocational choices.* Englewood Cliffs, NJ: Prentice-Hall.

Hoppock, R. (1967). *Occupational information.* 3rd ed. New York: McGraw-Hill.

Isaccson, L. E. (1977). *Career information in counseling and in teaching.* 3rd ed. Boston: Allyn and Bacon.

Lathrop, R. (1977). *Who's hiring who?* Berkeley, CA: Ten Speed.

Maslow, H. (1954). *Motivation and personality.* New York: Harper and Row.

Menninger, W. (1964). The meaning of work in Western society. In H. Borow (Ed.), *Man in a world at work.* Boston: Houghton Mifflin.

Miller, A. (1949). *Death of a salesman.* New York: Viking.

Morrow, L. (1981). What is the point of working? *Time,* 122, 94-95.

Otte, F. (1972). Tips on career development activities. *Elementary School Guidance and Counseling,* 7, 52-53.

Pate, R. H. (1980). The counselor in a psychological society. *The Personnel and Guidance Journal,* 58, 521-524.

Ridener, J. (1973). Careers of the month program. *Elementary School Guidance and Counseling,* 8, 235-236.

Roe, A. (1956). *The psychology of occupations.* New York: John Wiley and Sons.

Rost, P. (1973). The career pyramid. *Elementary School Guidance and Counseling,* 8, 52-53.

Splete, H. H. & Sklare, A. R. (1977). Career guidance in the elementary school. *Elementary School Guidance and Counseling* 12, 309-315.

Splete, H. H. & Hill, P. L. (981). Career education at Meadowbrook Mall. *Elementary School Guidance and Counseling,* 16, 47-50.

Super, D. 91956). *The psychology of careers.* New York: Harper and Row.

Taube, C. A., Burns, B. J. & Kessler, L. (1984). Patients of psychiatrists and psychologists in office-bound practices. *The American Psychologist,* 39, 1435-1447.

Tiedeman, D. V. & O'Hara, R. P. (1963). *Career development: Choice and adjustment.* New York: College Entrance Examination Board.

Tolbert, E. L. (1980). *Counseling for career development.* 2nd ed. Boston: Houghton Mifflin.

Tuckman, B. W. (1974). An age graded model for career development education. *Journal of Vocational Behavior,* 4, 193-212.

Wilensky, H. L. (1964). Varieties of work experiences. In H. Borow (Ed.), *Man in a world at work.* Boston: Houghton Mifflin.

Williamson, E. G. (1950). *Counseling adolescents.* New York: McGraw-Hill.

Wrenn, C. G. (1964). Human values and work in American life. In H. Borow (Ed.), *Man in a world at work.* Boston: Houghton Mifflin.

Zeller, B. J. (1975). A vocations week program. *The Personnel and Guidance Journal,* 53, 107-108.

CHAPTER IX

FOSTERING PSYCHOSOCIAL DEVELOPMENT THROUGH PLAY

THIS CHAPTER is designed for the reader who uses play therapy as a contributor to psychosocial development as well as the reader who uses concepts drawn from play therapy to facilitate psychosocial development in the classroom. The eclectic play activities described in the following chapter can be used by either professional.

THE POWER OF PLAY

The extraordinary power of play in one's psychosocial development is clearly articulated by Caplan and Caplan (1973), who cite some exceptional and unique features of play which are paraphrased as follows:

Play is a voluntary activity. It is intensely personal. Self-powered, it embodies a high degree of motivation and achievement. Play is an autonomous pursuit through which one assimilates the outside world to support one's ego.

Play offers freedom of action. Play is always free in the sense that each act can be performed for its own sake and for its immediate results. During play, one can carry on trial-and-error activities without fear of ridicule or failing.

Play provides an imaginary world one can master. Play is a voluntary system that admits both reality and fantasy. The one who plays is in full control. In the world of play, one can reduce one's world to a manageable size so that it can be manipulated to suit personal whims.

Play has elements of adventure in it. It has uncertainty and challenge which can prompt one to be exploratory. In play, the ordinary laws of life do not count, since play is larger than life.

Play provides a base for language building. The earliest years are non-verbal. Words come from a foundation of play experiences, from encounters with people, objects, and events which make up our world. Play nourishes reflective thinking, associative memory, and the naming and labeling necessary for the eventual mastery of reading.

Play has unique powers for building interpersonal relations. Play provides contacts with others while letting us engage in natural behaviors. Much of play aids our psychosocial development by helping us to define ourselves and fit that definition into a social context.

Play offers opportunities for mastery of the physical self. One can learn body control through active physical play. Physical play helps us to improve our laterality, directionality, and coordination.

Play furthers concentration. One's power of concentration in the here-and-now world is improved through play. That improved ability to concentrate can be generalized to activities outside of play.

Play is a way to learn about ourselves. Play helps us to learn how we'll respond to a certain set of circumstances. Connections are made between stimuli and responses during play, and we can see equivalent stimuli outside of play which generate similar responses. We begin to see a unity to how we respond to certain stimuli both in play and outside of play.

Play is a way of learning about roles. In early play, children imitate the behavior, attitudes, and language of the important adults in their lives. Play may be considered a rehearsal for adult roles and anticipatory to adult life. Adults learn about the similarities and differences in role expectations in play and outside of play.

Play is always a dynamic way of learning. The layers of meaning implanted by play often include conscious organization of the environment, explorations of physical and social relationships, and deep levels of fantasy. One's perceptions of reality often evolve out of play requiring fantasy.

Play refines one's judgments. Play is often an accepted vehicle for expressing one's feelings and thoughts. Through play one analyzes which feelings and thoughts can be expressed and accepted by others and which cannot.

Play is vitalizing. Play has important neurophysiological effects on us. Play is a diversion from routines, demands, and pursuits. For a period of time, play permits one to reverse one's behavior and do the opposite of what one has been doing. Play is essential in order to bring renewed vigor to the formal and required activities of our lives. Play enables us to engage in natural and spontaneous behaviors so necessary to freeing us from the pressures of life.

PLAY AND COGNITIVE DEVELOPMENT

According to Piaget (1951), play is an indispensable step in the child's cognitive development. Play is the bridge between sensory-motor experience and the emergence of respresentative or symbolic thought. In his study of play, Piaget concluded that there are three main categories of play: practice games, symbolic games, and games with rules.

Practice games appear first and are an outgrowth of the imitative activities which are characteristic of the sensory-motor period of development. Such games may lead to improved motor performance or to destructive performance (e.g. knocking over blocks). They may develop into constructive games like building or weaving which are viewed by Piaget as a bridge between play and work.

Symbolic games imply representation of an absent object and are both initative and imaginative (Piaget, 1951). Insofar as these games symbolize the child's own feelings, interests, and activities, they help the child to express the self creatively and to develop a rich and satisfying fantasy life. Between the ages of two and four, symbolic play is at its peak. One type of symbolic play identified by Piaget is compensatory play which involves doing in make-believe what is forbidden in reality. Closely related to compensatory play is play in which emotion is acted out in gradual degress, so that it becomes bearable. Often, children will use play to act out unpleasant scenes or actions. In reliving them by transposing them symbolically, they reduce some of the unpleasantness and make the situations more tolerable. The function of symbolic play is seen in the "make-believe" games of children from two to four. According to Piaget (1951), symbolic play frees "the ego from the demands of accommodation" (p. 134).

Games with rules. After the age of four or five symbolic play becomes increasingly social, according to Piaget. Symbolic games lessen as socialization progresses. Around the age of seven or eight there is a definite decline in symbolic play coinciding with increased interest in school and in socialized activities. The child becomes involved in games with rules which are essentially social, leading to increased adaptation. Piaget believes that since these games persist even among adults, they may provide the explanation of what happens to children's play; that it dies out in later years in favor of socialized games through which the child develops social skills and attitudes (Pulaski, 1971). The child is required to share, to cooperate, and to assume different rules and consequently learns the first lessons of mutuality in social relations and begins to build more complex relationship skills.

THE PSYCHOSOCIAL VALUE OF PLAY

Play is the child's natural medium of expression (Axline, 1969). "In his talk and his toys are his words" (Ginott, 1961) and this form of communication gives the adult a tool with which to understand and relate to the child with confidence and warmth (Schiffer, 1969; Moustakas, 1973; Jernberg, 1979). Indeed, Allen (1942) observed that it would be difficult to establish a relationship with a child without play activity. Axline's (1964) book, *Dibs: In Search of Self,* provides a good example of play as an accepting, reflecting, clarifying, and communicating relationship with a child.

Amster (1943) was one of the first to identify the values and benefits coming from play:

1. Play can be used for diagnostic understanding of the child . . . . We can observe the child's capacity to relate to the self and others, the child's distractibility, rigidity, areas of preoccupation, areas of inhibitition, aggression, perception of people, wishes, and the child's self-perception. In the child's play, the child's behavior, ideas, feelings, and expressions help our understanding of the child's problem and how the child sees it.
2. Play can be used to establish a working relationship. This use of play is helpful with the young child who lacks the adult's facility for verbal self-expression and with the older child who shows resistance or inability to articulate.
3. Play can be used to break through a child's way of playing and the child's defenses against anxiety. This is helpful as an additional way of treating distortions in a child's way of playing.
4. Play can be used to help a child verbalize certain conscious material and associated feelings. This use is helpful when a child blocks in discussing certain material and an impasse is created.
5. Play can be used to help a child act out unconscious material and to relieve the accompanying tension. This cathartic use of play deals with symbolic material which may have dangerous significance to the child. The child helper must be aware of how much release in play the particular child can tolerate without panic and

must be aware of the kind of participation and interpretation in which to engage.
6. Play can be used to develop a child's play interests which the child can carry over into daily life and which will strengthen the child for the future. This use of play has particular importance because of the correlation between the play and work capacities of an individual (pp. 63-67).

Erickson (1964) indicates the psychosocial value of play when he says that "the child's play is the infantile form of the human ability to deal with experiences by creating model situations and to master reality by experiment and planning . . . . To 'play it out' in play is the most natural self-healing measure childhood affords" (pp. 10-11).

Nelson (1968) indicates that many of the elements and principles of play therapy are appropriate to helping all children with their psychosocial development. He cites the work of Moustakas (1959) and Axline (1969) on play therapy with "normal" children as supporting the concept of helping all children through play activities.

Meeks (1968) has a firm conviction that play should not be used to diagnose emotional problems or to bring about predetermined personality changes. Meeks (1968) indicates that any process of helping should be compatible with the goals of Axline's concept of play therapy (i.e. non-directive play therapy): (1) it offers a most favorable condition for children to experience growth; (2) it allows the child to face feelings through a natural medium of expression; and (3) by facing feelings, it assists the child to control them or to abandon them. Through play the child is able to realize the power possessed by the self; to be an individual, think, make decisions, and become psychosocially more mature. In presenting a theoretical basis for the use of play to help children, Nelson (1968) points out that play provides a vehicle for the individual to explore thoughts and feelings and evoke self-enhancing courses of action, behavior patterns, or attitudes. This process may take place on a non-verbal as well as on a verbal level. It is the function of play to facilitate psychosocial self-exploration and clarification and is consistent with the goals of a program of psychosocial development.

GENERAL CHARACTERISTICS OF PLAY THERAPY

Although there is a variety of approaches used in play therapy, there are certain general basic characteristics (Ellis, 1973). First, play therapy involves the use of play media ranging from unstructured materials such as sand and clay to more structured toys such as dolls and playhouses. Second, through the use of play materials and through talking, the child expresses feelings and experiences. Third, as a result, the child experiences a solution to a problem, a reduction in tension, or a release of emotion (pp. 120-127).

What magic function does play possess that enables it to work so well as a therapeutic tool? Through play the child: expresses forbidden, physical impulses in a symbolic way; releases anxiety and hostility; tells stories about traumatic situations thus relieving tension; and symbolically manipulates toys in such a way as to test out possible solutions to problems. And, finally, through play the child externalizes or projects painful feelings of shame and inferiority, bridges the gap between dreams and reality, and even assumes a role different from the child's normal life role.

BRIEF HISTORY OF PLAY THERAPY

The purpose of this section is to help the reader understand the roots of play therapy. Such an understanding will enable one to sense the rationale and process of play therapy as it was originally conceived and developed.

The beginnings of play therapy appear to have emanated from a Freudian or psychoanalytical attempt to deal with children and their emotional concerns. One of the primary goals of Freudian therapy was to bring repressed and denied ideas and experiences into conscious awareness. This was usually accomplished through free association which worked well with adults but not as well with children who would refuse to free associate. Viewing this as a significant problem, Anna Freud modified the classical psychoanalytic approach by indicating that children do not generally have transference problems and could therefore interact with an adult therapist. To reach a child, she would often play with the child. Such play, however, was considered preliminary to the real work of psychoanalysis and not central to it.

Independently of Anna Freud, Melanie Klein began developing her own techniques with children, which also evolved from theories of Freud. She assumed that a child's play activities were as motivationally determined as free association in adults and could thus be interpreted to the child. The term used to describe this process was "play analysis" and it became one of the first approaches in the deep interpretations of children's behavior.

Soon after Klein and Freud, Jessie Taft began applying Otto Rank's theories to play therapy, bringing about some important changes in the goals and procedures of therapy with children. Rank's focus was on "relationship therapy." The relationship (between therapist and client) was seen as growth producing in its own right, and emotional problems, as they exist in the immediate present, were more important than the past experiences of the client. Out of these streams of thought emerged "non-directive" play therapy which reflects the Freudian concepts of: permissiveness and catharsis, repression, play as natural language of the child, the meaningfulness of apparently unmotivated behavior, the Rankian emphases on expressed feelings rather than content, and on the diminution of the authoritative position of the therapist.

These were the early thoughts and ideas of play therapy. These thoughts and ideas began to take on more breadth and depth, research regarding their effectiveness was started and the following formal approaches to play therapy emerged.

APPROACHES TO PLAY THERAPY

Psychoanalytic

The psychoanalytic approach uses interpretations of the child's behavior in the play therapy sessions. Interpretation consists of making connections for the child where the child sees none. Sometimes these connections are between a defense and a feeling, sometimes between a fantasy and a feeling (Ellis, 1973). The psychoanalyst hopes, through interpretation, to help the child achieve some insights into the child's behavior and problems. In the process of achieving this, the therapist tries to make the unconscious conscious to the child for the purpose of enabling the child to learn enough about the self to recognize personal feelings and defenses and deal with them directly (Levy, 1978). Psychoanalysts work on the child's past in order to provide a cleared and improved ground for future development (Kessler, 1966). Psychoanalysts are convinced that their treatment process is essential for alleviating certain kinds of symptoms, such as acute anxiety, and a sense of helplessness and inadequacy.

Release Therapy

Release therapy is an approach developed by Levy (1939) as a particularly useful way of relieving severe anxiety, fear reaction, or night terrors precipitated by traumatic experiences (surgical operations, accidents, divorce of parents). In this approach, the therapist supplies the child with dolls and other play media and depicts a plot concerned with what the therapist feels is the child's major problem (e.g. separation from mother). This aproach is advocated by Levy as most appropriate for children under 10 who present a recently acquired symptom generated by a specific event in the form of a frightening experience. Levy (1939) indicated that it is important for the appropriate use of this approach "that the child is suffering from something that happened in the past and not from a difficult situation going on at the time of treatment" (p. 916).

Existential Approach

Moustakas (1959, 1973) borrows a phrase from Otto Rank and entitles his form of play therapy, "relationship therapy." Moustaskas characterizes play therapy as a unique growth experience created by one person seeking and needing help and another person who accepts the responsibility of offering it.

A sense of relatedness of one person to another is an essential requirement of individual growth. For children, as well as adults, this involves an internal struggle. But the struggle must take place within a relationship where the child eventually feels free to face the self, where the child's human capacity is recognized and cherished, and where the child is accepted and loved. The child will then be able to become more and more individualized. The focus lies in the present living experience—the existential moment. The child is able to see the therapist as a new reality in the *present* world, and from this relationship, the child reclaims the powers of the child's individual nature and affirms the real self. The helping relationship is one in which the adult maintains a deep concern for the psychological growth of the child, is sensitive to the child's individuality, and possesses the ability to explore the child's psychosocial experiences with the child.

Moustakas has found that the best setting for relationship therapy with children is a play room. The toys and materials form a part of the setting and, to some extent, influence the nature of the child's play.

Three basic attitudes which Moustakas feels should be conveyed to the child are faith, acceptance, and respect.

Moustakas feels that a child who has *faith* knows:
1. Personal growth
2. What can be done, when an adult says to the child, "That's up to you," or "You're the best judge of that."

3. What will be done in the future, when an adult says to the child, "It is important that you do what you want."

In the matter of *acceptance*, there must be a commitment on the part of the helping person to accept the child's feelings, the child's personal meaning and perceptions. A statement on the part of the helping person such as: "Mmm," "I see," "That's the way you feel," "You're really afraid of him," "It can be anything you want it to be" conveys acceptance of the child's viewpoint.

In the matter of *respect*, the therapist has concern for the individual child as a person and wants the child to be self-helping. One does not probe or otherwise violate the child's privacy. One empathically follows the child in play.

Moustakas outlines stages of the play therapy process as follows:

1. The child starts with undifferentiated behavior that is hostile, anxious, and/or regressive.
2. The clarification stage in which the child's actions become more specific.
3. Stages of ambivalence by the child about the child's traditional or characteristic actions.
4. Undifferential positiveness on the part of the child (anger mixed with positiveness).
5. Modified and moderated reactions by the child.

Client-Centered Approach

According to Axline (1969) there is a powerful force within each individual which constantly strives for complete self-realization. This may be characterized as a drive toward maturity, independence, or self-direction, and it needs good "growing ground" to develop. For the child, Axline views the "growing ground" to be the playroom.

The playroom atmosphere grants the child the permissiveness to be open and honest in the process of play. The child is accepted completely, without evaluation or pressure to change. The therapist recognizes and clarifies the expressed emotions or feelings of the child through a reflection of the feelings behind the child's words. This offers the child an opportunity to learn to know the self and to chart a course for attitudinal and behavioral change. All suggestions, restraints, and criticisms are absent from the helper's behavior in the playroom and are replaced by a complete acceptance of the child and a permissiveness for the child to feel, think, behave, and play in a personally honest manner.

In a child's playing out of feelings (e.g. tension, anxiety) the child brings these to the surface, gets them into the open, faces them, learns to control them or abandon them. When the child has finally achieved an emotional catharsis in the helping process, the child begins to realize that one can be an individual—to think, make decisions, become psychosocially more mature and, in so doing, to realize "selfhood."

Group Play Therapy

Ginott's (1961) main emphasis is on group psychotherapy with children—working with children in groups within the playroom setting. Ginott indicates that in group play therapy the presence of other children seems to diminish tension and stimulate activity and participation. The group induces spontaneity in children. They begin to relate to the group's therapist and trust that person more readily than in individual relationships outside the group. This observation is confirmed by Schiffer (1969).

Ginott feels that the medium which is best suited for children is play. In therapy, this "is equivalent to freedom to act and react, suppress and express, suspect and respect." The *group* setting further provides a tangible *social* setting for the discovery of new and more satisfying ways of relating to peers, for the aim of play therapy, according to Ginott, is to help to develop behaviors in children which are consistent with society's standards.

GROUP VS. INDIVIDUAL PLAY THERAPY

When is group play therapy more useful than individual play therapy? Group play therapy is generally a better method to use when the child's problems are primarily social (Schiffer, 1969). A child who has difficulty in relating to others may benefit from a group experience. On the other hand, individual therapy is deemed more useful for individualized emotional problems. The only difficulty with this approach may be the fact that individualized emotional problems are often expressed socially. There are times when a combination of individual and group therapy is useful. For example, individual therapy may be given for the first session and group therapy for subsequent sessions. Some therapists will have individual therapy with a child and then, upon request, permit the child to invite friends to a group therapy session. Such a group may be even more valuable for therapy than a group chosen by the therapist, because often the child will invite withdrawn youngsters who are not particularly troublesome and hence unlikely to be referred for therapy by adults.

There are a number of other distinct advantages in the group approach. For one thing, *there is the sharing of a problem* and the realization that a particular problem is not unique. This factor makes the problem seem less "earthshaking" to the child. Also, *there is the interplay of personalities* which adds a new dimension to therapy. In a group play session one may find significant emotional fluctuation from person to person ranging all the way from smiles to tears. There is some doubt that such a wide range of emotions would occur in individual play therapy. In addition, as a result of the rapt attention which members show toward the activities of their peers, the group may notice one child forging ahead at a particular task and try doing the same. This results in a positive reinforcement for certain activities. However, in individual therapy each child separately involved would not have similar catalysts. Sometimes, in group play it is not even necessary for other group members to "try out" a particular behavior, because they can vicariously experience it by watching it being expressed by one of their play therapy peers.

PRINCIPLES OF HELPING THROUGH PLAY

The effective use of play, based on the following eight principles derived from Axline's (1969) historic work, will help the reader to use play as an effective contributor to the student's psychosocial development.

1. The helper must develop a warm, friendly relationship with the child, in which good rapport is established as soon as possible.
2. The helper accepts the child as the child is.
3. The helper establishes a feeling of permissiveness in the relationship so that the child feels free to express feelings.
4. The helper is alert to recognize the *feelings* the child is expressing and reflects those feelings back to the child in such a manner that the child gains insight into the meaning of such feelings and their relationship to behavior.
5. The helper maintains a deep respect for the child's ability to solve problems if given an opportunity to do so. The responsibility to make choices and to institute change is the child's.
6. The helper does not attempt to direct the child's actions or conversations in any manner. The child leads the way; the helper follows.

7. The helper does not attempt to hurry the play process along. It is a gradual process and is recognized as such.
8. The helper establishes only those limitations that are necessary to anchor the helping process to the world of reality and to help the child develop a sense of responsibility in the relationship.

When using play, the helper must become sensitive to the pitfall of functioning as a "playmate." Helping children through play requires empathic personal and professional qualities. It is not meant to be a maudlin, sugarcoated, or sentimental approach to working with children. Play is used to facilitate communication, self-awareness, and to put the child in contact with the reality of the child's behavior. To help the child move in these directions the helper must be genuine, empathically understanding, warm in a non-possessive way, concrete, and possess skills in reflecting and clarifying feelings (Moustakas, 1973).

In the helping relationship, the child learns that one can do anything that one likes in the room—that it is a time in which there is an absence of pressure—that this is the child's room and the child's hour. The helper accepts the child as the child is at the moment and does not try to mold the child toward socially approved behavior. The child is not forced or manipulated to play with certain toys and is freely permitted to remain silent and inactive if the child chooses. The helper accepts the meaning of the child's symbols at the child's level and works at the child's level of communication even when the meaning appears obvious. The helper, by being accepting, observing, and understanding, learns something of how life is going for the child—from the way the child handles materials we learn something about the child's level of maturity—from verbalizations made while the child is at play we learn something about the child's feelings about the self and others.

The helper makes no interpretation of the child's behavior or selection of play materials. The child is not reduced to an object to be analyzed. In using play media, the helper works with the child's current behavior. There is no reliance on historical or case history information about the child. This here-and-now view stresses the importance of seeing the child's world in the present. The child in play shows personalized ways of seeing, choosing, and acting at this moment in time. No matter what the child has endured in the past, a positive, facilitating, *present* experience contributes to the child's psychosocial stability. Providing positive, present experience does not depend on knowing the child's past experiences or on the subjective and sometimes biased interpretations of the meaning of those experiences.

Catharsis and insight, which occur for the child during the process of play, are not by themselves therapeutically curative. Catharsis in children usually involves mobility and acting out. Acting out has no curative effect beyond pleasure and release and it does not usually lead to self-evaluation, awareness of motivation, and attempts to change behavior. This is particularly true in young children for whom acting out becomes just fun. Insight also has its limitations. For children, there is no direct relationship between insight and behavior change. Often, insight is a result rather than a cause, attained by children who have grown emotionally ready through the play process to become acquainted with denied elements of their experiences.

Beyond catharsis and insight, the use of play gives the child an opportunity to try out new behavior in the safety of an accepting and permissive atmosphere created by an adult helper. By allowing the child the opportunity to be, the child is encouraged to experiment with new roles and behaviors and to experience vicariously the kind of psychosocial behaviors that the child would like to move toward and own.

SELECTION OF PLAY MATERIALS

Nearly any toy, as Nelson (1968) points out, has expressive possibilities in the eyes of the child, but he suggests three key criteria for selection of play materials for use with children: (1) select materials that may be used in a variety of ways such as clay, paints, and pipe cleaners; (2) select materials that promote communication such as toy telephones and a typewriter; and (3) select materials (toy gun, punching bag, hand puppets) that encourage the expression and release of aggressive feelings. Generally, the more unstructured and flexible the toys, the more readily the child can express his or her imagination and feelings through them.

Ginott (1961) indicates that there are five major criteria for selecting and rejecting materials for play therapy, stating that a play therapy toy should: (1) facilitate the establishment of contact with the child by the helper; (2) evoke and encourage catharsis; (3) aid in developing insight; (4) furnish opportunities for reality testing; and (5) provide a vehicle for sublimation.

The toys used with children should be within each child's realm of play. If exposed to toys that are too old for the child, the child won't be able to express true emotions through them. By using toys the child is used to playing with, the child will feel free to be imaginative and reveal psychosocial needs and feelings (Moustakas, 1973).

Beiser (1955) studied the free choice of a selected group of toys of 100 children (79 boys and 21 girls), ranging from 2 to 12 years of age, who had been referred to the Chicago Institute for Juvenile Research. Each toy was tabulated according to the total number of children who played with it (popularity), a ratio of popularity and total dynamic interpretations stemming from play with a toy (communication value), frequency with which the toy stimulated fantasy on the child's part (fantasy stimulation), the breadth or number of dynamic intepretations that could be made from a child's play with an individual toy (dynamic spread), and a combined total ranking of toys. In terms of highest combined total rankings, toys were listed in the following order: (1) doll family, (2) soldiers, (3) guns, (4) clay, (5) paper and crayons, (6) animals, (7) planes, (8) Nok-Out Bench, and (9) trucks. The lowest combined total ranking toys were: (1) pencil, (2) paste, (3) scissors, and (4) ball.

The particular toy used by a child should not be an issue for the helper. It is more important that it is something which will motivate the child to see the toy as having meaning, see it as something which can be incorporated into play, and see it as a vehicle through which feelings can be expressed. Helping the child to select facilitative toys is an important early step in the helping process.

PLAY MATERIALS FOR PSYCHOSOCIAL DEVELOPMENT

The following play materials have been used with varying degrees of success by Dorfman (1951), Ginott (1961), Axline, (1969), and Moustakas (1959, 1973).

Doll family/doll house. — A spacious dollhouse appropriately furnished and peopled with dolls depicting male and female, children and babies. The treatment accorded by the child to a parent and sibling dolls can give the helper an understanding of the child's perceptions of self and others within the family context. The sleeping patterns in the dollhouse may be of some interest (Ginott, 1961) as well as the targets of anger and affection. In some studies, it has been found that the child most often selects the doll family as play material. There are some who feel that through the use of dolls the child is best able to express feelings. It should be borne in mind that all acting out with dolls or puppets is not significant. It is only significant when the child uses these media to help express the self or to work through feelings that are troublesome.

Toy animals. — Some children find it difficult to express aggressive feelings against people even through the make-believe world of dolls. They do, however, find they can express aggressive feelings in safety against "bad" animals. It should also be pointed out that toy animals can elicit feelings of affection and love.

Block party. — Blocks satisfy children's need for risk and adventure and may also serve as a substitute object for hostility. Blocks enable children to build and destroy without dire consequences and are very amenable to a rapid rebuilding. The child can destroy a block building over and over again and learn in the process that one's aggression is not catastrophic.

Water play. — Water play can involve pouring water, blowing bubbles, squeezing sponges, washing, soaking, and rinsing anything that can be immersed. Water, according to Ginott (1961), is perhaps the most effective of all playroom materials. It does not require any special skills, so every child can play with it with success. It enables even the meekest of children to experience a sense of accomplishment. The materials make so little demand and offer so little resistance that every child can manipulate them. It allows for cleansing or it can become, in the child's imagination, an agent for messing. Water play is limited only by the child's imagination. Materials for water play are inexpensive, readily available, and a delight for children.

Sandbox. — Sand is another excellent medium for the child's aggressive play. It can be thrown about with comparative safety; dolls and other toys can be buried in it; it can be "snow," "water," or a "burying ground." It can also elicit creative impulses and provide excellent opportunities for the use of the child's imagination.

Easel and finger painting. — These offer a suitable outlet for the satisfaction of the child's need to mess. They are non-threatening media which allow children to translate feelings into color and movement. Even for the over-controlled and inhibited child, the contact with soft, colorful, mercurial-like substances encourages spontaneity and a free flow of fantasy.

Clay. — Clay allows for success at any level of a child's develoment and skill. It provides an outlet for both creative and destructive urges. It lends itself to random manipulation; it requires no intermediary; it can be used by aggressive children to punch and pound; it gives a sense of accomplishment in the child's mastery of pliable material.

Aggressive Toys. — These should be chosen with care to avoid physical harm to the child. Cap guns, rubber knives, punching bags, and pounding boards provide harmless oulets for expressing hostility. Noise-making toys such as drums and xylophones can also be used by children for a non-destructive expression of hostility.

Puppets. — Many children find that they can use the anonymity of puppets to express their feelings in safety. Puppets are a delight to work with and can be manipulated by the child to express a wide range of psychosocial needs and feelings.

Many other toys can be used to enhance the psychosocial development of the child (Caney, 1972). It should be noted that almost every toy which can evoke a destructive response can also produce a positive response. This was brought about in a graduate course when students who were experientially learning about play began to talk about their personal reactions to the spring-back punching bag. During the time the graduate students played with the materials, nearly all of them had a chance at the punching bag and expressed delight in hitting the bag as hard as they could. However, a few students stated that when they approached the punching bag, rather than hit it, they hugged it. What emerged in the ensuing discussion was that toys and other play materials are neutral objects and whatever feeling is expressed with a toy is a reflection of the person using it rather than the toy itself. It is not surprising, then, when a child picks up a toy gun, looks at it momentarily, and then puts it aside, saying, "I wish people would stop hurting each other." For the child, the toy gun may bring forth a feeling of sadness rather than aggression. It is wise to put aside stereotyped images about the emotional valences of toys and to encourage the child to share perceptions and feelings as these are evoked by the toy or medium used in play.

THE PLAYROOM

The necessity of having a special room set aside and furnished for helping children through play is questioned by Axline (1969), who believes there are many possibilities for using the medium of play within limited budget and space appropriations. A small rug, an easel, and a toy box located in a corner of a classroom would constitute an adequate play-media environment. In the toy box would be a doll family, a few pieces of furniture, nursing bottle, telephone, puppets, crayons, drawing paper, water colors, finger paints, a toy gun, and some transportation toys such as cars and trucks. These materials would be sufficient for play helping relationships and could fit a space as small as a suitcase.

If a special room is to be put aside for play, it should have the following features. The playroom should be kept simple. Other than basic furniture, the only things which should be there are toys. The floor and walls should be washable and easily cleaned. The room should have acoustical ceiling tile and wall materials which will absorb and reduce sound. It would be useful to protect the windows with screening. The room should be bright and attractive, well lighted, well ventilated and play materials should be visible and available. There should be a sink with running hot and cold water, a sandbox, and a wooden bench for use as a table or work area. Materials should be kept on shelves which are easily accessible to the children. Regardless of the mess made in previous play sessions, the room should be put in order so that it is always neutral and free from the suggestive indicators regarding which play materials were used by a previous individual or group using the playroom.

It would greatly enhance the child's sense of freedom if the child were provided with a smock, an old shirt, or some sort of coverall to protect clothing. The child will then have the freedom to be messy.

ESTABLISHING LIMITS

Rationale for Limits

In his discussion of play therapy, Ginott (1961) offers five reasons for establishing limits:

1. Limits direct catharsis into symbolic channels.
2. Limits enable the helper to maintain attitudes of acceptance, empathy, and regard for the child and not be distracted from those attitudes.
3. Limits assure the physical safety of the child.
4. Limits strengthen ego controls.
5. Limits are set for reasons of law, ethics, and social acceptability (pp. 103-105).

Axline (1969) indicates that limits consistently anchor the play experience to the world of reality, give the child a sense of responsibility in the relationship, and safeguard the helping process from possible misconceptions, confusion, guilt feelings, and insecurity (pp. 128-135).

The use of durable and inexpensive media in a playroom which is easily cleaned will obviate the need for limits relating to materials (with a few exceptions). It is evident that some limits bearing on the relationship are required if the child is to learn how to deal with the real world and if the purposes of the play experience are to be met. There appears to be general agreement (Dorfman, 1951; Ginott, 1961; Axline, 1969; Moustakas, 1973) that the following limits serve to improve the psychosocial quality and effectiveness of play experiences.

Appropriate Limits

Time Limit. — A time limit is determined and held to. The helper tells the child of the time limit and toward the end of the session reminds the child that there are only a few minutes left to play. Extending time at the request of the child is not wise. When the child learns that time limits are part of everyone's reality, the child will begin to make profitable use of the time available for play.

Taking Toys from the Playroom. — Toys should remain in the playroom. Broken toys should also remain in the playroom, otherwise some toys would be broken for the purpose of taking them home. If a child wants to show a toy to a parent or teacher, then the child may ask the parent or teacher to the playroom to see it. Children should be allowed to take home paintings and clay work that they themselves create.

Breakage of Toys/Destruction to Room. — Children's destructive urges and feelings should be recognized, reflected, and respected, but limits on action should be invoked and implemented. It is more a help to the child to let the child face the limits that human relationships require them to let the child give rein to destructive *actions*. There is little self-enhancing value in permitting a child to break playroom equipment or toys. The child's negative actions should be channeled toward materials in the playroom designated for the purpose.

Physical Assault — There is little if any psychosocial benefit in letting a child physically assault another child or the helper. It is generally agreed that this is a limit which should not be modified under any circumstances. It is more helpful for the child to channel aggressive feelings through symbolic actions against play materials which are there for that purpose. Permitting a child to attack another person can cause harm not only to that person but also to the child who needs to learn that mutual respect requires some control of feelings and that the unbridled expression of anger through physical assault is no solution for the child's psychosocial problems.

Limits should not be mentioned before the need for them arise. If limits are kept to a minimum and are introduced only when the need emerges, then the play experience progresses more naturally. There appears to be little advantage in beginning the play experience by prescribing limitations on actions that may never occur. Children's everyday experiences usually prepare them for some prohibitions upon their actions, and it is better to wait until the need for limits comes up before identifying them.

PARENTS AND PLAY

As a consultant to parents, the staff member responsible for play experiences can help parents to use play to facilitate the psychosocial development of the child. The value of play as a vehicle for fostering the psychosocial development of the child cannot be underestimated. The school and parents can work together to use the extraordinary power of play to enhance the psychosocial maturity of children (Moustakas, 1973). One vehicle for doing this is a toy-lending program for parents and children.

The toy-lending program is based on two basic idea: that play activities should be self-rewarding so that a child participates because of the enjoyment the child receives, not because the child is coerced or coaxed; and that psychosocial development cannot take place without free expression. The goal of a toy-lending program is to create psychosocially helpful play environments in the home and to encourage play between parents and children as a medium for getting to know each other and learning about each other's psychosocial needs. In play at home the child should also be free to give vent to feelings of anger and frustration and be able to talk to the parent(s) about the experiences and circumstances which cause these feelings.

Initiating a toy-lending program is not difficult. The components are simple: a meeting place, a group of interested parents, a presentation on the psychosocial purposes of play, demonstrations on how play elicits feelings, an identification of the play materials which evoke feelings, role-playing opportunities to engage in play, and the formation of a support group atmosphere in which parents can be encouraged in their play efforts to contribute to the psychosocial development of their children.

In conclusion, the psychosocial benefits of play cannot be underestimated. Play is the child's natural language for expressing a wide range of feelings. When the adult helper attempts to assist a child to express feelings just through verbal interactions, the experience can be frustrating for the child, who typically does not possess the language to express those feelings. But when the adult helper establishes a play relationship with the child, the child is able to express feelings which are more accurate, honest, natural, and spontaneous. The feelings which previously could not be expressed are now expressed because of the stimulus provided by play materials and the child's psychosocial development is well served.

REFERENCES

Allen, F. H. (1942). *Psychotherapy with children.* New York: Norton.
Amster, F. (1943). Differential uses of play in treatment of young children. *American Journal of Orthopsychiatry,* 13, 62-68.
Axline, V. (1964). *Dibs: In search of self.* Boston: Houghton Mifflin.
Axline, V. (1969). *Play therapy.* New York: Ballantine Books.
Beiser, H. R. (1955). Therapeutic play techniques: Play equipment for diagnosis and therapy. *American Journal of Orthopsychiatry,* 25, 761-770.
Caney, S. (1972). *Toy Books.* New York: Workman.
Caplan, R. & Caplan, T. (1973). *The power of play.* New York: Anchor Books.
Dorfman, E. (1951). Play therapy. Chapter 6 in C. R. Rogers, *Client-centered therapy.* Boston: Houghton Mifflin.
Ellis, M. J. (1973). *Why people play.* Englewood Cliffs, NJ: Prentice-Hall.
Erickson, E. H. (1964). Toys and reasons. In M. R. Haworth (Ed.), *Child psychotherapy: Practice and theory.* New York: Basic Books.
Ginott, H. G. (1961). *Group psychotherapy with children.* New York: McGraw-Hilll.
Kessler, J. W. (1966). *Psychopathology of childhood.* Englewood Cliffs, NJ: Prentice-Hall.
Levy, D. M. (1939). Release therapy. *American Journal of Orthopsychiatry,* 9, 113-136.
Levy, J. (1978). *Play behavior.* New York: John Wiley and Sons.
Meeks, A. R. (1968). *Guidance in elementary education.* New York: Ronald Press.
Moustakas, C. C. (1959). *Play therapy with children.* New York: Harper.
Moustakas, C. C. (1973). *Children in play therapy.* New York: McGraw-Hill.
Nelson, R. C. (1968). Play media and the elementary school counselor. In D. C. Dinkmeyer (Ed.), *Guidance and counseling in the elementary school.* New York: Holt, Rinehart and Winston, 267-270.
Piaget, J. (1951). *Play, dreams, and imitation in children.* New York: Norton.
Pulaski, M. A. (1971). *Understanding Piaget.* New York: Harper and Row.
Schiffer, M. (1969). *The therapeutic play group.* New York: Grune and Stratton.

CHAPTER X

ECLECTIC ACTIVITIES TO FOSTER PSYCHOSOCIAL DEVELOPMENT

THE ACTIVITIES identified in this chapter can be used as an adjunct to play therapy with small groups. The activities can also be used by classroom teachers. In both cases, the activities are designed to facilitate and further the psychosocial development of youngsters.

This chapter describes eclectic activities which can be used by the teacher to help students in their psychosocial development; to help students in their self-awareness and their awareness of others; to build positive self-concepts; to help clarify personal values and priorities; to develop relationship and problem-solving skills; to identify and understand psychosocial behavior; to encourage positive group interaction; and to learn something about the cause and effect of behavior patterns. We urge responsible and prudent use of their activities.

RATIONALE

The earlier literature of education abounded with suggestions and descriptions of exercises, activities, experiences, and games to help young persons with their psychosocial development (Bessell, 1970; Borton, 1970; Brown, 1971; Gunther, 1968, 1971; Otto, 1967; Lyon, 1971). More recent publications expand this literature, and particularly useful resources have been developed by Brown (1975), Casteel and Shahl (1975), Fromkin and Sherwood (1975), Howe and Howe (1975), Selfman and Hermes (1975), Canfield and Wells (1976), Hendricks (1976), Powell (1976), Dickman, Weiss, and Morrison (1977), and Cerio and Cerio (1979). The rationale for the use of such psychosocial development activities is expressed in the following principles:

1. The student's natural and spontaneous interest in play make the use of games and exercises especially appropriate for psychosocial development.
2. The student's need for structure and clearly defined goals can be served through the use of games and exercises with clearly defined rules.
3. Games and exercises establish a vantage point from which to view and learn about interpersonal processes and relationships.
4. Games and exercises magnify experiences — they also make something happen in short order, demolish or diminish same inhibition or resistance, or permeate some defense.
5. Games and exercises offer a change of pace — a means for relieving tension.

GUIDELINES FOR SELECTING PSYCHOSOCIAL ACTIVITIES

We recommend that teachers use the following guidelines, derived from Trotzer and Kassera (1973), as useful and appropriate criteria for selecting psychosocial activities to use with students:

(1) Select Activities on the Basis of Their Efficacy in Terms of Purpose, Relevance, and Desired Outcome. This is the top rule. No activity should be attempted because it might be fun, exciting, or produce an emotional high. The impact of the technique should be considered above all else. All too frequently popularity or familiarity with the characteristics and instructions of a particular activity are the basis for selection rather than the why and the wherefore of its use.

(2) Select Activities That Are Familiar and That Are Comfortable For You to Use. If the teacher is hesitant, confused, or uncomfortable with an activity, this will be picked up by the group and could cause resistance or failure in its use. Activities which you have experienced should take precedence over those you may have read about or observed. Do not use activities with a group that you have heard about just to see what will happen. To augment new activities, first attempt them under controlled and comfortable conditions where the process and outcome will have little possibility of being disruptive.

(3) Select Activities That Are Primarily Verbal Rather Than Physical. Physical contact is often the first issue raised against the use of psychosocial activities with groups and should be guarded against. Most desired outcomes can be attained either by verbal exercises or by nonverbal activities involving a minimum of physical contact. For example, leading by the hand in a trust walk is acceptable, but the extended physical contact of an activity such as body sculpturing is better avoided.

(4) Select Activities Which Do Not Require Labels or Can Be Labeled With Terms Which Do Not Carry Some Type of Stigma. Often, the same activity can have many different labels. For example, the statement, "Let's see if you can show us how you reacted in that situation" could be termed psychodrama, sociodrama, or role playing. However, there is a considerable difference in connotation between the label of psychodrama and the label of role playing. Activities selected should lend themselves to being explained in everyday langauge or in rather neutral terms.

(5). Select Activities Which Are Commensurate With the Age and Maturity Level of the Group Members. The students' ability to comprehend and immerse themselves in an activity without undue tension, stress, or embarrassment is extremely important to the effective use of any activity. The use of puppets to aid third graders in exploring their feelings may be more appropriate and effective than role playing. Eighth graders, however, may feel puppets are childish and may prefer and gain more from role playing.

(6) Select Activities Which Are Adaptable to the Physical Setting in Which the Group is Meeting. If the physical setting does not allow for an activity to be fully experienced or interferes with its being carried out, the activity should be avoided. Using dyads in a small room for a verbal activity requiring high concentration may simply create confusion rather than accomplish a useful purpose. Similarly, techniques requiring students to leave the room should be avoided, because they may result in loss of control and may create misunderstanding by others.

(7) Select Activities Which Allow for Maximum Member Participation. Some activities may require physical skills or endurance which may be frightening, distasteful, or overtaxing to some group members. Activities which require some type of physical involvement should always be prefaced with a caution to members and an option of observing rather than participating. Strenuous activities are best avoided. Other activities which involve elements of embarrassment (wearing a skirt versus slacks) should be used only when students have been advised in advance of these factors.

(8) Select Activities Which Allow Group Members to Control Their Own Involvement. Avoid activities which force students to do something they are not ready for, cannot do, or are threatened by. Members should be allowed to decide how they will involve themselves in the activity and to what depth they will go. Communication techniques should promote freedom, not restrict it.

(9) Select Activities That Will Result in Outcomes You Are Sure the Group and You as a Teacher Can Handle. Activities which precipitate or facilitate the expression of strong feelings and emotions are always risky and should be used with extreme caution. If the possibility of loss of control is evident in the use of any techniques, it is best avoided. Teachers must always consider their own capabilities and the composition of the group in selecting activities to be used in the group.

(10) Select Activities Which Can Be Completed in the Time Available. Do not select activities which cannot be presented, experienced, and discussed during the time limits of the group. Similarly, do not begin an activity if it cannot be fully worked through before the group session ends. If an activity has not been completed, it is often better to hold the group over than to allow members to leave with feelings and misunderstandings that have not been resolved.

ACTIVITIES FOR THE PSYCHOSOCIAL DEVELOPMENT OF STUDENTS

1. *Now I Am Aware* (personal awareness of here and now). Students are asked to pay attention to the things around them, to let their eyes roam around the room, settling on any objects they want to see. They are then asked to state specifically what they see. What do they smell, what do they taste, what do they hear (Lewis & Streitfeld, 1970)?
2. *Loosen Up.* Have everyone let out a mighty roar and bang and stamp the floor. (A lot of tensions and frustrations may be brought into the group meeting.) This is a good way to let them out as well a "loosen up" all members (Lewis & Streitfeld, 1970).
3. *Lungs Alive* (yelling helps get the old air out, along with held-in feelings). Members are instructed to vigorously slap their chests, without causing pain, and the yell "Ahhhhh" as loudly as possible. After half a minute or so, let the yelling and slapping subside.

"Think about how you feel." Now, members take an enormous breath. They are told to keep their lungs filled for a long time, then to slowly let the air out until they can't force any more air out of their lungs. Finally, they are told to allow the air to rush in. Exhilaration and vigor will follow. (This exercise in hyperventilation, like many others, should be well supervised) (Lewis & Steitfeld, 1970).

To Promote Awareness of Self and of Others

4. *Getting Acquainted.* Students mill about informally to meet as many people as possible (within a given period of time) without use of any verbal communication. This technique can also be formally structured using inner and outer circles of students rotating to greet members in the opposite circle.

5. *Who Are You?* Group members are paired, members are instructed to sit opposite their partners, and for three (more or less) minutes one partner asks the question, "Who are you?" The other person must come up with a different answer each time. After a few moments, partners change places. After both partners have experienced the exercise, discuss what happened.

6. *Alter-Ego Technique.* Have one person stand behind another, trying to put himself in the place of the other and periodically stating how he thinks the other must feel (Schutz, 1967).

7. *Mirror Talk.* Pairs of students sit facing each other and alternate as leader and follower to pantomime and "mirror" responses to gestures and facial expressions communicated to each other through direct eye-to-eye contact.

8. *Modified "Simon Says."* A way to use make-believe language is to ask the partners to take turns making noises, then to let the partner imitate the sound, then in turn to imitate the partner's ("Simon Says" is probably familiar to the children; this modified version is fun and will help in icebreaking) (Lewis & Streitfeld, 1970).

9. *Private World.* Students react silently (with eyes closed) to a vivid descriptive passage designed to stimulate self-awareness through experiencing a series of changing environmental situations. This activity emphasizes individual needs for security, privacy, and self-respect.

10. *Fantasy World.* Similar to the preceding but less structured and formal, this exercise encourages freedom of expression and individuality in response to the colorful imagery created by a

narration of fantasy. This technique is helpful in stimulating self-evaluation of personal needs.

11. *What's in a Name?* We identify closely with the names. It was probably the first word we were able to spell and read. This constant companion, our names, can help increase awareness of feelings. Have group members write their names as slowly and carefully as possible. Discuss how they felt while writing (Schutz, 1967).
12. *Ideal Family.* Group members are asked to think of an imaginary family they would like to be a part of, then to talk about the "ideal" family.
13. *My Family.* Group members are asked to choose one word to describe each member of their family. Perhaps fill in the blank, "He/She is the _____ one." Descriptive words are first written down, then shared. What words would family members use in describing themselves?
14. *Self-Portrait.* Begin by asking group members to draw their own portraits. Then they are asked to look at themselves in a full-length mirror. They should *really look*. How does their mirror image compare to their drawings? Why? (Lewis & Streitfeld, 1970)
15. *When I Grow Up.* Members share their fantasies of what they would like to be when they grow up; what they would like to do and be.
16. *Special Name.* Ask group members if there is a "special name" they would like to be known as in the group sessions. Then those that choose names (and those who also prefer their own) are asked to tell the group why they chose the name. It is useful for the group leader to also choose a name.
17. *Be an Animal.* Members pretend to be the animal they feel most like today, at this time (not their favorite animal) (Huxley, 1963).
18. *What I Am Like.* Group members are asked to choose partners, then to sit back-to-back with them. They are instructed to talk about themselves to the partner. "What I am Like . . . . " They are then to face one another and, without talking, continue the interaction. Finally, they talk face to face and when the group is brought together, they introduce their partners using only the information from the activity.

To Build and Strengthen a Positive Self-Concept

19. *"All About Me" Folder.* Individual work folders provide a private place for students to collect and preserve prized papers and projects about

themselves. These folders serve as a continuing project to encourage individual growth and development of a positive self-image (Items 20-23 below are excellent activities to initiate and develop self-image folders.)

20. *Self-Portrait.* Student self-protraits (in any art medium) are effective image builders. Signed portraits can be exhibited regularly by using them as name tags to identify an individual student's papers and projects that are on display.

21. *Personal Time Line.* Each student records memorable life experiences on a vertical line which represents the student's life span from birth to the present. Entries may be either written or drawn and should include all events which the student remembers as a meaningful part of his or her life.

22. *Being Breath.* Members are instructed to close their eyes (again, it is all right for those who choose not to close their eyes to participate) and to become aware of their breathing without interfering with it. Then, they should try to feel where their breathing begins. "Feel the air coming from your nose; feel your chest rise then fall. Feel the temperature of the air. Be aware of the air going into your nose (and mouth); just see how it feels and don't try to control it. Think about how you feel while you're breathing. Open your eyes." This exercise can be used for personal self-awareness of shared experience or as a relaxation activity (Gunther, 1971).

23. *Three-Dimensional Self-Impression.* Have a bunch of "junk" (collect miscellaneous materials such as papers, pictures, blocks, string, marbles, scraps of wood, pieces of cloth, and any other odds and ends) and ask students to construct a picture, a representation of themselves, out of the materials.

24. *Notebook Diary* Students keep individual running records of their feelings and impressions of weekly happenings both in and out of school. Entries are limited to short and informal comments, and time is provided each week for bringing the diaries up to date.

25. *Serial Autobiography.* Students "build" an autobiography over a period of weeks by completing a series of worksheets covering a wide variety of personal information ranging from vital statistics and interests to future aspirations and goals. The finished worksheets are bound together with artwork to complete the autobiography.

26. *Collage of Self.* Students create composite images of themselves by selecting and assembling an individual assortment of meaningful

pictures, words and phrases which represent and express ideas and things which are important to them. The collage may be assembled in any shape or form desired.

27. *Martian Language.* Ask the group members to spell out their first names in reverse on paper. Next, pretend that this is a word in Martian language and define it as it would appear in the Martian dictionary (Lewis & Streitfeld, 1970).

To Help Clarify Personal Values and Priorities

28. *Values Voting.* A non-threatening group activity which permits students to express positive and negative feelings in response to a series of thought-provoking statements about values. Hand voting allows three possible responses ("yes," "no," and "pass") to each question.

29. *Values Ranking.* A non-judgmental activity in which students participate in ranking groups of alternatives in the order of their individual preferences. This is an excellent device to explore, defend, and justify differences in priority selections.

30. *Values Continuum.* Students individually locate their own positions between the extremes on a continuum (line) in order to complete a profile of class feelings on a selected issue. This technique is very useful in exploring current events and in introducing controversial topics for discussion.

31. *Public Interview.* A student volunteer is questioned at length about a wide variety of personal interest topics. The student has the option to pass on any question the student does not wish to answer and, at the conclusion of the interview, may ask the interviewer any of the questions which were asked of the student.

32. *Group Interview.* Similar to preceding except that the interviewee is asked questions by the entire group. The interviewee may pass on any question which the interviewee does no wish to answer. The interview can be terminated at any time by the interviewee.

33. *Interview Whip.* This is a fast-paced variation of activities 31 and 32. The teacher moves about the class asking a different question of each child in turn. Clarifying questions may be used wherever necessary, and any pupil may pass on any question the pupil does not wish to answer.

34. *Proud Whip.* Each student is given the opportunity to publicly state some recent event or accomplishment of which the student is

proud. Responses begin with the statement, "I am proud . . . ." and are limited to a specific category.

35. *Sentence Stub.* Students are encouraged to reflect upon their own values and feelings to provide meaningful endings for provocative unfinished sentences. Responses may be either oral or written.
36. *Major Event.* Members share their most important happenings, happy or sad, with the group.
37. *Image of Yourself.* Members are asked to choose a great person, living or dead, that they admire and to become that person. They are then instructed to think about the qualities that they admire in the person and try to express them. (Keep away from historical fact telling.)

To Broaden Perspective in Intepersonal Relations

38. *Flat Picture.* Pictures illustrating common problem situations are used to stimulate responses and motivate group discussions of feelings, attitudes and behavior. This is an excellent vehicle for developing role-playing situations.
39. *Open-Ended or Unfinished Story.* Students provide and explore alternative endings for unfinished problem stories in this versatile activity which serves as a springboard for discussions, debates, written responses and role playing.
40. *Role Playing.* A non-threatening, interpersonal activity designed to broaden a student's experience and perspective through assuming the role of another in a problem situation. This technique is especially useful for involving all students in open discussions in conflict areas. Role playing can vary from a highly structured situation, with predetermined characterizations and dialogue, to a flexible and impromptu activity with a minimum of structure.
41. *The Fantasy Game.* This technique helps to uncover the factors that enter into making a decision. It affords a greater insight into what is happening in "inner space," the feelings inside the body. The leader asks for volunteers, then asks group members to think about their experience in deciding whether to volunteer or not. "Imagine two people inside your head. One of them is telling you to volunteer; the other one is telling you not to. Picture a conversation between these two in which they try to convince each other, until finally one of them wins. After they talk, have them meet each other without speaking. See what happens. Close your eyes for a couple of minutes and imagine what happens."

42. *Concrete Poetry (Symbolic Word Pictures).* Discussions of problems in interpersonal relations are stimulated by differences in individual interpretations of pictures created from artistic patterns of words and language symbols. Concrete poetry is designed to convey a wide variety of meanings as determined by individual experiences and environments.

43. *Folk Music.* Traditional and modern folk songs based upon significant social problems are used to elicit responses and to initiate group discussions of relevant issues in interpersonal and intergroup relationships.

44. *Triad.* Working in groups of three, students analyze and discuss, in turn, a specific problem of each member of the group. The roles of helper, helpee, and observer are interchanged so that each member of the group serves in all three positions. This is an excellent technique for prompting group cooperation in problem solving.

45. *Inner-Outer Circle.* Discussion of controversial issues is facilitated by a circular seating pattern which permits alternate listening and speaking roles for opposing points of view. Each group has a turn to speak openly and unchallenged to the inner circle, while the opposing group in the outer circle listens without comment or interruption.

46. *Fishbowling.* This technique is a modification of a panel discussion in which a group of 5 or 6 students engage in an impromptu debate of a controversial issue. Throughout the discussion, panel members are replaced by new participants selected from the listening audience. The frequent changing of speakers permits exposure of a wide variety of opinions and provides continuing impetus for the discussion.

47. *Brainstorming.* This activity is used to provide the class with an exhaustive working list of ideas relative to a particular problem. The objective is to explore all possible avenues of solution by freely accepting all contributions without regard to merit or feasibility.

To Illustrate Cause and Effect of Behavior Patterns

48. *Closed Circle.* A circle of students, with arms interlocking, act in concert to keep two or three "outsiders" from breaking into the circle. This simple demonstration vividly illustrates the behavior and attitudes of "in" and "out" groups in school, business, and society.

49. *Breaking Out.* The group forms a tight circle, interlocking arms. One person stands in the middle and must break out. Members try to keep the person in the circle. This exercise is valuable for those individuals feeling constricted or tyrannized by the group. The feelings present in the escaping behavior can serve as the basis for discussion.

50. *One-Way, Two-Way Communication.* Guided solely by verbal instructions, students attempt to reproduce two separate designs of geometric figures. For the first demonstration, the instructor is unseen and there is no opportunity for questions. For the second situation, the instructor faces the group and will answer any questions. Results of the two attempts are compared and discussed.

51. *Rumor Clinic.* An ambiguous picture is shown to all but five members of the class. A reporter then verbally relates the incident to the first non-witness, who passes the story to the second, and so on, until each of the five, in turn, have been informed. The class has the opportunity to watch the effects of stereotyping and rumor development.

52. *The Lady (Perception Activity).* A picture conveying two widely divergent illustrations of a woman is used to demonstrate the inhibiting influence of "mind set" on visual perception. This exercise illustrates the difficulty encountered in seeing the second of two equally obvious illusions once the first has been identified by the viewer.

53. *Blue Eyes-Brown Eyes.* The class is divided into two groups which are determined by some arbitrary characteristic such as eye color. An artificial superior-inferior situation is created by the deliberate preferential treatment of one group at the expense of the other. This activity involves students in experiencing the feeling and attitudes generated by prejudice and discrimination.

54. *Superior-Inferior.* A variation of activity 53 in which the class is divided into two groups which are assigned specific superior and inferior roles. Working in pairs (one of each group), the students are required to complete a joint rank-order listing of priority items. This experience dramatically illustrates the effects of superior and inferior status in interpersonal relations.

55. *To experience dominance.* The person experiencing dominance stands on a chair and continues interacting from that position.

56. *To experience subordinance.* The person experiencing subordinance sits on the floor while the other group members remain seated in chairs.

57. *IALAC.* A dramatic presentation of the erosion of self-concept resulting from negative exeriences in daily interpersonal relations. A sign with the acronym "IALAC" is used to present the concept, "I am lovable and capable." For each negative incident which occurs, a piece of the sign is torn away until only a small portion remains intact. This technique vividly illustrates how people can unintentionally injure the feelings of others.

58. *Group WALAC.* An adaption of activity 57 which uses the group concept, "We are lovable and capable." A piece is torn from the class sign for evey individual incident which mars the group concept. This activity relates the role of individual behavior to the group image.

To Motivate and Encourage Positive Group Interaction

59. *Sing-Along.* Singing is a natural form of interaction which provides an excellent vehicle to promote a sense of group togetherness. A sing-along is an ideal ice-breaker and it is especially helpful in initiating other group activities.

60. *The Wheel.* Pairs of students write first impressions of each other on individual "what" wheels. The wheels are exchanged and read, and then each student selects one item about the self for which further elaboration is desired. This information is written on a "why" wheel. An optional third wheel can be used to explore the "how" aspects if additional development is desired.

61. *Group Creative Task.* Students are divided into work groups in complete separate group construction projects. Tools and materials are distributed in such a way that no one group has the necessary equipment to complete the task. Only through cooperation, planning, and sharing among the groups can the projects be successfully completed. This is an excellent activity for developing cooperative group interaction.

62. *Group Fantasy.* Two or three members most involved with each other are asked to lie down on their backs with their heads together and their bodies stretched out like spokes on a wheel. All members are asked to close their eyes. one of the floor participants begins by telling whatever pictures comes to mind, or someone may start the person off with a specific image. Everyone else tries to enter this person's fantasy and carry it on in whatever way it happens inside their on heads. Each person on the floor is to enter verbally at any time so that the fantasy continues. Other

group members may join those on the floor. (The mechanism through which the group fantasy operates is still relatively unknown. Apparently, it is similar to communication at a different level of awareness, as with the unconscious. It frequently leaves the participants with close feelings for each other.)

63. *Blind Milling.* Pupils standup, shut their eyes, put out their hands and just start walking slowly around the room. When people meet, they concentrate on their explorations of one another. Are they afraid to touch? Can they guess who they've touched? Also, in the follow-up discussion, how did they feel when others explored, touched or walked away from them? This method may enhance cohesive ties within the group in addition to enhancing and sharpening awareness of the other people.

64. *Group Agreement Task.* Student work groups are assigned the task of agreeing upon a priority rank-order listing of space survival equipment. Representatives from each group are then selected to meet as a committee to develop a mutually agreeable rank-order list for the class. This technique involves students in the process of decision making determined by group consensus.

65. *Propaganda Game.* Groups of three or four students work as teams to accumulate points in a multiple-answer selection game. Each team must agree on a common answer in selecting the appropriate category for various types of propaganda. The accepted answer for each round is determined by the majority team response. This activity is helpful in stimulating positive group interaction.

66. *Feeling space* (how to make contact with others). Group members are asked to gather close together. They are then asked to close their eyes and, stretching out their hands, "Feel the space"—all the space in front of them, over their heads, behind their backs, below them, and then begin to be aware of their contact with others as they overlap and begin to touch one another. This continues for about five minutes, until group members tire. The follow-up discussion usually opens up the area of feelings about aloneness and the need for contact.

67. *Strength Bombardment.* Group members are asked to tell the member who is the focus of their attention all the positive feelings they have about that person. The focus person is to listen only.

68. *Here and There.* Members are asked to close their eyes and to go away, in make-believe, to a place where they feel happy and safe.

They are then instructed to return to the here and now and to compare the two situations. Members are asked about the situations, which was better, why? Again, members are instructed to close their eyes and to go away. Members are told when to open their eyes, then to tell about the pictures, including the way the people looked, how their voices sounded, how big they were, what they said, where they were, and what happened. They are instructed to notice any changes in their fantasy place since their last visit. Shuttling between the here and now and the fantasy "there" continues until members feel comfortable in the here, the present situation. The difference between the here and there can demonstrate directions members want to move in their psychosocial development and/or life goals.

69. *Dyad Communication* (when two people can't understand each other)

    a. *Verbal Method.* Each participant is asked to stop talking and to try to state the adversary's position as clearly and sympathetically as possible: "Okay, there must be some reason why X is getting so upset; can't you try to figure out why? Let's pretend that if you were X, why would you say those things, why would you feel the way X does?" It is important to insist (if mocking occurs) that it be stated as if it were a reasonable position to take. "We realize that you disagree, but try to pretend that there are good reasons to feel the way X does."

    b. *Non-Verbal Method.* Ask the two members to continue to communicate but without using words. "Keep talking, but don't use your mouths." The defensive, obscuring function of the words is eliminated and the feelings are directed toward the body. The benefit of this activity can also be maintained by asking what fantasies or pictures immediately come to mind. In both non-verbal and verbal methods it is helpful to ask adversaries to sit facing each other.

70. *Trust Walk.* Members are asked to choose partners, perhaps those used in a previous activity, and instructed that the eyes of one member should be closed and the other partner is to be a guide. The guide "shows" the blind person things that can be experienced without being seen—things to touch and smell. The walk should last about fifteen minutes, then when both partners have experienced being "blind" (and being the guide) they may talk about the feelings they had. If some participants are hesitant to

close their eyes or are obviously peeking, that's acceptable. The purpose of this activity is to develop a trust feeling for the partner as well as to experience the world around us without sight.

To Help Identify and Understand Emotional Behavior

71. *Weekly Reaction Sheet.* This activity allows students the opportunity to openly express their feelings and opinions about the school week by completing a short, written evaluation form. A series of seven to ten open-ended sentences (or sentence stubs) is used to encourage expressions of satisfaction, dissatisfaction, and areas of improvement or change.
72. *Depict Your Feelings.* Students are instructed to think of an object that seems to describe themselves and are encouraged to express and evaluate their feelings through the object.
73. *Feelings Card.* A variation of activity 71, the feelings card is an individual written comment of a student's feelings about a particular aspect of school about which the student has strong positive or negative feelings. Cards may be voluntarily submitted to the group and are intended to help group members explore their feelings.
74. *Imitation of Life* (to sense how easily we assume roles). Group members are asked to transform themselves into inanimate objects (a road, a car, a football, a TV set) and to describe how those objects might feel if they were brought to life. One can realize the strength of this activity when group members are asked to describe the feelings of alcohol and drugs if they were given life.
75. *Five Faces (Feelings Pictures).* Students are encouraged to interpret and evaluate their own feelings through the use of pictures or drawings portraying five different kinds of emotions as revealed by facial expressions. This activity is primarily directed to self-understanding and it is an excellent supplement to self-concept building techniques.
76. *Happy Clown-Sad Clown.* Similar to activity 75, this technique utilizes pictures of opposing emotions to help students identify and evaluate behavior which represents their own attitudes and feelings.
77. *In a Word.* Students are asked to take a word that means a lot to them (for example, love), to close their eyes and to repeat this word to themselves over and over for three to five minutes (probably less time). After, ask them to keep their eyes closed and to experience how they feel.

78. *Gibberish Conversations.* Break up into pairs and have members have a conversation using only non-sensical, rather than real words. Ask participants if they can get angry, be happy, sad, surprised, and demonstrate these without using our language.
79. *Emotional Charades.* Useful in demonstrating how we "show" our feeling to others and how we interpret others' non-verbal behavior. Each group member has a slip of paper on which the member writes a feeling like sadness, anger, or happiness. The slips are then mixed and distributed among the members. The group is asked to think of the kinds of things that make them experience the emotions on the papers. Then, individually, members nonverbally act out the emotions on their slips. Other members may, after several seconds, try to guess the feeling.
80. *Role playing Via Creative Writing.* This is a non-threatening activity to encourage self-expression with students who are reluctant to write. By assuming the role of an inanimate object, students are motivated to project their feelings and attitudes into a personalized representation of the object.
81. *Socio-Drama.* This is a short, open-ended playlet (with formal script) which deals with current social issues. The socio-drama is specifically designed to provide in-depth interaction and discussion.
82. *Classroom Geography.* A variety of classroom seating patterns are tried in an effort to find out which one will maximize interactions among group members. The best and poorest seating patterns are discussed in order to identify their interactive strengths and weaknesses.
83. *Leadership Styles.* This adaptation of the superior-inferior technique is specifically designed to demonstrate the effects of three different styles of leadership behavior: dominant, cooperative, and indifferent. Pairs of students enact and evaluate three separate decision-making situations in which each student plays each of the three leadership roles.
84. *Group Discussion Analysis.* This activity can be correlated with any group discussion topic for the purpose of analyzing and identifying the various task and maintenance roles played by individuals in group decision making. Observers are supplied with uniform descriptions of various role functions and are asked to evaluate and discuss each participant's behavior.
85. *School Distance Ranking.* Individual rank-order selection of ethnic and racial groups is effectively used to illustrate the influence of

group stereotyping on social distance concepts. This activity is normally used in conjunction with other activities, such as superior-inferior (activity 54), in order to understand the roots of prejudice.

86. *Sociogram.* Designed primarily for teacher information, the sociogram is an informal written survey which indicates individual social interaction patterns within the classroom. This instrument can be helpful in determining individual status in peer group associations or in the formation of various committees to work on a class project.

REFERENCES

Bessell, H. (1970). *Methods in human development: Theory manual.* El Cajon, CA: Human Development Training Institute.

Borton, T. (1970). *Reach, touch, and teach.* New York: McGraw-Hill.

Brown, G. I. (1971). *Human teaching for human learning.* New York: Viking.

Brown, G. I. (Ed.). (1975). *The live classroom: Innovation through confluent education and Gestalt.* New York: Viking.

Canfield, J. & Wells, H. C. (1976). *100 ways to enhance the self-concept in the classroom.* Englewood Cliffs, NJ: Prentice-Hall.

Casteel, J. D. & Stahl, R. J. (1975). *Value clarification in the classroom: A primer.* Pacific Palisades, CA: Goodyear.

Cerio, N. G. & Cerio, J. E. (1979). Loving relationships, life-styles, and needs: Exploring values through group process. *Journal for Specialists in Group Work,* 4, 40-44.

Dickman, L., Weisse, E. & Morrison, K. (1977). *How to develop creativity.* Oshkosh, WI: McAllister.

Fromkin, J. L. & Sherwood, J. J. (Eds.). (1975). *Intergroup and minority relations: An experiential handbook.* La Jolla, CA: University Associates.

Gunther, B. (1968). *Sense relaxation below your mind.* New York: Macmillan, Collier Books.

Gunther, B. (1971). *What to do till the messiah comes.* New York: Macmillan, Collier Books.

Hendricks, G. (1976). *The centering book.* Englewood Cliffs, NJ: Prentice-Hall.

Howe, L. W. & Howe, M. M. (1975). *Personalizing education: Values clarification and beyond.* New York: Hart.

Huxley, L. A. (1963). *You are not the target.* New York: Farrar, Strauss and Giroux.

Lewis, H. R. & Streitfeld, H. S. (1970). *Growth games: How to tune in yourself, your family, your friends.* New York: Harcourt Brace Jovanovich.

Lyon, H. C. (971). *Learning to feel—Feeling to learn.* Columbus, OH: Charles E. Merrill.

Otto, H. A. (1967). *Guide to developing your potential.* New York: Charles Scribner's Sons.

Powell, J. (1976). *Fully human, fully alive: A new life through a new vision.* Niles, IL: Argus Communications.

Schutz, W. C. (1967). *Joy: Expanding human awareness.* New York: Grove Press.

Seldman, M. L. & Hermes, D. (1975). *Personal growth through groups: A collection of methods.* San Diego, CA; The We Care Foundation.

Trotzer, J. P. & Kassera, W. J. (1973). Guidelines for selecting communication techniques in group counseling. *The School Counselor,* 20, 299-302.

NAME INDEX

A

Allen, F.H., 212, 228
Allen, V.L., 62, 76
Alschuler, A.S., 11, 21, 22, 24, 25, 26, 28, 29, 54, 75, 77
Altman, H., 169, 186
Amster, F., 212, 228
Anderson, K.A., 31, 32, 79
Apolloni, T., 61, 77
Arbuckle, D.S., 12, 13, 25, 81, 82, 84, 107, 156, 164
Asch, M.J., 68, 78
Aspy, C., 74, 75
Aspy, D.N., 10, 25, 52, 74, 75, 93, 107, 168, 174, 185, 186
Axline, Virginia, 60, 212, 213, 217, 219, 222, 224, 225, 226, 228

B

Baker, 6
Baker, S., 74, 75
Baldwin, W.P., 4, 25, 26
Bardon, J.I., 13, 25
Barth, R.S., 84, 107
Beene, J., 132, 140
Beiser, H.R., 222, 228
Bejarano, Y., 160, 165
Belkin, G.S., 155, 164
Berenson, B.B., 104, 107, 109
Berenson, B.G., 60, 75, 88, 104, 105, 107, 108
Berg, C.D., 25
Bessell, H., 49, 75, 229, 245
Biddle, B.J., 167, 186
Blocher, D.H., 129, 140, 149, 164
Blocksma, D.D., 68, 75

Borow, H., 208
Borton, T., 44, 45, 75, 229, 245
Boy, Angelo, V., iii, vii, 11, 12, 25, 27, 70, 75, 77, 85, 91, 95, 107, 108, 123, 124, 125, 129, 131, 133, 137, 138, 139, 140, 150, 151, 154, 157, 164, 165, 167, 170, 172, 175, 182, 183, 184, 185, 186, 187, 190, 207
Boyer, 8
Brammer, L.M., 13, 125
Brandt, R.S., 172, 186
Bratton, E.C., 172, 186
Bronfenbrenner, V., 8, 25
Brooks-Gunn, J., 26
Brophy, J.E., 135, 140, 167, 186
Brown, G.I., 12, 13, 25, 229, 245
Buhler, J.H., 168, 185
Bumpass, L., 4, 25
Burns, B.J., 190, 208
Burton, A., 109
Buscaglia, L., 13, 25
Butterworth, A., 27

C

Caney, S., 224, 228
Canfield, J., 229, 245
Caplan, R., 209, 228
Caplan, T., 209, 228
Capuzzi, D., 5, 25
Carkhuff, Robert R., 13, 25, 60, 75, 88, 104, 105, 107, 108, 109, 124, 125
Carlson, J., 35, 76
Cash, R.W., 104, 108
Casteel, J.D., 229, 245
Cerio, J.E., 229, 245
Cerio, N.G., 229, 245
Chasnoff, R., 164

Cohen, J., 74, 75
Colingsworth, 174
Collingswood, T., 187
Combs, A.W., 136, 137, 140, 176, 177, 186
Conley, J.E., 6, 25
Cooke, T.P., 61, 77
Coombs, A.W., 52, 75
Copeland, E.J., 91, 108
Corey, G., 88, 89, 108
Coulson, W., 96, 108
Courtois, C.A., 26
Cox, P.D., 62, 78
Crisci, P., 8, 62, 64, 65, 75
Cristiani, T.S., 112, 125
Curtis, J., 169, 186
Curwin, R., 149, 164

D

Danish, S.J., 118, 125
D'Augelli, A.R., 118, 125
Danzberger, J., 6, 26
David, H.P., 26
Davis, J.U., 84, 108
DeLeon, P.H., 13, 28
Devin-Sheehan, L., 62, 76
Dickman, L., 229, 245
Dinkmeyer, D.C., 33, 34, 35, 37, 75, 76, 228
Dinkmeyer, D., Jr., 33, 34, 76
Dockstrader, M.F., 72, 73, 79
Dorfman, E., 222, 226, 228
Drake, E.A., 26
Dreikurs, R., 33, 34, 76
Dymond, R.F., 109

E

Eckardt, M.J., 5, 26
Egan, G., 121, 124, 125
Eichmanns, 7
Eliot, George, 190
Ellenburg, F.C., 7, 26
Elliott, L.C., 149, 165, 170, 187
Ellis, A., 65, 66, 76, 84, 108
Ellis, M.J., 213, 215, 228
Ellis, S., 62, 76
Emerson, 144
Emery, R.E., 4, 26
Erickson, E.H., 213, 228
Espenshade, T., 4, 26
Etzioni, A., 8, 26

Evertson, C.M., 135, 140

F

Fagan, T., 6, 26
Fantini, M.D., 12, 28, 50, 51, 79, 84, 109
Farley, J.R., 13, 26
Faw, V.E., 68, 76
Feldman, R.S., 62, 76
Fenstermacher, G.D., 31, 76
Field, J., 177, 186
Fink, A.M., 60, 76
Flynn, E., 84, 108
Forsythe, L.B., 206, 207
Foster, C.D., 26
Foster, K., 172, 186
Freud, Anna, 214, 215
Freud, Sigmund, 190, 214
Fromkin, J.L., 229, 245
Fromm, Erich, 143, 164
Frymeir, J., 175, 186
Furstenberg, F., 5, 26

G

Gazda, G., 107, 108, 140
Gelatt, H.B., 13, 26
Gendlin, E.T., 109, 132, 140
George, R.L., 112, 125
Gerene, 133
Gerler, E., 62, 76
Gibbons, Maurice, 39, 40, 41, 76
Gibran, Kahil, 190
Gill, G.D., 207
Ginn, R., 27
Ginott, H.G., 7, 26, 212, 218, 221, 222, 223, 225, 226, 228
Ginzberg, E., 192, 193, 207, 208
Glaser, B., 63, 77
Glass, G.V., 74, 78
Glasser, W., 43, 76
Gmelch, W.H., 185, 186
Good, T.L., 167, 186
Goodlad, J.L., 7, 31, 76
Goodman, P., 47, 77
Goodyear, R.K., 12, 27
Gordon, Thomas, 102, 103, 108, 116, 125
Gorman, A., 57, 76
Goslin, D., 77
Graves, D.H., 150, 164
Green, D., 140

Gresham, F.M., 61, 77
Gross, L., 68, 77
Grunwald, B., 34, 76
Gunn, 5
Gunther, B., 229, 235, 245
Gutmann, A., 148, 164

H

Hadlock, W., 107
Hahn, A., 6, 26
Hall, R.T., 84, 108
Hamachek, D.E., 171, 186
Hammond, J., 172, 186
Hamrin, 71
Handel, L., 205, 206, 208
Hansen, J.C., 111, 113, 125, 134, 140
Hanson, A.R., 61, 62, 78
Hart, J.T., 78, 88, 108
Hatfield, T., 47, 77
Hauer, A.L., 118, 125
Haworth, M.R., 228
Hazel, E.R., 189, 208
Hefferline, R., 47, 77
Heibert, B.A., 84, 108
Hendrick, I., 191, 192, 208
Hendricks, G., 229, 245
Hermes, D., 229, 246
Hersch, R., 73, 77
Hertz-Lazarowitz, R., 160, 165
Hesse, Hermann, 145, 164
Hicks, L.H., 52, 75
Hill, P.L., 206, 208
Hobbs, N., 59, 77
Hodgkinson, H., 4, 6, 26
Hofferth, S.L., 4, 26
Hoffman, A., 165
Holland, J.L., 198, 199, 208
Holmes, D., 177, 186
Holmes, N., 177, 186
Hoppock, R., 198, 208
Howe, H., 6, 8, 26
Howe, L., 71, 78
Howe, L.W., 229, 245
Howe, M.M., 229, 245
Huxley, L.A., 234, 245

I

Isaccson, L.E., 201, 208
Ivey, A., 11, 26, 54, 77

Iwanicki, E.F., 182, 187

J

Jacobs, A., 108
James, William, 172, 186
Jeghelian, A., 26
Jernberg, 212
Jersild, A.T., 171, 186
Johnson, D.W., 160, 161, 164, 165
Johnson, L., 6, 28
Johnson, R.T., 160, 161, 164, 165

K

Kagan, N., 145, 165
Kassera, W.J., 230, 246
Kearney, A., 132, 139, 140
Kerr, M.M., 61, 78
Kessler, J.W., 215, 228
Kessler, L., 190, 208
Kiesler, D.J., 109
Kildahl, J.P., 171, 186
Kindsvatter, R., 149, 165
Kirkpatrick, J.S., 26
Kirschenbaum, H., 63, 71, 77, 78
Klein, Melanie, 214, 215
Klopfer, C., 27
Kohl, Herbert R., 169, 186
Kohlberg, S., 73, 77
Kraft, A., 135, 140, 177, 186
Kremer, B., 13, 26
Krumboltz, J.D., 187
Kussell, P., 160, 165

L

Ladd, G.W., 77
LaFaso, J.F., 84, 108
Larson, D., 108
Lathrop, R., 191, 208
LeCoq, L.L., 5, 25
Lee, E.E., 26
Lee, R.E., 27
Leehan, J., 26
Leeper, R.R., 140
Lefhowirz, B., 6, 26
Lepper, M.R., 133, 140
Levy, D.M., 215, 216, 228
Levy, J., 215, 228
Levy, S.M., 17, 27

Lewis, A.C., 8, 27
Lewis, H.R., 232, 233, 234, 236, 245
Lifton, W.M., 27
Little, Rick, 62
London, P., 4, 5, 6, 27
Long, J.D., 131, 140
Long, L., 147, 165
Losoncy, L., 35, 76
Love, W.E., 13, 27
Lyon, H.C., 13, 27, 229, 245
Lyons, V., 164, 165

M

Martin, J., 66, 67, 68, 77, 84, 108
Martin, W., 66, 67, 77
Marx, R.W., 84, 108
Maslow, H., 193, 194, 195, 208
Mayer, G.R., 27
Maynard, P.E., 134, 140
McKay, G.D., 33, 76
McMullen, R.S., 30, 77
Meeks, A.R., 213, 228
Menninger, W., 198, 208
Milgram, 5
Miller, Arthur, 191, 208
Miller, G.M., 26
Miller, T.I., 74, 78
Mitchell, K.M., 104, 107
Mize, J., 77
Mooney, W.T., 27
Morgan, S.P., 5, 26
Morris, V., 134, 139, 140
Morrison, D.M., 5, 27
Morrison, K., 229, 245
Morrow, L., 191, 208
Mosher, R.L., 11, 27, 45, 72, 77, 78, 79, 84, 108
Moustakas, C.C., 168, 186, 212, 213, 216, 217, 220, 222, 226, 227, 228

N

Nadenichek, P.E., 74, 75
Nelson, R.C., 213, 221, 228
Neubert, G.A., 172, 186
Newberg, N.A., 13, 27
Niles, J.A., 172, 187
Noad, B.M., 168, 187
Nolte, Dorothy Law, 177, 187

Norton, F.H., 27
Novak, J.M., 58, 59, 77, 136, 139, 140, 150, 165

O

O'Hara, R.P., 189, 197, 208
Otte, F., 206, 208
Otto, H.A., 229, 245

P

Pallack, M.S., 13, 28
Palomares, U., 49, 75
Paquette, M., 171, 187
Passons, W.R., 48, 77
Pate, R.H., 189, 208
Patterson, C.H., 88, 108, 134, 137, 140
Peck, C.A., 61, 77
Pepper, F., 34, 76
Perls, Fritz, 47, 60, 77
Peters, T.J., 75, 77
Piaget, J., 211, 228
Pierce, R.M., 107, 108
Pietrofesa, J.J., 158, 165
Pine, Gerald J., iii, vii, 11, 12, 25, 27, 69, 70, 75, 77, 85, 91, 95, 107, 108, 123, 124, 125, 129, 131, 133, 137, 138, 139, 140, 150, 151, 154, 157, 164, 165, 167, 170, 172, 175, 182, 183, 184, 185, 186, 187, 190, 207
Pines, M., 185, 187
Pinto, D., 165
Popowicz, C.L., 74, 75
Porter, E.H., 68, 75
Powell, J., 229, 246
Price, J.M., 77
Pulaski, M.A., 212, 228
Purkey, W.W., 58, 59, 77, 136, 139, 140, 150, 165

R

Ragland, E.U., 61, 78
Rank, Otto, 215, 216
Rathbone, C.H., 84, 107
Raths, 71
Raviv, S., 160, 165
Remer, R., 48, 77
Ribner, N., 27
Riccio, A., 185, 187

Ridener, J., 205, 208
Ringness, T.A., 13, 27
Roark, A.E., 144, 165
Roe, Anne, 193, 194, 195, 208
Roebuck, F.N., 10, 25, 74, 75, 93, 107, 174, 185, 186
Rogers, Carl R., 10, 13, 27, 58, 59, 60, 68, 69, 70, 77, 78, 84, 86, 102, 104, 105, 109, 111, 112, 114, 117, 125, 129, 130, 131, 132, 136, 138, 140, 146, 148, 149, 151, 153, 165, 228
Rogoff, B., 62, 76
Rosner, Hilda, 164
Rost, P., 205, 208
Rothrock, D., 31, 78
Rubin, D., 180, 187
Ryan, K., 27, 65, 78

S

Sanche, R.P., 44, 78
Schappi, A.C., 4, 27
Schiffer, M., 212, 218, 228
Schrader, L.A., 48, 77
Schultz, E.W., 169, 187
Schunk, D.H., 60, 61, 62, 78
Schutz, W.C., 233, 234, 246
Schwab, R.L., 182, 187
Schwebel, M., 68, 78
Seldman, M.L., 229, 246
Seuss, 45
Shakespeare, 190
Shapiro, S.B., 52, 78
Sharan, S., 160, 165
Sharan, Y., 160, 165
Shaw, M.C., 12, 27
Sherwood, J.J., 229, 245
Shostrom, E.L., 113, 125
Silberman, C.E., 170, 187
Simon, S.B., 71, 78, 151, 155, 165
Sklare, A.R., 201, 208
Skovholt, T., 10, 27
Slavin, R.E., 160, 165, 171, 187
Smith, David, 190
Smith, M.S., 74, 78
Smith, S., 171, 187
Soradahl, S.N., 44, 78
Sparks, D., 182, 187
Splete, H.H., 165, 201, 206, 208
Sprinthall, Norman A., 11, 13, 27, 45, 60, 72, 77, 78, 79, 84, 108

Stahl, R.J., 229, 245
Stanford, G., 144, 165
Stefflre, B., 168, 187
Steinbeck, John, 73
Stensrud, K., 6, 28
Stensrud, R., 6, 28
Stevic, R.R., 111, 113, 125
Strain, P.S., 61, 77, 78
Streitfeld, H.S., 232, 233, 234, 236, 245
Strother, D.B., 6, 27, 32
Sullivan, P.J., 72, 73, 79
Super, D., 195, 196, 208
Sweeney, T.J., 132, 140
Swisher, J.D., 74, 75

T

Taft, Jessie, 215
Takanishi, R., 13, 28
Taube, C.A., 190, 208
Tavantis, T.N., 27
Thompson, A.P., 28
Tiedeman, D.V., 189, 197, 208
Tolbert, E.L., 200, 208
Tomlinson, T.M., 78, 108
Trotzer, J.P., 230, 246
Truax, C.B., 109
Truax, C.G., 104, 105, 109
Tuckman, B.W., 199, 208
Turock, A., 124, 125

W

Wagschal, P.H., 6, 28
Walberg, H.J., 31, 32, 33, 79
Wallace, A., 6, 26
Wang, M.C., 31, 32, 33, 79
Warner, R.W., Jr., 111, 113, 125
Waterman, R.H., 75, 77
Waxman, H.C., 31, 32, 79
Weinhold, B.K., 149, 165, 170, 187
Weinstein, G., 12, 21, 22, 24, 25, 28, 50, 51, 79, 84, 109
Weiss, E., 229, 245
Wells, H.C., 229, 245
Wildman, T.M., 172, 187
Wilensky, H.L., 190, 208
Williams, H., 174, 187
Williams, R.L., 131, 140
Williamson, E.G., 192, 208
Wolf, J.G., 169, 187

Wood, J., 109
Woods, E., 28
Woody, R.H., 28
Wouk, Herman, 73
Wrenn, C.G., 190, 208

Wynne, E., 28

Z

Zeller, B.J., 206, 208

SUBJECT INDEX

A

Adaptive education, 31-33 (*see also* Adaptive instruction)
Adaptive instruction
  basis of, 31
  characteristics, 31-32
  generalizations regarding, 33
  positive results of, 32
  summary, 33
Adlerian psychology applied within classroom, 33-39
  basic principles of human behavior, 33-34
  C-Groups, 35-37
    definition, 36
    procedures for improving communication, 36-37
    skills in, 35
  directing destructive to positive goals, 34
  DUSO (*see* DUSO)
  encouragement process, 35
  goals of students' misbehavior, 34
  role of teacher, 34-35
Adulthood, skills for, 63-64
Affective education, 84 (*see also* Counselor teacher)
Alcohol and drug use by children, 5
America's psychosocial crisis, 4-7
  alcohol and drug use by children, 5
  births to unwed females, 4-5
  child neglect and abuse, 5
  child poverty, 6
  children's suicide, 5-6
  family problems, 4
  high school dropouts, 6
  number affected by, 6
  sexual behavior, 4-5
  variety of, 6

C

Career awareness, 189-207
  activities for developing, 204-207
    career corner, 205
    career pyramid, 205
    careers of the month club, 205
    field trips, 204-205
    hat exhibit, 206
    interviewing workers or parents, 206
    real world participation, 206, 207
    seminars, 206
    using resource persons, 206
    vocations week, 206
    workbooks, 207
  and psychosocial development, 189-191
  and the teacher, 201-204
  as process identifying and implementing a self-concept, 195-196
  career development model stages, 199-200
  career development points of view
    Ginsberg, 192-193
    Holland, 198-199
    Hoppock, 198
    Menninger, 197-198
    psychoanalysts, 191-192
    Roe, 193-195
    Super, 195-197
    Tiedeman and O'Hara, 197
    Tolbert, 200-201
    trait and factor, 192
    Tuckman, 199-200
  comparison role of to hierarchy of needs, 193
  conclusions, 207
  definitions, 190
  dissemination career information
    through bulletin board displays, 202

253

through language arts curriculum, 202-203
through mathematics and science curriculum, 204
through social studies curriculum, 203-204
hypothesis of Hoppock, 198
impact ego on, 197
integration occupational information with curriculum, 201-202
meaning of work (*see* Work)
organization of psychosocial needs, 193, 194
relation personality types to careers, 198-199
role of teacher in relation to, 201
stages in process of, 192-193
theory of occupational choice, 198
trait and factor approach, 192
viewpoint of Tolbert on, 200-201
Career Pyramid, 205
Challenge education, 39-43
advantages of, 42-43
basic modes of, 41-42
basis of, 40
fields of study, 42
need for, 39
process of, 40
use of working journal, 41
Child neglect and abuse, cases reported annually, 5
Child poverty, incidence of, 6
Classroom meetings
guidelines for conducting, 43-44
types of, 43
Client-centered approach to play therapy, 217-218
Client-centered counseling
counseling process, 92-93
development of, 84-85
goals of, 87-88
rationale for applying, 85-92
applicability of, 89
comprehensive, 89
enables behavior changes in natural sequence, 91-92
evidence supporting effectiveness of, 88-89
focuses on student, not problem, 89-90
focuses on teacher-counselor attitudes, 90
goals for students, 87
has systematic response pattern, 90
is flexible to go beyond feelings, 90-91
is individualized, 91
methods of individualizing counseling, 91
positive philosophy of person, 86
possesses definition of counselor-teacher's role, 88
possesses achievable human goals, 87-88
propositions regarding human personality and behavior, 86-87
role of teacher, 85, 86 (*see also* Teacher-counselor)
Cooperative learning group, 160-164
definition, 160
elements of, 160-161
role of teacher, 163
stages of, 161-163
summary, 164
Counseling
basic concepts, 101
client-centered (*see* Client-centered)
human resources development (*see* Human resources development)
peer (*see* Peer counseling)
person-centered, 84-92 (*see also* Person-centered counseling)
process of, 92-93 (*see also* Counseling process)
school (*see* School counseling)
teacher (*see* Teacher-counselor)
Counseling process
concepts, 101
conclusions, 101-102
foundation of, 92-93
from phase one to phase two, 95-97
phase one
advantages, 93
attitude of teacher, 93
attitudinal foundations, 94-95
communication, 95
relationship teacher-student, 92, 93
teacher attitudes, 93-95
time needed for, 96-97
transition to phase two, 95-97
phase two
choices of, 97
guidelines, 97-100
positive outcomes, 92
response patterns, 96
student response, 96
transition from phase one, 95-97
phases of, 92
Counselor teacher (*see* Teacher-counselor)

Creative teaching, signs of, 52-54
Curriculum of concern
  need for, 44-45
  tiers of, 45

D

Dignity
  belief for self and others, 143
  definition, 143
Drug abuse prevention, role of Quest, 64
DUSO
  basis of, 37
  definition, 37
  Kit D-1 themes, 38
  Kit D-2 themes, 38, 39
  objectives of, 38-39
Dyad communication, 242

E

Eclectic activities to foster psychosocial development, 229-245
  for positive group interaction, 240-243
  for students, 232-233
  guidelines for selecting, 230-232
  principles of, 230
  purpose of, 229
  rationale, 229-230
  to broaden perspectives in interpersonal relation, 237-238
  to clarify personal values and priorities, 236
  to identify and understand emotional behavior, 243-245
  to illustrate behavior patterns cause and effect, 238-240
  to promote awareness of self and others, 233-236
Education
  adaptive (*see* Adaptive instruction)
  challenge, 39-43 (*see also* Challenge education)
  humanistic, 50-52
  individualized instruction (*see* Adaptive instruction)
  interactive process of, 57-58
  invitational, 58-59
  rational-emotive (*see* Rational-emotive education)
  student-centered teaching, 69-70
Effective teaching, characteristics, 143

Ego identity
  definition, 197
  focus of career development, 197
  impact upon career development and maturity, 197
Emotional education (*see* Teacher counselor)
Ethical Quest in a Democratic Society Project, 73

F

Feeling
  behavior as reflective of feelings, 14-15
  effect on behavior, 16
  effect on thinking, 18-20
  expression of, 18-20
    enables one to examine motives, 18-19
    involves risk, 18
    leads to personal freedom, 20
    leads to self-responsibility, 19-20
    serves as a release, 19
  influence on thinking and behavior, 14-21
  results repressing of
    interpersonal conflict, 16-17
    negative physical consequences of, 17-18

G

Gestalt units
  basis of, 47-48
  expressing feelings, 49
  external awareness unit, 48
  internal awareness unit, 48

H

High school dropouts, 6
Human Development Program
  basis on prevention, 50
  description, 49-50
Human relations and intentionality
  focus of approach, 55
  in academic life, 55
  in social life, 55
  objective of curriculum, 54
  teaching of, example, 55-57
Human Resources Development Model, 104-107
  core dimensions, 105
  development of, 104-105
  helping process, 105-107

Humanistic education
  characteristic value principles, 52
  concerns of children, 50
  counselor teacher (*see* Teacher-counselor)
  major elements of, 51-52
  signs of creative teaching, 52-54

I

Individualized instruction, definition, 31 (*see also* Adaptive instruction)
Invitational education self-concept approach, 58-59
  principles of, 58

L

Latch key children, number of, 4
Learning, 127-139
  as affective, 132
  as cognitive, 132
  as cooperative and collaborative process, 131
  as evolutionary process, 131
  as sometimes painful, 131-132
  atmosphere needed, 135-139
    ambiguity tolerated, 137
    creation learning conditions, 139
    feeling of being accepted, 138
    need for respect, 138
    open self not closed self, 137-138
    personal meaning of ideas, 136
    personal, subjective nature of learning, 136
    right to make mistakes, 136-137
    teacher as a learner, 139
    trust in self, 138
    use self-evaluation, 137
  behavioral change and experience as, 130-131
  changing behavior in positive directions, 129
  conditions which facilitate, 135-139
  control of, 129
  cooperative, 160-164 (*see also* Cooperative learning)
  definition, 128, 130, 134
  expressing values as, 133
  goal of, 129
  importance of work, 133
  integration psychosocial development and academia, 127-128
  joy in accomplishment, 132
  learner as free, responsible agent, 134
  learner as resource for, 132
  optimal conditions for, 132
  personal meaning of ideas and, 130
  personal styles of, 134
  principles and conditions of and psychosocial development, 128-129
  principles which facilitate, 129-135
  role of learner, 129
  subliminal curriculum, 130
  teaching as, 134-135
  use by teacher, 128-130
  use of term, 128
Listening
  empathy defined, 146
  non-evaluative, 145
  sensitive listening, 146
Living School
  description, 65-66
  purpose of, 65

M

Moral development, stages of, 73
Moral education, 84 (*see also* Teacher-counselor)

N

National Mental Health Association Commission, goal of, vi

O

Open education, 84 (*see also* Teacher-counselor)

P

Peer counseling, 59-62
  definition, 60
  development of, 59-60
  effectiveness of, 60
  exposure students to, 46
  illustration, 60
  outcomes of, 60
  peer modeling, 60-61
Peer modeling
  advantages, 60-61, 61-62
  classroom application of, 61
  use by teachers, 61-62

Subject Index

Person-centered counseling, 84-92 (*see also* Client-centered counseling)
Play
  and cognitive development, 211-212
    games with rules, 211-212
    practice games, 211
    symbolic games, 211
  conclusion, 228
  features of, 209-211
  general characteristics of, 213-214
  materials for psychosocial development, 222-224
  non-directive play therapy, 213
  parents and, 227-228
  play therapy (*see* Play therapy)
  playroom, 224-225
  power of, 209-211
  principles of helping through, 219-221
  psychosocial value of, 212-213
  selections of play materials, 211-222
    criteria for, 211
    toys selected by children, 222
  values and benefits from, 212-213
Play therapy
  approaches to, 215-218
    client-centered approach, 217-218
    existential, 216-217
    group play therapy, 218
    psychoanalytic, 215
    release therapy, 215-216
  criteria for selecting and rejecting materials for, 221
  eclectic activities (*see* Eclectic activities)
  establishing limits, 225-227
    appropriate limits, 226-227
    reasons for, 225-226
  group vs. individual, 218-219
  history of, 214-215
  non-directive, 213, 215
  relationship therapy, 215
Pregnancy
  of married teenagers, 5
  of unwed teenagers, 5
  race and, 5
Project LEAD
  goals of, 65
  teams used, 64-65
Psychoanalysts, attitude toward work, 191
Psychological education, 84 (*see also* Teacher counselor)
Psychology, rational-emotive approach, 65-66
Psychosocial crisis of America (*see* America's psychosocial crisis)
Psychosocial development
  America's psychosocial crisis (*see* America's psychosocial crisis)
  aspects of, 8
  definition, v
  eclectic activities to foster, 229-245
  feelings influencing thinking and behavior, 14-21 (*see also* Feelings)
  fundamental principles, v-vi
  goal of educators, vi
  importance of today, 3
  principles of, 176-177
  rationale for fostering, 3-25
  schools as contributors to, 7-13 (*see also* Schools and psychosocial development)
  self-knowledge education (*see* Self-knowledge education)
  teaching and educational approaches to fostering (*see* Teaching and educational approaches)
  teaching for, 167-185 (*see also* Teaching for psychosocial development)
  through career awareness (*see* Career awareness)
  through play (*see* Play)
Psychosocial information
  assumptions regarding, 152-153
  consideration problem, 154
  factors affecting a student group's processing of, 153-155
  factors affecting teachers use of, 155-157
  feelings of group, 153-154
  guidelines for processing in groups, 157-159
  perceptions of group, 154-155
  processing with student groups, 151-152
  self-concept, 154
  student group's problem, 156
  teacher's feelings, 155-156
  teacher's perceptions, 156-157
  teacher's self-concept, 156
  teacher's values, 157
  values of group, 154-155
Psychosocially sensitive teacher, 141-164
  assumptions regarding information, 152-153
  challenge for, 151
  characteristics of teaching style, 143

characteristics of typical, 141-143
  ability to listen, 145
  concentration on needs, problems, feelings of students, 147
  deep respect for learner, 143-144
  develops effective communication, 144-146
  empathic acceptance of student, 146-147
  liberality, 148
cooperative learning, 160-164
effects psychosocial learning experiences, 148-151
factors affecting processing of information, 153-155
factors affecting use of psychosocial information, 155-157
processing psychosocial information with student groups, 151-152
  definition psychosocial information, 152
self-actualizing, 143-148

Q

Quest
  effectiveness of, 64
  formation of, 62
  need for, 63
  Project LEAD, 64-65
  skills involved, 63-64

R

Recreation as psychosocial experience
  aspects of teaching to obviate, 173
  need for 172-173, 174
Reflecting feelings process
  advantages of, 95, 113
  concept of, 111
  conditions for, 114-118
    attitudinally emphatic, 116-117
    feelings influence thinking and behavior, 115-116
    patience with reflective process, 116
    possession affective vocabulary, 117-118
    student has power to change, 115
    veracity student's presenting problems, 116
  continuation or limitation, 124-125
    guidelines, 124-125
  expanding effectiveness of, 123-125
    confrontation, 124
    interpretation, 124

function of teacher-counselor, 112
need for positive self-concept, 113
process of, 114, 118-123
  discipline in applying reflective responses, 122-123
  reading feelings accurately, 119-120
  reflect primarily, but clarify, 121
  sensitivity to corrections of feelings, 121-122
  sensitivity to feelings, 120-121
response patterns of teacher, 96
roots of, 111-113
use as therapeutic technique, 114, 116
Relationship therapy, 215
  attitudes conveyed to child, 216-217
  basis, 216
  stages of play therapy process, 217
Release therapy, 215-216

S

School counseling (*see also* Teacher counselor)
  beginning of, 82
  development of as profession, 82-83
  purpose of, 82
School's role in psychosocial development
  advantages to student, 10
  approach to school to, 11-12
  curriculum of caring, 8
  desirable school year psychosocial qualities, 13
  influence school upon, 13
  negative outcome, 11-12
  objective of, 11
  practical outcome of, 12
  responsibility of school, 9-10
  results approach to education of, 10-11
  student-centered teachers, 10
Self-actualizing psychosocial educator (*see* Psychosocial educator)
Self-instruction skills
  definition, 66-67
  knowledge sources activating, 67
  levels of competence, 67
  teaching of, 67-68
Self-knowledge education, 21-24
  definition self-knowledge, 22
  development, theory of, 21-22
  elemental, 22, 24
  goal of, 21
  pattern, 23, 24
  scientific model creation of, 21

Subject Index

situational, 22, 24
transformational, 23-24, 24-25
Sexual activity, of teenagers, 4-5
Single parent families, statistics regarding, 4
Skills for Living Program (*see* Quest)
Student-centered counseling (*see also* Client-centered counseling)
  basis of, 68
  characteristics interpersonal relationship facilitating, 69-70
  principles and hypotheses, 68-69
  responses students to, 10
  teaching approach of, 10
Suicide, by children, 5-6

T

Teacher
  as a counselor (*see* Teacher-counselor)
  career awareness (*see* Teacher-counselor)
  need for sense of humor, 174
  need to be physically fit, 174
  psychosocially sensitive (*see* Psychosocially teacher)
Teacher rights, 180-185
  evaluative problems, 182
  freedoms of, 180
  need for sense of humor, 174
  to a professional role, 181-182
  to be fairly evaluated, 182
  to equalized staff relationships, 184
  to fair administrative practices, 183
  to implement a teaching model, 184-185
    criteria for, 184-185
  to school climate free from politics, 182-183
Teacher-counselor
  beginning of, 81-82
  communication, 95
  concept of, 84
  conclusions, 101-102
  counseling process (*see* Counseling process)
  effectiveness training, 102-104 (*see also* Teacher effectiveness training)
  movements involving, 84
  person-centered perspective (*see* Client-centered counseling)
  reflective process (*see* Reflective process)
  teacher attitudes, 93-95
  value uncertainty into the classroom, 83
Teaching (*see also* Education)
  definition, 129
  good, definition, 58
Teaching and educational approaches to foster psychosocial development
  achievement motivation, 29-31
    characteristics experience in, 30
    effectiveness of, 31
  adaptive education (*see* Adaptive education)
  Adlerian approach (*see* Adlerian psychology)
  classroom meetings, 43-44
  curriculum of concern, 44-45
  deliberate psychological education, 45-47
    child development, 47
  counseling component, 46
    definition, 45-46
    improvisational drama, 46-47
  effectiveness primary prevention approaches, 73-75
    results studies of, 73-74
    summary, 75
  Gestalt approach, 47-49 (*see also* Gestalt units)
  Human Development Program, 49-50
  humanistic education, 50-52 (*see also* Humanistic education)
  intentionality and human relations, 54-57 (*see also* Human relations)
  interactive process of education, 57-58
  invitational education, 58-59
  peer counseling (*see* Peer counseling)
  peer modeling (*see* Peer modeling)
  Quest, 62-65 (*see also* Quest)
  rational-emotive approach, 65-66
  self-instruction, 66-68
  student-centered teaching, 68-70
  values clarification, 70-73 (*see also* Values clarification)
Teaching for psychosocial development, 167-185
  and the self, 168
  classroom experiences
    gains for pupil, 177-178
    principles of, 176-177
  creation enriching psychosocial experiences, 169-170
  experiences provided by administrators, 175-176
  friendship experiences, 170
  guidelines of teaching/learning process, 179-180
  importance of teacher, 167, 168
  positive attitude within self, 178-180

recreation, 172
relationships with others, 171-172
rights of the teacher, 180-185 (*see also* Teacher rights)
teachers need for enriching psychosocial experience, 169
teaching as expression of psychosocial values, 168-169
Toy-lending program
  goal of, 227
  initiation of, 227-228
Training effectiveness training
  functions of teacher, 102-103
  new skills required, 103
  purpose, 103
  skills taught, 103-104

V

Values clarification, 70-73
  events prompting public interest in, 72-73
  goal of, 71
  issues in conflict, 71, 83
  of student groups, 155
  stages of moral development, 73
  teacher strategies, 71-72

W

Work
  attitude psychoanalysis toward, 191
  attitudes toward, 190
  contribution to psychosocial stability, 191
  definition, 190
  meaning of in life of a person, 190-191
  negative attitude to work, 133
  therapeutic value of, 197-198
  theory of occupational choice, 198
  work principle, 191-192
Work principle of Hendrick, 191-192